D1145891

BETWEEN STONE AND SKY

To Piers,
with my warmest
wishes for
Happy Christmas
and New Year

— Dom

17 XII 2011

Between Stone and Sky

Memoirs of a Waller

WHITNEY BROWN

Constable • London

CONSTABLE

Some names and details have been changed to protect the privacy of others.

First published in hardback in Great Britain in 2018 by Constable

13 5 7 9 10 8 6 4 2

Copyright © Whitney Brown, 2018

The moral right of the author has been asserted.

All rights reserved.
No part of this publication may be reproduced, stored in a retrieval system,
or transmitted, in any form, or by any means, without the prior permission in
writing of the publisher, nor be otherwise circulated in any form of binding or
cover other than that in which it is published and without a similar condition
including this condition being imposed on the subsequent purchaser.

A CIP catalogue record for this book
is available from the British Library.

ISBN: 978-1-47212-733-4

Typeset in Sabon by Hewer Text Ltd. Edinburgh
Printed and bound in Great Britain by Clays Ltd, St Ives plc

Papers used by Constable are from well-managed forests and other responsible sources.

Constable
An imprint of
Little, Brown Book Group
Carmelite House
50 Victoria Embankment
London EC4Y 0DZ

An Hachette UK Company
www.hachette.co.uk

www.littlebrown.co.uk

To Jack, who gave me his craft, his countryside and his love.

To Rose, who was for a time my fiercest ally, and who will always be my favourite swimming companion.

And to darling Kate, who kept me afloat when rough waves threatened and pushed me along, strong and steady as a spring tide.

These three, each in their own way, led me into a world of magic and wonder, and more importantly, into myself. I will be forever in their debt for their love and faith, and for all the quiet moments we shared in places too beautiful to be believed.

And this our life, exempt from public haunt,
Finds tongues in trees, books in the running brooks,
Sermons in stones, and good in everything.
I would not change it.

William Shakespeare – Act II,
Scene 1 *As You Like It*

Introduction

Iwas sitting in a grubby pub near Bethnal Green station across from a guy named Steve. He was reserved at best, disinterested at worst. I couldn't quite tell. Pelham, our mutual friend, was at the bar getting a round of drinks before we all headed off to an exhibition opening at the V&A Museum of Childhood. Steve and I were forced to make small talk, having arrived only minutes before and quickly losing our friend to the taps. I'm always nervous with strangers and the getting-to-know-you game – tenfold if I'm sober – and Steve was not making it any easier. He was completely straight-faced, impenetrable. British manners – though I'd soon find out he's a long-time Irish Londoner – don't exactly help me relax. Even at thirty-three, I'm like a big, goofy puppy, slightly too friendly and slobbery even though I mean well – even more so when I'm anxious – which can be a bit bewildering to many I meet on the eastern side of the Atlantic. And I get weary of awkwardly explaining what I do for a

1

living, especially to strangers whose frame of reference and level of interest I don't know. I prepare myself for blank stares and boredom, though I am often pleasantly surprised.

Straight-faced Steve's eyes suddenly lit up as I mumbled something dismissively about being a dry-stone waller, hoping to play it down so he wouldn't make me explain what that was.

'I've heard you on the radio,' he said.

It took me a minute to process this sentence. There was no way this guy had heard me on the radio in 2009, let alone still remembered it. I said about ten words total in that segment, and it had been almost eight years.

Jack and I were interviewed for a programme that aired so early in the morning only farmers would be awake and tuned in. It was my first trip to Wales, and I just happened to be working with Jack as he repaired a lime-mortared wall at a disused quarry near Llandybie when the interviewer showed up with John the Rocks, a.k.a. Professor John Davies, noted geological scholar. He stuck a mic in my face just to be polite, I think. I have no idea now what I said – hopefully nothing too idiotic – and I had nearly forgotten it happened at all.

I did finally manage to say aloud, 'There's no way you heard that!'

'It's your voice,' Steve said. 'I remember it. When you said you were a dry-stone waller it reminded me.'

'But that was *ages* ago,' I said, shocked.

He told me that he just had Radio 4 on in the background all the time. I still couldn't believe it. Apparently, he also had quite a good memory. Probably helps that I have a curious accent. (Mountain South doesn't get out in the world a whole lot. My experience of Brits is that they think we all talk like John Wayne or characters from *The Godfather*.)

The night just got better and better from there, ending at The Approach Tavern with long-time East Londoners regaling me with tales of a more sinister but lively time in Bethnal Green . . . And encouraging me to say all sorts of words for their enjoyment. Steve, as it happened, turned out to be really cool.

I should tell you that Lydia Noble is the best female dry-stone waller in the Anglophone world – possibly the whole world. Everyone in my trade knows that. She was born into a family of Yorkshire wallers, probably wielding a hammer from the get-go, and she is amazing. She was building master-fully long before I ever laid eyes on my first dry-stone wall at age twenty-six. And she's younger than I am, by the way.

I am not Lydia Noble.

This is not the story of mastery in a craft. It is the story of struggle, of becoming, of love across two continents and two generations. It is the story of an ongoing obsession with a place where I don't belong . . . except that somehow I have come to, slowly, and with many bruises and nettle stings along the way.

I am not the only or the best female dry-stone waller. I may simply be the one who talks the most.

Eight years have come and gone since I first came face to face with a dry-stone wall, and nothing has been the same since. I daresay no one could have predicted what followed. Certainly *I* didn't have a clue what was coming.

It's amusing now to think that my life was changed by a temporary wall on the National Mall in Washington, DC, but it's true. That encounter, with a wall and its maker, was the start of a very good story.

I have no desire as I tell it to paint myself as some kind of feminist hero or pioneering icon. You must understand: when the journey began, I only set out to be happy. I had a good dose of critical thinking about labour and philosophy in graduate school, but any feminist awakenings I had came much later as I worked and moved through the world as a woman in overalls. At least three people have said to me over the years, 'I'll be so happy if my daughter turns out just like you', and while I am flattered, I also wince ever so slightly. Much of what I have done has been completely self-indulgent, but if people feel inspired by that in a feminist way or even a 'Take this job and shove it' kind of way, that's OK. We all look for inspiration in the world around us. I know I did. And perhaps I have moved into those political spaces now, but they were not part of my original decision-making. I didn't have an agenda except to be happy. I made my choices bravely (sometimes still quite fearfully) within the framework I was given, but I have been lucky, too. So far, I have always landed on my feet, pulled it off, healed in time, met the right person at the right moment. Stars have aligned and oceans have been crossed to make me what I am today: a person whose voice is recognised in a pub in Bethnal Green.

Much of this story seems like a distant dream now. If I sound a bit mystical at times about what happened to me, it's because I can't figure out any logic in how or why it happened . . . Chance meetings, gut feelings, leaps of faith, and incredible generosity. Jack and I have often wondered aloud why we met, why all of this came to be. I don't have an answer, but I will tell you the story.

Some of the people in my tale are presented 100 per cent as they are in life: real names, real personalities. A few names have been changed to protect the most private individuals who were part of my life in these years – people who were so wonderful I wish you could know them yourselves – yet I want to keep them just for me.

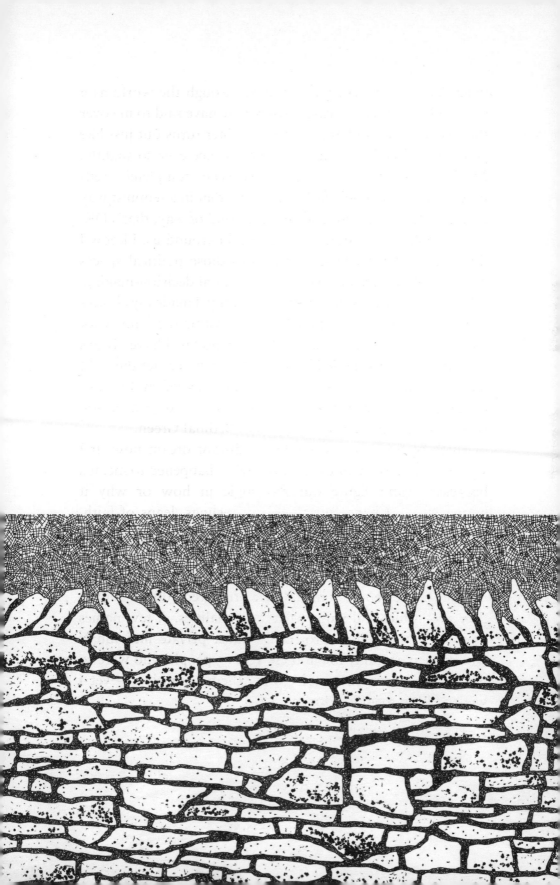

Washington, DC

In the beginning, I wasn't particularly interested in him or his stone walls. I was just stressed out and wanted to smash some stuff with a sledgehammer instead of disappearing into the tiny space between my office trailer and the security fence to cry for the umpteenth time that summer. Jack was kind enough – and perhaps amused enough – to indulge me when I stopped by.

It was the summer of 2009, and I had returned to Washington, DC, for my second year of work at the Smithsonian Folklife Festival. I had just completed my coursework for a Master's degree in Folklore at the University of North Carolina at Chapel Hill, and I was supposed to be chipping away at my thesis that summer. What I did instead was work about seventy hours a week to help produce an international cultural festival on the National Mall that would be visited by over a million people in the course of ten days, and I played just as hard as I worked. Every night I came home exhausted. There was no time to write. I would get to the thesis later. (*Much* later, actually.)

In any given year, the festival always features a seemingly mismatched collection of cultural groups. They might include a specific ethnicity or tribe, an American state such as Virginia or Texas, a foreign country such as Mali or Peru, or a group that is otherwise culturally linked, like the people who live along the length of the Silk Road in Eurasia. In 2008, we'd hosted Bhutan, and it would be difficult to be more exotic and enchanting than that. This year, there was a Latin American music programme that drew musicians and dancers from a variety of regions and styles, one on African-American oral traditions, and a big section of the festival that would be devoted to the little country of Wales. I had spent a lot of my academic career studying African-American expressive culture, and Latin American programmes were always lively and fun . . . but *Wales*? It just didn't hold the same intrigue for me. It seemed a bit . . . tame? What would it be – a few people making stuff out of wool and someone singing melancholy songs?

As a young graduate student simply working a summer gig, I held the essential but unglamorous job of Supply Coordinator, which meant I was responsible for providing almost everything festival participants needed for demonstrations and performances. Sometimes what they needed from me was as simple as honey and lemons for the singers, but inevitably there are complications and wild goose chases each year. These become the stuff of legend among the festival staff. That year I had to figure out how to borrow, load, deliver into a tent, set up, secure in said tent, and safely return a 360kg-plus irreplaceable letterpress that would be used by a bookbinder from the National Library of Wales. Some people put up the tents and build stages. Some people run the demonstration

8

kitchens and book the flights and arrange the hotels. I got the stuff.

I lived and died by my lists and spreadsheets, and I spent hours and hours driving frantically in a white van, sheet after rumpled sheet of hastily printed maps and itineraries flying all over the dashboard. I traipsed miles a day up and down the Mall in my steel-toecap boots tending to various people and storage trailers. At all times I was saddled with two mobile phones and a radio in addition to my desk phone and computer. There was never quite enough time to eat. Sleep fell by the wayside, too. What kept me going was a yellow legal pad (my back-up brain), waves of adrenaline and *gallons* of coffee.

It wasn't a glamorous job, but most days were an adventure, and I got to mingle with world-class talent on a daily basis. Most nights, we danced and drank and shared stories into the wee hours with little regard for how the morning might feel. For staff, the festival is always a mix of extreme stress and euphoria, a time when lifelong bonds form between people who otherwise might never have met at all. I took the bad with the good just like everybody else around me. I knew, too, that I was laying track towards something more lasting at the Smithsonian if I could just get through my Master's thesis.

Wales was the biggest programme that year, occupying the most extensive and elaborate physical space on the Mall and boasting the largest number of participants . . . a new wave of Welsh colonisation in one of the most visible and symbolic spaces in all of America. As a programme, it would ask a lot of me. There were dozens of artisans. Many of them didn't communicate by email. They needed things like boat varnish, raw sheep's fleeces, stone-carving tools, bookbinding leather (and the aforementioned printing press), potter's wheels, slabs of alder, and medicinal leeches. Sometimes I knew these things ahead of time, and sometimes I didn't. We made it work.

The Welsh were the first to arrive on site. An advance team of five – three artists and a dry-stone waller plus one cameraman – appeared on the Mall a few weeks before any other participants. Angharad, a blacksmith and installation artist, had designed an elaborate festival site that physically wove together symbols of the Welsh landscape and culture, and she and her team were here to pull it all together in what would be a marathon of creative construction. There were dry-stone walls to be built, gates of forged steel to be hung, traditional North Walian slate slab fences to be installed, red rugby goalposts to be erected, and a few other key items to be displayed that were still stuck somewhere in a sea container in US customs in the port of Baltimore.

I was hastily introduced to the Welsh team as their programme curator, Betty Belanus, gave them a tour of the festival site and I happened to be passing by. They seemed nice enough, but I was in a hurry. (I was *always* in a hurry.) To boot, it wasn't at all clear to me if they all spoke English. That's how little I knew of a country where, actually, *everyone* speaks English, and only about 20 per cent of the population speak Welsh. But I clocked Angharad straightaway, and I wanted to know who on earth she was. This confident woman striding up and down the Mall with all her tools and her men-in-waiting did not compute in my brain – my staid, responsible, academic brain – and I needed to know more. It would be a while before I had time and courage to ask. I simply studied her every chance I got, fascinated.

These five didn't ask me for much in English or in Welsh, but as the weeks went on and we all worked in circles around each other as the festival came together, I caught glimpses of

Angharad as she did some cold-bending and welding for installation pieces and watched in awe as she commanded her team of men. She was *so* intimidating. Much to my relief, she was also friendly and welcoming. Eventually, I got up the nerve to ask her to give me a one-on-one welding lesson in the festival's workshop tent. You would have thought I'd won the lottery when she said yes. In stifling 90-degree heat, I donned the heavy, protective leathers over my bare arms and legs and put on the helmet for the first time. Even the gear made me feel powerful.

'It's quite like icing a cake,' she said. 'Have you ever done that?' It had been my chief hobby in graduate school, I said proudly.

I'd never thought much about these things before, but it was the first real moment of feminist empowerment in my life – putting on the kit, picking up the tools, and doing so in the company of a woman who knew it all like the back of her hand, who made it seem approachable. As both a woman and an intellectual I had never imagined learning any sort of manual trade. It simply wasn't suggested at any point in my life. It seemed not to occur to the world that I might enjoy it.

At a house party hosted by a Smithsonian undersecretary one night just before the festival opened, Jack, the big, friendly dry-stone waller, whisked me out onto the makeshift dancefloor, twirling me so enthusiastically that I thought we might fall into the pool as we traced our way around to the sounds of Sam Cooke's 'Bring It On Home to Me'. I don't even think we'd had a proper conversation yet, but it was clear that he sang and danced just as well as he built. Multiple times a day for weeks I had walked past as he worked, but I usually slowed my pace only enough to hurl a polite hello his way. There were always fires to put out, some phone or another ringing, someone grabbing me by the arm to ask for something.

It wasn't until the festival opened and things relaxed a bit for me that I really had much time to get to know anyone. I stopped by sometimes to spend a few minutes with Jack's sledgehammer in order to improve my attitude, and eventually I became as interested in the creative aspects of his work as much as the destructive ones. He taught me a bit about building, and one afternoon on the Mall he supervised a wall-building competition among two teams of festival staff. To my horror, my team lost, which only made me more determined to figure it out. I hated to lose.

One morning when I meant to be catching up on spreadsheets and reconciling budgets, Jack appeared at my office trailer door, and instead we sat together zooming down on Google's satellite photos of his house and mine, each of us wondering about places we might never visit ourselves. He gave me more place names to type into the search box – he wanted to show me his walls, too – and as he spelled them slowly aloud my face contorted in disbelief. Did these letters really go together?! I laughed, though I felt a bit rude for it. (Way to be culturally sensitive, folklorist!)

And there they were: long, brownish lines traversing the great expanses of green flattened across my screen. You could even see them from space. How beautiful they must be in person, I thought.

There was something special about Jack. He was a mountain of a man and considerably older than me . . . a bit mysterious, too, but always friendly and charming. I found him intriguing – and a bit unnerving.

I met Jack and Angharad at a crucial moment in my life: with two years of graduate school under my belt, I was beginning to feel like I had been in some sort of quarantine. I had learned so much, and I was grateful, but I was ready to get back out into the world. I had spent the last two years virtually glued to a laptop, and I wanted to do anything but parse, analyse, and type. I wanted desperately to be outdoors and out from under deadlines, and I wanted to be the person *doing* something instead of the person *writing* about other people doing things.

At the same time, I was aware that my coursework on sense of place and material culture was precisely what made Jack's and Angharad's work so meaningful to me. The intricate mix of traditional Welsh boundaries and gateways they erected on the Mall was beautiful, yes, and so was watching them build it, but it did more than visually conjure the landscape of their homeland. Modern Welsh culture is still rooted deeply in what its land could yield historically, from coal and slate to sheep and steel. Angharad's design told that story: the close and evolving relationship between people, land and labour. Moreover, it spoke to the lasting beauty and relevance of traditional, local craftsmanship in a world so often filled with cheap, plastic, Chinese imports, manufactured on a grand scale in grim conditions. Transporting these old-style walls, fences, and gates – ubiquitous features of the Welsh landscape that are simply part of the backdrop of life – some 4000 miles from home and suddenly juxtaposing them in a grand, non-native public space had transformed them into powerfully evocative symbols.

These were precisely the things I'd been studying in graduate school: how place, identity and tradition intertwine in the present and in the stories we tell about ourselves. The folklorist in me was delighted – and it was nice for me to think about these things without having to regurgitate theoretical essays for once.

My new Welsh friends had impressed me in so many ways during the handful of weeks we were together in America. They had worked tirelessly in extreme conditions, were finely

13

attuned to aesthetic details most would never notice, and they never missed a chance at a joke – in English or in Welsh. They were beautifully articulate about their work and happy to talk about it on practical or intellectual levels. They were so clever about so many things, and *they worked with their hands*. These were some of the warmest, most dynamic and inspiring human beings I had ever encountered.

On the last Sunday morning of the festival I stood on the National Mall with tears running down my cheeks as I listened to dozens of Welsh men and women singing hymns in their mother tongue. A mix of strangers, curious passers-by and new friends stood in a semi-circle bathed in morning sunlight, and our ears filled with the sounds of a traditional Gymanfa Ganu – a gathering of Welsh-language sacred music in a kind of four-part harmony that made me melt. I was exhausted and emotional after weeks of endless work and intense experiences. Many of us were, and hungover to boot. I was struck as I always am when faced with strong, sincere singing voices, overwhelmed by the simple beauty of it. My people, I knew, would be too timid, too self-conscious to make such proud and joyful sounds, but the Welsh *love* to sing. These farmers and artisans were singing from some-where deep inside, and the thick July air seemed to hang even heavier with the enormity of their voices.

The last Sunday is always emotional, but the group I was least excited by in the beginning had made this festival a very special one for me. Wales and its people had touched my core. For three weeks I had watched the Welsh greet the world with huge, loving hearts and the greatest enthusiasm – and I wasn't ready to say goodbye to them yet. We had one hotel party left to go that night, and that was it. The tents would soon be taken down, the stone walls disassembled, the steel gates lifted off their hinges. I felt bereft already, keenly aware that something very special was about to vanish from my world.

Jack had invited me during his last few days in America to come share his home in Wales and try a bit of dry-stone walling with him out in the hills, but I was too exhausted and too busy at that point to consider his offer, which – frankly – I hastily dismissed as crazy and probably too good to be true. No one is *that* kind. We *all* believe at the end of *every* festival that we will keep in touch with all our wonderful new friends. It has been an intoxicating and magical few weeks we've shared together. No one wants it to be over, but eventually we all return to real life, where we usually find we have far less time, energy and emotional investment available for that sort of thing than we'd hoped. I'd already been through it once on the previous year's festival (the Prince of Bhutan and I were not, in fact, still in touch). So when the time came for Jack to go home, I bade him a sad, uncertain farewell.

We kept emailing in the weeks that followed, unable to let the magic of the festival die. Jack sent me long, entertaining emails, full of anecdotes and – importantly – photos of a very beautiful countryside. I felt like I was getting to know him in a different way – without the frenzy of the festival as a distraction – and the images looked so alluring on my laptop screen, especially since I was otherwise faced with the hundreds of pages of notes that I was painstakingly turning into a Master's thesis. He made sure I knew his offer of room, board and work was genuine. There it was in writing.

Before long, he sent news that Angharad, Goddess of the Forge, would also open her doors to me if I turned up in Wales. My hero – my stereotype-smashing, swashbuckling feminist hero – was waiting to show me the ropes. And introduce me to her kids.

Was I this lucky? Was I crazy enough to go?

15

I still wasn't sure – but I also couldn't get it out of my head.

As a parting gift in Washington, Jack gave me a model dry-stone wall that he had built in his spare time. I put it on my desk alongside a few other festival trinkets when I got back home, and as I sat trying to focus on my thesis, the wall kept catching my eye. It was an incredibly poignant little thing, built to technical perfection with tiny fragments of stone chipped off the big pieces he used to build on the Mall. Set on a hillside of plywood scrap, he had meticulously stuck together each tiny piece with a dab of wood glue. One end is unfinished, tumbling down like a field wall waiting to be restored after a sheep or a snowstorm or simply gravity had opened a gap.

Angharad's sculpted steel tree sat behind me, its 2-metre-wide boughs awkwardly squished into a corner of my top-floor flat. I had loved this tree since I watched her do the cold-bending to make its curling branches. I'd helped her carry it out across the Mall, where it sat in a tent so that children could hang leaves of paper on it, scribbled with their ideas of Wales. After being deemed too big to be transported to Wales in the sea container (by which I mean another of the advance team made that decision because he knew I wanted it) it appeared like magic by my trailer door one afternoon. I came back to find it after a series of stressful errands, and I wept. I rented a truck and drove it all the way to my apartment in North Carolina, where it now sat in a setting far too inelegant for its beauty.

I had to go to Wales.

It made absolutely no sense to do so. I tried to be honest with myself. Was I just a victim of the post-festival blues, refusing to close the door on a magical experience and return to real life? Was I simply burned out from two years non-stop at a laptop and looking for any excuse to run away? Maybe.

I didn't have any money, really, and there was still a very long slog ahead to finish my MA. My committee would surely be furious. This reeked of procrastination. Probably my parents wouldn't be too happy either.

Exactly what plan did this fit in with, and did it make any sense financially? Everyone was nervous about my graduation and my finances. (I was, too, but less than most.) It's true that I wasn't tied to a job after the festival was over, but I would need one before long, so shouldn't I be focused on that? on responsibility? I had a lease on an apartment that still had to be paid, and student loans that would come into repayment before long. Wales did not have money to offer me – but what it did have was adventure and intrigue. And, to be honest, money has always bored me. I'm not a very good capitalist, American though I am.

But I wanted to go, and in my core I knew I *had* to – I had a sense that I would regret it forever if I let the opportunity pass me by. So what if I got my diploma a little later? Besides, I was sure I'd have quiet nights to work on my thesis while I was away. How much distraction could there possibly be in the middle of nowhere?

My parents, as I expected, weren't exactly enthusiastic about my decision to put aside my graduate study and take off across the ocean for . . . what exactly? I thought they were being mistrustful. I'm sure they must have thought I was being naïve and irresponsible. After twenty-six years with me, however, they could be certain of one thing: I was incredibly headstrong once I made up my mind to do something. Six or twenty-six, I was determined.

Let's be clear: before I'd made the decision to go to Wales that first time I'd done all the things I was supposed to and only a few of those that I wasn't. (Most of the latter were my little secret anyway.) I had been dutiful. I had networked

17

and achieved. I had played by the rules and been mostly responsible. A+ student, valedictorian, 'Most Likely to Succeed', Phi Beta Kappa, Dean's List, *summa cum laude*, et cetera. I had a plan, and it followed on logically from all of my previous, predictable, easily digestible achievements. I had been unimpeachable thus far. I always played it safe, and I was terrified of imperfection. Wales was the first thing tantalising enough to compel me out of living so cautiously. I had begun to wonder at last what I would miss if I were to continue my obsession with ticking all the right boxes and hitting all the traditional markers of success and achievement right on time. In Jack and Angharad, I had seen another way to live.

My mother was unsure of my decision, but my father outright disapproved. Mom had been out shopping for tough new work trousers with me despite her reservations because, as she would later tell me, she admires how brave I am. Dad, on the other hand, barely spoke to me for a month after I announced I was going to Wales. He wasn't thrilled about my decision to cross the ocean to live with people I barely knew. After weeks of giving me the cold shoulder both at home and on our family beach vacation, he finally decided to bring it up as I was walking out the door to drive back to my apartment. 'I need to talk to you,' he said.

I was already annoyed with him about this stalemate. His timing did not help his case.

'How would you feel if I told you I didn't want you to go?' he asked, doing what protective fathers do.

Why, I complained silently to myself, must we talk about this right now? As I'm walking out the door in a rush? After all this time at home? I was exasperated. I stifled as much of my sighing and eye-rolling as I could. I knew that he meant well.

'I would say I'm going anyway,' I replied in as measured a tone as I could muster, 'and it would be nice if we could find a way for you to feel better about it.' I remember feeling quite proud of this answer, shocked by my deft and polite rebuttal. (Words generally fail me in conversations that matter. I am a slow thinker no matter how quickly my mouth may move. I'd just managed to sound formidable and clear for once.)

He was not satisfied. There were more questions. 'How would you feel if I went to Wales for three weeks and brought home someone your age?' Why, he prodded, was this significantly older man being so kind to me by inviting me to live and work with him? Did he have an ulterior motive?

Dad had met Jack briefly when he visited the festival, watching us dance at a packed-out evening concert under one of the huge white tents. But I had danced that night with everyone from a fifty-nine-year-old Welshman to a twenty-year-old female intern. I just liked to dance, and despite being built like a very strong and frightening rugby player, Jack moved with an amazing amount of grace and no shortage of enthusiasm. I had shaken off the reserve of my Southern Baptist roots. Beer helped, and so did the festival atmosphere. No one ever cut loose at home. People didn't revel unselfconsciously. This had obviously unsettled my father.

What is it, I wondered to myself, about the sight or even *thought* of older men and younger women that is so threatening in the eyes of the world?

In answer to his second question about how I would feel if roles were reversed, I said, 'I might not understand, but I would try, because obviously you would have seen something in her, and I love you.' Besides, I was not romantically interested in Jack at all, so why did any of this matter? It was the work I longed for – stone and metal – and a countryside I could only imagine. And, frankly, I just wanted this

19

conversation to be over. We don't do direct confrontation in my family. This was a rare moment, and I was getting very squirmy.

Dad was not satisfied with these answers, but he did relent. In the end, we simply did our normal, understated goodbye in the kitchen, a ritual we'd been through many times over the years as I'd driven off to one distant school or another.

'Love you,' I said.

'Love you, too,' he said. 'Be careful.'

And with that, I was out the door and on the road. Thank *God*. Ten minutes had been more than enough time in the hot seat for me. That's the thing about having been so well behaved all my life: I wasn't at all used to being scrutinised over impropriety or recklessness. I wasn't sure if I had felt more infuriated or humiliated as I sat through those awkward questions – especially at twenty-six rather than seventeen – but I was relieved that it was at least over.

I was glad, too, that I was getting on the plane if not with my father's blessing then at least with his speaking to me again. Who knew what was to come? It's not as if I had steely nerves about my upcoming adventure to begin with. There was a lot I didn't know. I didn't need him rattling me to boot.

Anxiety is my background noise. Has been my whole life. Public speaking, parties full of strangers, ordering at the drive-thru window, not knowing the right answer in class – it's all unnerving for me. You wouldn't know it to talk to me, but it's always there, lurking, taunting, ruffling feathers. The strange blessing of it – which I don't think of in the worst moments, when I feel as though I am on a runaway raft in a frighteningly dangerous river with lots of jagged rocks – is that in my brain ordering at the drive-thru window is not so different from getting on a plane across the ocean to go live and work with strangers for four months. They're all sort of

20

the same, these scenarios, from the everyday to the extraordinary. In a way, being anxious about everything emboldened me for bigger things – for adventures. When *everything* is scary, it's no big deal to choose the crazy option.

That first trip to Wales would be only the beginning.

Croeso i Gymru – Welcome to Wales

Waiting at Detroit airport on my layover between Greenville and London, I was hit by a wave of last-minute terror. What on *earth* had I done?! This was crazy! I imagined all manner of worst-case scenarios, and I worried about how I might save myself when I had no close contacts in Britain, not much money, and no mobile phone. But I was in motion, and I could not turn back now.

I landed in London the next morning, and Jack picked me up. By the looks of him, he was just as nervous as I was. He must have been wondering what on earth he'd been thinking, too, when he asked me to come . . . last-minute jitters in the face of encroaching reality. He looked thinner. We hugged gladly, but slightly awkwardly. He insisted on taking my absurdly heavy luggage as we walked to the car. Once we got everything into his little white Ford Fiesta, he couldn't figure out how to work the machine that would raise the mechanical arm and free us from the bowels of Heathrow's Terminal 4 car park. Eventually, with traffic backing up behind us, a shockingly patient attendant helped us get out. Jack must have been mortified at how incompetent he seemed in the eyes of his young visitor, but I laughed it off. I was more intrigued that he was sitting on the *right* side of the car and driving on the *left* side of the road.

We headed west through the English countryside, chatting nervously, each being uncharacteristically formal and polite. We stopped at a pub somewhere between the Cotswolds and the Forest of Dean for a proper Sunday roast lunch, complete with Yorkshire pudding (a strange blobby thing that didn't look anything like any pudding I'd ever had, but soaked up gravy nicely). I was relieved to have a drink. The wine that steeled my nerves in Detroit was long gone, and though things were going fine so far – I'd been picked up on time, and Jack hadn't suddenly seemed like an axe-murderer – I welcomed a top-up of liquid courage.

Soon after lunch we crossed the border into Wales. I remember even now that everything seemed to become more beautiful in an instant (and the Cotswolds aren't exactly an eyesore). Even through my bleary-eyed jet lag I could see that it was a very pretty place, more vivid and romantic than any photos could show, and I had looked at plenty beforehand.

Jack drove me to his cottage via a slower and more scenic route. We wended our way along tiny, curving lanes, lined by hedgerows and holloways so ancient and deep they sometimes felt like tunnels, enveloping us and blocking out the light. The sky, when I could see it, seemed always to be changing, and the light had a completely different quality – a sort of tenderness and drama – from anything I'd ever seen at home. There were a *lot* of sheep. I mean, sheep were *everywhere* – even lying lazily in the road in some places! It was cold already, and the leaves were just beginning to turn from green to yellow with the arrival of October.

The roads hardly seemed big enough to be two-way, and in fact they weren't. (So many particularities of Welsh country life became apparent to me on day one.) There were regularly positioned wide spots that one car would reverse into if two met nose to nose, or one might politely pull in ahead of time if the other car – or perhaps an enormous tractor towing an even more enormous implement – was spotted in time. I sometimes had to get out and open a gate, let Jack drive the car through, shut the gate, and then get back in. It was a complete novelty.

Eventually, we got to Beulah, Jack's village. I'd only seen it in those satellite photos he and I had browsed through in my office trailer some months before. Located in the county of Powys in Mid Wales, Beulah sits about four miles up the A483 from Llanwrtyd Wells, home to the World Bog Snorkelling Championship, and about eight miles from Builth Wells, home to the Royal Welsh Agricultural Show. I have to say it was noticeably less picturesque than many places we'd seen that day. There wasn't anything quaint about it from the main road. I wouldn't say I felt disappointed, but I wasn't exactly charmed by the smattering of modern bungalows, the one lonely petrol station or the thoroughly modern brick and pebble-dash pub across the car park. It wasn't until we turned off the main road and then took a right by a picture-postcard village church that things began to look as magical as I'd hoped.

After a few more gates and a slow drive up his bumpy gravel track, we finally arrived at Jack's little stone cottage in the late afternoon. I would never have guessed there was a house at the top of these fields, hidden amongst several hills and visible only from one. It felt incredibly protected, as if no one would or even *could* find us unless we wanted them to. In truth, we were only a mile out of the village and surrounded by working farms and a 4000-acre estate, but as a child of suburbs and subdivisions, I had never known such glorious privacy or space. Perhaps others in my situation might have been slightly unnerved by such comparative isolation, but I simply felt relieved. No one knew where to find me! As I stepped out of the car and into the open air, responsibility suddenly felt very far away. Danger felt impossible. Jack's gravel track might as well have been a drawbridge over a moat full of angry alligators. I could exhale, and I did.

A grey tabby cat greeted us. Sheep bleated peacefully over the beech hedges, and unfamiliar little birds skittered here and there. Unruly yellow roses framed the indigo blue door, and the plastered front side of the house was painted rather prophetically the colour of butter. There were various bits of heavy, rusty metal strewn about the garden ... old ploughs and chaff cutters, cast-iron wheels from some enormous machine long gone. These were nearly lost amidst untidy tangles of lush, damp grass. There were Land Rovers in varying states of disrepair, bits of carved stone and old roofing slates Jack must have picked up over the years. There was something elemental about the place – honest, perhaps – and I found beauty in its rustic simplicity. I distinctly remember there was no traffic noise – a marked absence compared to any soundscape I had ever known. What I was aware of more than anything else was the overwhelming scale and grandeur of the land itself. It felt like he and I were on a small island of civilisation in the middle of an enormous rolling ocean of green.

Inside, Blaen Cammarch was a tidy, cosy little place. Jack told me his sister had done a marathon clean in preparation for my arrival, horrified that a young American woman would be coming to stay in his house. 'She was very distressed over the state of my floors,' he laughed. His kitchen, I learn, is normally filled with various old tools and antiques in some phase of restoration. It smelled like it still, some combination of beeswax and fossil fuels and toast. I found it strangely comforting. There was an oil-burning Rayburn in the kitchen, plus a wood stove in the lounge across the small foyer.

'Would you like some tea, Miss Brown?' I was nearly catatonic by the time we arrived, having spent a solid twenty-four hours both awake and in motion. This would be my initiation to tea's restorative powers.

Upstairs, my bedroom window was situated in the front gable of this sixteenth-century house with its walls that stood an astonishing foot-and-a-half thick. It looked out over a beautiful, sloping field and up towards a wooded hillside. It would get gorgeous morning sun, I could tell already.

As I looked out, Jack joined me at the window. He told me that the River Cammarch ran below the house, just down to the left and across a field. He pointed, but it was shielded from view by the stands of hazel and oak that lined its banks. A steep and densely wooded hillside rose from what must have been the other side of the river. At its top rested an Iron Age burial chamber, Jack said, long ago ruined by enthusiastic but slightly haphazard Victorian excavation. 'We'll walk up sometime.' He paused to admire the swifts nesting in his eaves, swooping in and out of their temporary home.

Jack had run me a bath, and there I relished the first alone time I'd had in very long while. I sank down into the welcoming tub, exhausted, and grateful for safe passage, for generosity, for beauty and true quiet. Again, I looked through a window towards the woodland above the Cammarch and I knew that I was exactly where I needed to be. 'Thank God,' I murmured, lips just above the water's surface. I shut my eyes, sank deeper, and let the water fill my ears, blocking out the world. I lost all sense of time. I simply stayed until the water got cold.

I can't remember now if I napped after the bath that day, but I remember putting on warmer clothes and walking with Jack up the hill behind the house that evening as the sun began to set. I remember how incredibly charmed I was that we could literally walk out of his door, through the back fields, and up a mountain. No trails, no parks – just well-established, perfectly bucolic British rights-of-way and farm tracks. In America, we would have been trespassing.

We climbed stiles, opened and shut yet more gates (sometimes battling baling twine knots that substituted for a working latch), and inevitably scared a few sheep farther off into the fields as we walked. After we passed through a hanging oak wood on our way up, I found myself in an undulating, treeless wonderland. Soon, we reached the top of the hill, and I stood agape at the patchwork green that stretched out below me, bathed in more and more golden light as we lingered there. The scene evolved quickly, hurtling towards the sublime until eventually the threatening darkness forced us back downhill. It was so beautiful I felt as if I'd been watching some sort of panoramic film, not looking with my very own eyes. I was in a state of disbelief, virtually drunk on a cocktail of pastoral glory and jet lag. We saw not a soul.

The next day Jack drove me south towards the Valleys, a misleadingly named region since most of Wales is hills and valleys, but the Valleys proper were home to the mighty steel furnaces and coal mines that helped build and power the British Empire. We were on our way to visit some of his old walls around the farms of Carmarthenshire. While we were down that way, we paid a visit to Angharad, too.

She put the kettle on immediately. Being new to Welsh homes and still a bit foggy-headed from jet lag, I hadn't quite got the tea ritual down yet and honestly just didn't need as much caffeine as these people seemed to, but the folklorist in me knew that I was experiencing an important gesture of hospitality. Was I doing it correctly? Being polite enough? Taking my tea the right way? Eating the appropriate number of biscuits? I would realise before too many more days that it's like *breathing* to Welsh people, serving you tea. It's automatic. Important, but unceremonious. I needn't have worried. So long as you say yes to tea you're OK.

We drank Earl Grey, as we would do every single day we were together after that. (I believe at any given time she has more Earl Grey than blood in her veins. Coal fuels the forge, but bergamot-scented tea fuels the blacksmith.) I couldn't tell you what we talked about that afternoon, but I remember being fascinated by everything around me: sights, sounds, colours, accents, manners. Importantly, I got my first glimpse of her workshop. I would join her there closer to Christmas.

As we drove to and fro on the famously winding roads of Mid Wales, I kept staring out the window saying 'Wow', forever impressed by some beautiful scene along the roadside. I realised, too, why it can take six hours to drive the 150 miles that stretch between this tiny country's north and south coasts: one is forever applying the brakes, downshifting, heeding the endless sharp, chevron-marked bends. The occasional car-sized hole in the hedgerow, strung across with police tape, served as a cautionary tale for the speeding driver. Jack seemed to know the roads like the back of his hand, and I was sure he could have driven them in his sleep. He even had the gear changes memorised.

It was clear that I would not have to learn Welsh – even the road signs were bilingual, much to my entertainment – but it was time to learn the language of walling . . . a new visual and physical way of understanding the world and interacting with it. That was why I had come. I had taken in the scenery and the rituals of this new place, and I'd bought the gear I would need. Now, it was time to get down to work.

Those first few days in Wales, making preparations and imagining what wonders and delights lay ahead, had all the anticipation of Christmas Eve.

Y Mynydd – *The Mountain*

A day or two later, after I had slept off some of my jet lag, we headed south along the A470 past Talgarth and Pengenffordd towards a farm called Grafog ('wild garlic' in Welsh, I learned). It was tucked away in a narrow valley, hidden from most of the world. The wall we were reconstructing ran up the slope of a mountain, a boundary between a family farm and the open hillsides of the Brecon Beacons. After nearly an hour in the car, we walked almost a mile through the fields from the farmyard where we parked, passing cattle and sheep, stepping across streams and climbing fences, with picks and shovels balanced over our shoulders and lunch boxes, flasks and waterproofs in our rucksacks.

Here on this first job site, I would begin stripping out an eighteenth-century mountain wall so that we could rebuild it. No one had touched this wall since it was hastily constructed by great gangs of wallers several hundred years ago after the Acts of Enclosure, and as we took it apart I found the broken clay pipes that had belonged to the original builders, still hidden within, cast aside when they'd outlived their usefulness. It was a moment of surprising intimacy. I felt connected to these anonymous men (as they surely would have been in those days) whose craft I was beginning to learn. I wondered who they were, whether they enjoyed their work . . . To add to my amazement, Jack explained to me that this was the exact same type of stone that had supplied the materials for the walls he built in Washington. This was the local stone – Old Red Sandstone – but the same seam from Pennsylvania runs along the floor of the Atlantic Ocean and pops up again in Wales. I found a certain symmetry and poetry in this image, and it seemed yet another sign that I had come to the right place.

There was much to learn. This wasn't like stopping by Jack's post at the festival to pick up a sledgehammer and relieve a bit of stress through what I affectionately termed 'smash therapy'. Across the ocean on a working farm, this was the real thing. I had to fit all the pieces back together, and what I built would be tested by leaping ewes, scratching cattle, driving winds and drifting snows. Real field walls take a beating day in, day out, all year long . . . for centuries.

There were the technical parts of a wall: foundations, courses, throughstones, coverbands, cope stones and hearting. I had to learn to recognise them all so that I could strip out properly, sorting and arranging the components into their appropriate classes and locations. As I stripped out I learned a wall's parts in reverse, starting from the top and working towards the foundations. (This one wasn't a total collapse. It was still recognisable as a wall, just slumped.) Not every stone could be used for every purpose – they were not necessarily interchangeable parts, depending on the style of wall, I learned – so some special kinds had to be grouped and conserved for the right application. Hearting went into piles nearest the wall so it could be constantly accessed. It was the small stuff – scraps and shards – that went in between the bigger pieces, filling any internal gaps and functioning as shims would for a carpenter. Copes, coverbands and foundations tended to be particular shapes suited to their purpose, so they were all separated out from the primary building stone. Copes were placed furthest away since they were used last in building. Coverbands went on the wall just before the copes, so they went out to the furthest edges of the sorting, too. Foundations went nearest the wall since they were first to go back in and heaviest to move. You wanted to move them as little as possible so you weren't wasting energy, and if the foundations were sound, we didn't disturb them at all. The regular building stone – and there was an awful lot of it – was laid out in long rows like books on a shelf, roughly grouped by size. I was astounded by how much work it was just to get ready to build. I was exhausted before we started.

Once the wall was stripped out, we were ready to begin rebuilding. I learned to dig stepped foundation trenches to work with the steep hillside. If we let the tops of the foundations run with the pitch of the hill, the wall atop them would be more likely to slip, so we essentially dug out stairs in mud so that the top of each stone – or several stones in a row – sat level. It made for much easier and sturdier building afterwards. Setting the foundation stones themselves was no easy task in a mud pit that was both sticky and slippery. It was a bit like a mud-wrestling match, only just one of the opponents is grunting and swearing. It can be slow and a bit frustrating at times, and it sometimes takes clever manoeuvring with shovels, picks and bars to get them *just so*. They *have* to be right, or the rest of the wall above it is compromised from the start. Do it right the first time, I learned.

31

Foundations in, I learned to add one course at a time (again, more complicated due to the steep slope we were working on), which meant moving back and forth along the wall like a typewriter, and always leaving a stepped, ragged edge ('racking back') so that the next section would tie in nicely. This was a complete rebuild and hundreds of metres long in total, so we broke it down into smaller sections, building perhaps 3 to 5 metres at a time after a 15-to-20-metre strip out. Tying all the pieces together properly meant always being careful to cross my joints from course to course. I could get away with a few near misses, but I had to keep an eye out for something called a rip seam or running joint – a line that runs up through multiple courses where joints either have not been crossed or have been crossed too closely to one another. This is where the wall may shear off in a collapse. It's a weakness that can be easily avoided with careful attention, but there are so many factors to juggle as you build that sometimes even experienced wallers can miss one creeping up.

I learned how to use hearting all along to make sure there's no empty space or room for settlement – to pack the middle and give the wall its strength. As I built each level, I was supposed to try to course them with consistent thicknesses, generally using the thicker stones towards the bottom and gradually moving on to thinner ones as I moved up in height. This type of stone allowed for that, but Jack said other geologies meant that the walls had random coursing. I would find it very challenging at this stage, he said, so that was a good wall to learn on.

Halfway up, we put in throughstones, ideally spaced about a metre apart, which reach all the way from one face of the wall to the other, helping to tie together the load. They're like a belt or a back brace for the wall. Dry-stone walls, really, are two walls leaning against each other – the lean is the batter – and if you look down on them from above, each side should be at least a third of the total thickness of the wall, reaching deeply towards its other half. I observed to Jack that it looked like a zipper if done well. All along we packed with hearting, carefully filling any little gaps under or between the bigger stones that made up the faces of the wall. Later, I learned at last to heave up the flat, heavy coverbands that give the wall a clean top line and cast a regular shadow for the eye to enjoy, and atop those went the cope stones for the final bit of weight and height.

I had to learn how to hold a hammer, work on my aim, brace a stone so that it breaks where you want it to, rather than in a spot that ruins its usefulness. (There is a lot of heartbreak involved in Hammer Use 101 and 102. One usually gets it tragically wrong and must start again in the selection process, though the shards will be useful somewhere eventually.) I had to learn how to shovel with my whole body instead of just using my arms and back. I had to remember, no matter what, to bend my knees. I had to learn to dress against a subtle and penetrating chill, how to throw a stone away from myself to avoid getting pinned if I found suddenly that I were falling, and how to keep the mud on my gloves from getting *too* smeared across my face as I wiped my constantly dripping nose. I learned, too, that sphagnum moss and foxglove leaves made the best loo paper if you needed them, and I learned the hard way that what looks a bit like lovely wild mint to a hurried amateur is actually a cantankerous plant called a stinging nettle . . . Accordingly, I was introduced to dock leaves as a remedy for the lingering sting of having made their acquaintance.

One of the biggest problems I had to tackle on the hill was not eating enough. Wallers burn through an astonishing number of calories in a day, and not eating enough leads not only to poor job performance as a result of flagging energy, but also to mood swings and distraction for me. I was turning into a useless crazy person simply because I wasn't managing my blood sugar properly, but I'd never had to think about that before. I'd simply grown up thinking of myself as the outsize woman who really ought not to get fat or she will *really* scare all the men away. Eating was a thing to worry about rather than a necessity of work.

Jack ate like a hog, and on a very regular schedule, and he wasn't ashamed of it. Nor was he fat. But he was a *man*, and for the most part, men think of weight and eating very differently than women do. 'This is hard graft, Miss Brown. You've got to fuel your body,' he would say. 'Think of what you're asking it to do. You might be moving six to eight tons in a day, and you need *thousands* more calories to do that day after day.' I really thought he just liked as many excuses to eat cakes and pies and cookies and doughnuts as possible . . . And this *was* true, but he had surveyed wallers all over the country as he worked on his dissertation on the walls and wallers of Wales, and they reported in on their diets. His numbers *were* convincing, but eventually my own experience told me that he was right: my body was running out of fuel about midway through the day. I just didn't want to carbo-load on refined sugar at *quite* the masterful level that he did.

I was about to discover something that felt like a revolution. Something Jack called 'elevenses' soon began to fill the gap between breakfast and lunch at the exact time I'd been hungry my *entire* life. (In the days when I did have an office job, I was often laughed at by colleagues for eating lunch so early in the day. Americans don't do the official mid-morning snack, and we are not driven by clockwork cups of tea like the Brits.) At 11 a.m. Jack and I put down our tools, got out the flask, and had tea and coffee with something sweet. This would give us the bump of caffeine and energy we'd need to get to lunch at 1 p.m. And some days I was so hungry I'd eat part of my lunch then, too, which Jack found endlessly amusing since not long before I was so afraid to eat at all. We developed an amusing daily lunch routine whereby he was vocally, dramatically disgusted by my peanut butter, I by his 'fish with heads' – sardines – which reeked enough to stink me out even on the side of a windswept mountain.

Gradually, I began to figure out how much I needed to eat and when. I learned to eat without guilt as I finally began to understand I wasn't a pig. I wasn't fat. I wasn't going to gain weight except a whole hell of a lot of muscle. My body was the machine, and I had to learn to power it. Once I did so, it served me well on the side of that slippery, exhausting mountain. I was still crap at building, but I was soon strong enough to move big stones up and down the hill as we needed them.

So much of what I experienced in those first weeks on the hill in Wales was frustration. Eating did help, but the truth is that I wasn't used to being bad at anything, at having to work at something slowly, at exercising patience with the learning process. And I *was* bad back then. I'm sure I was – and have been told so time and time again by Jack – a complete pain in the ass most of the time. But there was something about it all that I loved despite clumsily smashed fingers, ungracefully bruised shins, a sore back and a frustrated mind. There was something about it that I wanted desperately to own despite the difficulty. I think walling spoke to something ancient and essential in me – I knew that this was where I was supposed to be no matter how many expletives I might utter each day, or huffing hissy fits I might throw when I couldn't get the right stone in the right place in what I felt was a perfectly adequate amount of time. And no matter how many times I fell in the mud.

'Look at your line,' he would say, often as I was physically tangled in it. Or, 'Have you stepped back to look at that recently? You should. You can't spot all the problems there, but they're obvious from back here. You'll see what I mean. You should be stepping back regularly.' Or, 'I see a letter-box.' (That's a space where you can fit your hand in above or below a stone, and it's not good. Sheep can use that as a foot-hold to climb over. Tight walls are good walls.) Or, 'Check the angle of the face on that one.' I was picking up, throwing back off, obsessing over the 'perfect' stone, or trying desperately to find a home for one I'd become attached to for some reason (usually not a good one). I'm not sure how he could bear to watch me work sometimes. Or cope with my moods. On the other hand, I'm not sure how I managed not to throw a stone at his head when he sang 'Sentimental Journey' or 'Bali Hai' for the seven hundredth time in a week. He had his annoying habits, too, for the record.

Still, no matter how prickly I was at times – especially in response to his perfectly justifiable critiques and corrections or my lulls in blood sugar – Jack usually admonished me with a laugh just to get on with it. He called me pedantic, frustrated at how I fixated on imperfections to the point that I would simply stop progress until I figured out exactly what went in the spot in question. 'Sometimes,' he said, 'the best thing is to leave it for a while. Walk away, and when you come back later it's much easier.' He also told me even then that my pride in my craft – my natural obsession with getting it right – is something that can't be taught. As ugly as my bits of the wall were, he reassured me once in an unusually sincere moment that he wouldn't let me work on his projects if he didn't think I could do it.

Oh, but he *loved* to call me a 'weak and feeble woman', not only because he took every possible opportunity to wind me up, but precisely because he was regularly impressed with my physical strength. 'But your lifting technique is terrible! You're going to hurt yourself if you're not careful.'

We moved *tons* of stone each day by hand in a place that, to me, felt like heaven, rough and exposed though it was. There were hillside streams, waist-high bracken, hawthorn trees turning red with the onset of autumn. Clouds tumbled and swirled above us. A gentle commingling of dank grass, lanolin and mud scented the air. Our only regular company were disinterested sheep, tearing away at the grass all day, or wary cattle, always with an eye on us. Sometimes we were visited by red kites soaring and circling high above, or we might find the occasional toad or newt in the wall that required gentle relocation to safe harbour while we worked. Once, on the other hand, I looked up, startled by distant mechanical noise, only to see a farmhand approaching on his motorbike with a full-grown ewe draped across his lap, freshly rescued from being left behind on the hilltop after autumn gathering. The absurd is never far away in Wales, however beautiful it may be.

The work was one thing, but I simply couldn't get over the astonishing, shifting beauty of the surroundings. As a suburbanite native to a much flatter, hotter place, I was gobsmacked by the beauty and intricacy of the Welsh countryside, especially as I began climbing fences and getting away from the roads more and more. My experience was only enhanced by the company of a man who had come to know the natural world so intimately during his years on the hill. There was much to learn. Every day a picnic, an adventure, a safari of sorts. I was fascinated by *everything* around me. Entranced, really.

Was this real? Every day I wondered. Who was lucky enough to work in this place? to come to this office every day? Jack was. Now, apparently, I was, too. I could not have felt further from the hustle bustle of Washington or the pressures of graduate school. It was another world altogether. I wasn't sure how I'd got here or why, but I wanted to linger a while.

All along I assumed I was simply picking up yet another eccentric interest that would have no role in my suburban life back home. As far as I knew, I was simply taking a moment to indulge my curiosity and have a little fun. Little did I know. I had not yet begun to understand that sometimes when you say things out loud to the universe, the universe hears you. Things transpire, dreams come to fruition as actual plans and events. Invisibly, slowly, the pieces fall into place. As the old saying goes, be careful what you wish for because you might actually wind up with it. And then what? The original plan goes out the window. If you're both lucky and brave, you'll be happy about that. Doesn't mean it's not scary as hell though.

I had an inkling as I sat eating my lunch on a damp, muddy hillside in Wales one memorable day that first October that I hadn't got it quite right in my life back home. How could I? It's not as if as a little girl in South Carolina I could look around me or even at the TV, or a book, or a career catalogue at school and say, 'I'd like to be a dry-stone waller. Yes, that's it! Sign me up! What courses? Which internships?' Same for, say, wine importer, or orchardist, or bad-ass lady blacksmith . . . any number of things. Those don't come up when you take formulaic quizzes designed to help you figure out what careers might suit your fledgling interests. No, you get lists like 'engineer, nurse, teacher' or 'lawyer, doctor, accountant'. And so it had gone for me for many years.

But I knew that day that I was in the right place now – there, that very second – and somehow sensed that the life I

38

would go back to in a few months' time would suddenly be wrong. What I was doing in Wales seemed on the surface completely *non sequitur* – perhaps even a bit irresponsible – yet I knew it was right. I was supposed to be in America writing my Master's thesis on local, sustainable food communities and then off to the sort of job I'd been networking towards for seven years, but here I was across the ocean, covered in earth and mist, learning to build dry-stone walls. I wasn't sure what I would do about all that awaited me at home, but for the first time in years, I was at peace, and that was enough for now.

Wye Valley

By the time November arrived the weather was demonstrating precisely how drab and horrid it could be. Jack and I were on our way to the Elan Valley for the first time together, but we had one stop to make en route. Turning off the A470 up in the Wye Valley, we soon found ourselves on a circular drive, surrounded by sheds and barns.

We weren't sure we were in the right spot, nor even which door to approach to find out. We were there to look at a job, having received a call from a woman who needed some walling work done. It was hammering down, so I was automatically leaning towards disinterested. This sort of cold, soul-crushing rain has a direct impact on one's curiosity.

As we sat in the Land Rover keeping dry and warm, I felt intimidated by this place, by the rain, by my Americanness. Maybe we should just go? The engine was still running, our resolve weakening. This lady surely wouldn't want to meet us in this horrible weather anyway. She might be relieved if we didn't show.

We spotted a woman in head-to-toe waxed canvas making her way towards us across the drive. God, she was clearly a hardy soul to be out in this mess. Unfortunately, the fact that she had appeared meant we couldn't run now. I felt so annoyed at her.

But then she opened her mouth to greet us when Jack wound down the window, and out came a kind, melodic and most intriguing voice. It caught me off guard. She spoke softly, and with *beautiful* tone and inflection. She was English, I could tell, and not of the Eliza Doolittle variety either. Very, very elegant, if a bit soggy. Not the average farmer's wife for this neck of the woods, I knew even then. She was not at all what I had been expecting.

We switched off the engine and got out of the Land Rover at last. I just kept my mouth shut and walked along behind Jack, trying not to get my leather boots too wet in the sopping grass.

She led us quickly into a field to the site of the wall collapse, where they'd decided they wanted to put in a gateway rather than close the gap. Did we think we could possibly do that for them? I strained to hear her gentle voice over the rain pounding my hood.

There was something very special about this woman. I couldn't put my finger on it, but I knew within minutes I wanted to make her my friend. I had got as far as 'Hello'. I don't think I caught her name on that first visit, and she certainly didn't know mine. I spoke so little that I'm not even sure she noticed I was American.

We would come back to work on the weekend following, we all agreed. As Jack and I drove off on our way to the Elan Valley, I wondered quietly to myself about that woman . . . Who was she? She seemed so out of place given what I knew about Wales so far.

Unsurprisingly, it was still raining cats and dogs ('sticks and old women', as the Welsh would say in their own language) when we returned the next Saturday. To add to the morning mire, I had crushed my left middle finger in the heavy, hinged gate closure as we left the house that morning, which left me slightly handicapped for work – and very cranky. I just didn't want to be there. Bear-with-a-sore-head, should-have-stayed-in-bed kind of day. Down a middle finger – key to grip and to prying things up from sticky mud – I was far less useful than normal. But we got stuck into the job because, well, we'd promised.

Before long, the woman appeared again to greet us, asking in her mesmerising voice whether we'd like coffee at 11 a.m. Jack half waved her off, saying we were used to being self-sufficient and had a flask with us. 'You don't want to be out in this,' he said. But she asked if we were sure. We soon gave in, and the tides turned when she plodded up a short while later with hot coffee in *real* mugs from the kitchen. It was only instant, but it was – I think – the best coffee I had ever had in my entire life. The gesture meant so much. I was cold and soggy, and my finger was miserable, and she had walked these steaming mugs a long way in foul weather with intrepid hospitality. It certainly made an impression.

She stayed and talked with us a few minutes, interested in our progress. She was as warm with strangers as I imagined she might be if we were old friends she was happy to see again after a long absence. She had a natural charm about her, which put me at ease, and something about her felt extraordinarily kind. We laughed at the mud, turned our palms up to the sky in amusement at the pitiless rain. Jack mentioned I'd hurt my finger. The kind woman reappeared before long with arnica, which I'd never heard of, and insisted that I put some on immediately. 'It will help with the bruising.' She had these little tablets, too, that she said I should dissolve under my tongue. I remember they were sweet and looked like tiny pearls. She invited us in for lunch later – brave given the state of us. We were hesitant at first to accept, as wallers are self-effacing creatures and don't like to impose, but she insisted. 'Come inside and warm up.'

I remember my relief as we bashfully entered the warm kitchen after stripping off our dripping waterproofs and muddy boots in the hall. The Aga was fired up, and it was nice and toasty inside. There were some family members about, who politely said hello before disappearing to another part of the house to make space for us at the table. I suddenly wondered how much mud I had on my face.

It wasn't a big kitchen, but we sat down at the cosy table with Kate and her husband Richard (names are easier to catch in groups) to a lunch of beef tongue, cheese, bread, butter and beer. I think there was chocolate after, too. I felt very shy in such close quarters, but these were lovely, generous people who did their level best to make us feel welcome and cared for. And it was a sweet, cheerful space, full of personality, with postcards and photographs and posters on every surface that would hold them. Dried flowers and herbs hung from the ceiling, well-used utensils on the walls. It was the kind of lived-in kitchen I wanted for myself, layered both with decades of memories and bustling activity.

Warmed, fed and grateful, Jack and I dressed and headed back to our mud pit. Before the day was over, he was literally face-down in the mud with his arm completely submerged in a hole, trying to remove a stone that stood in the way of our successfully sinking in one of the two gateposts we'd been asked to place. It was an absurd scene. Some of the foundation stones we needed to roll out of the way simply didn't want to be moved. This was unusually heavy stone, and the mud had a suction effect, holding them firmly in place. Jack soon howled expletives, having snapped a tendon in his right wrist as he struggled to shift an obstinate stone. 'Fuck! Fuck! Fuck, fuck, fuck . . .' He clasped his wrist in his other hand, holding it tight to his belly. Suddenly, we were both the walking wounded, but stubbornly we carried on with two-point-five good hands and arms between us. It was exhausting and frustrating to work in that much mud with such heavy, awkward stone – this geology forced the much more complicated random coursing Jack had warned me about at Grafog – and our injuries did not help our cheer. Still, it made all the difference to work for thoughtful, creative people who appreciated what you were doing for them. There were several moments of pain and outright irritation when we might have called it a day had we not liked Richard and Kate so much.

Injuries, mud and all, Jack and I finished the job the next day (aided in large part by Kate's faithful coffee and cake deliveries), and we bade the pair a friendly farewell, cheque in hand.

Kate and Richard had been exceptionally kind, and I felt sad to think I might never see them again. We remarked several times the next few days on how lovely they'd been . . . that we wished there were some way we could thank them.

I was constantly making cakes for Jack in those days – feeling very grateful to be housed and fed and taught a trade – and I managed to pry half of one out of his clutches to deliver as thanks to Richard and Kate. We showed up at their front door in darkness and rain one night later that week, cake in hand. It was chocolate, and soaked in whisky. They looked a little shocked to find us on their doorstep, but seemed touched. We simply bade them a warm goodnight at the door and headed on our way.

Brynaman

I saw Angharad off and on over the autumn. Any time she had a trip into the city, she'd invite me along, worried that a young woman in the countryside alone with a man more than twice her age might be losing her mind. We'd go off to places like Cardiff, Aberystwyth and Lampeter if she had Eisteddfod committee meetings or a bit of arts coverage to film for S4C, the Welsh language channel of the BBC. I'd wander these places alone, perhaps stopping into a café or sitting on a stark shingle beach to write my journal and watch the people go by.

We'd gossip like mad in the car on the way to and from. It helped me miss my friends less. Angharad was a bit older than me and already married with children, but she still loved to talk about boys and to party when she could work it in around metal and parenting. She regaled me with stories from her wild days living amongst the artists and musicians in Cardiff before her kids came along, and then about childbirth, too. I think I told her – at her enthusiastic request – about every boy who had ever been part of my life, and we spent time parsing various characters from the summer's festival. She gave me my first bits of feminist education, too, telling me stories from the early days of her career when she was learning to deal with the men who deliver the steel and trade out the gas cylinders. She was a true ally from the start, and we always had a good laugh together.

When I finally joined Har – as I was encouraged to call her to reduce 'Welsh language fatigue' for my goofy American mouth – in the blacksmith shop after Christmas, another piece of the puzzle fell into place. It felt right from the start. I had seen Har's workshop on film, and it was slightly surreal to be there myself and add in all the sensory extras that don't come through on screen.

Despite being inside, sheltered from the wind and weather, and with a coal fire in the forge, I shivered at times – at least until I really got to pounding on a piece of steel and my muscles generated enough heat from within. The chimney pulled not only the smoke but also much of the radiant heat up, up and away. Radio Two was forever nattering away in the background, and half-spent cups of Earl Grey gone cold were corralled on the shop table alongside welding magnets and soapstone sketches. The workshop had its own distinctive atmosphere, so different from the open hill, but charming in its own way. Really, though, it was the woman who ran the place that made it so special. I could not believe my luck.

Coal smudges on her face and always in a manner that inspired confidence from the start, she taught me how to form a point on both round and flat steel stock using the hammer and the anvil, then how to curve it. I would learn to split metal, to rivet. Buried in a helmet and gloves, I strained to decipher the bright blobs I was seeing through the darkened glass that shielded my eyes as I tried my hand at MIG welding or watched Har work. I remember how difficult it was to trust the protection of the helmet as I leaned in so close to such an incredible amount of heat and electricity, dazzling sparks popping everywhere as the pieces of metal fused together just inches from my face, but in time I got comfortable. (Sparks occasionally finding their way down the back of my neck were another story.)

Next, Har let me try my hand at the plasma cutter, which was even more impressive than the MIG. So powerful it seemed a form of black magic, it shot a precise arc of ionised gas through steel at 20,000 degrees Fahrenheit, cutting quickly and cleanly. With tools this fearsome and fast, I had to be aware at all times of the whereabouts of every part of my body – especially my hair – or I might soon find myself on fire or seriously injured. It was a little terrifying if you thought too much about it, but it was an amazing thrill to wield such power – to literally play with fire.

Mostly, I helped with far more basic tasks like fettling, grinding and drilling, but always with an eye on what Har was doing. In America she had impressed us all with her cold-bending technique, running lengths of steel through what looked like a heavy-duty tuning fork sandwiched in a vice and then using her body weight as leverage. It was like watching ballet, though she was more likely to make jokes about the movie *Flashdance*, which featured a dancer who had to make her living as a metalworker. (She confessed with zero embarrassment that this was her initial inspiration to try her hand at steel.) It was amazing to watch her work using such elegant and controlled movements. She produced perfection with what looked like minimal effort, and if she made a mistake, she always fixed it easily. Unlike me, she never seemed flustered. It was all just practice, she said. I wanted to

47

be that good. I was determined now. Inspired. And she was happy to share all that she knew.

Living with Har, a native North Walian and a Welsh speaker, I finally began to get a proper immersion in the language, too. Jack had grown up in an English-speaking part of Wales, and his generation would never have had the option to learn Welsh at school as so many do now.

Downstairs one morning as I sipped my first cup of tea, I listened through the ceiling as her two little boys had a very enthusiastic discussion in their bedroom, all in Welsh except the words 'poo' and 'poo face'. I had to stifle my laughter. Har told me on my first visit that although her children had learned Welsh first and went to a Welsh-language school, they thought it was much cooler to speak English. That was what they heard on telly most of the time, of course, and their father, Tom, was a native English-speaker. Their chat was always a mix of the two, and even Welsh adults can often be heard speaking 'Wenglish' these days, peppering long strings of Welsh with words like 'brilliant' or 'fantastic'.

Some modern Welsh is only loosely Welsh anyway, perhaps subbing out a letter or two in the English spelling of words like *bws* (bus) or *tacsi* (taxi). It is an ancient language, and accommodations have been made to incorporate the modern world. There's no X in Welsh (or *Cymraeg*, as it is in their language), and W is a vowel, whereas U actually makes a 'ee' sound. *Cymru*, the Welsh name for Wales, is pronounced 'COME-ree', with the emphasis on the first syllable, though it typically falls on the penultimate in a longer word. I still find the language absolutely fascinating. It's a difficult one, and even now I only have about as much of it as a child just learning to speak, but with a bit of swearing and toasting and traffic signs mixed in. I am a product of my environment: Jack, pubs, Har's children and the bilingual signs that facilitate my travel and groceries.

You mostly get used to the spellings and pronunciations. Y is also a vowel and sounds as a short U in English ('uh' or 'uhr', depending on its neighbouring letters). Then there's F, which sounds an English V, but the letters Ff sound as an English F. D is pronounced the same as in English unless you see two of them, in which case Dd sounds as a soft English Th, as in 'the'. These might be a lot to remember at first, but they aren't difficult to pronounce.

The double-L, however, is vexing, and I tried to avoid saying those if I could. For me, the Ll sounds roughly like someone hissing or clearing mucus from her throat while saying a loosely formed 'L' at the same time, yet in the mouth of a native it is beautiful. Much subtler. Unfortunately, a lot of town and village names begin with Ll, and many of them lie along my regularly travelled routes. I sometimes name an adjacent village in conversation instead, or conveniently forget where I mean until someone suggests the place aloud for me. If it's unavoidable, I say it as quietly as possible, putting what is probably a rather puzzling decrescendo in the middle of my sentence. If I am unlucky and someone says 'Sorry?' and puts his hand to his ear, I am forced to repeat the scary place name loudly and badly, and with great shame and blushing. I know perfectly well how it is *supposed* to sound. I just can't. It seems insulting not to try, yet it sounds a bit rude when one does . . . the conundrum for the non-native speaker. And so instead we simply revel in words like *popty-ping*, which is the comparatively easily pronounced onomatopoeic Welsh for microwave.

I bashfully played with the language around the house with Har and her family, often practising my single-digit counting with Bryn, the youngest. Har also gave me plenty of space to play with metal in the shop in those days. Any scrap was up for grabs for practising points and curves, which gave me the freedom to see through any ideas I might have. She encouraged me to sketch, and looking over my shoulder one night she told me quite enthusiastically that I drew well. I was heartened to have someone so supportive at my back who understood intuitively why I had come. This was a woman to whom I never needed to explain my attraction to craft, to big tools, to hard work.

She was also a woman who could not bear to look at the burn on my forearm that resulted from my catching my sleeve on fire while working a piece hot out of the forge. 'I'm sorry, Whitney,' she said, cringing, 'I'm so good about my own injuries, but I can't look at them on other people!'

In the evenings, we watched rugby or total trash TV – far more charming with a foreign accent – and we'd laugh and drink wine and cook dinner together. I got used to stepping on Lego pieces left in the rug, helping with the washing-up and the wood stove, and sometimes making pancakes (*crempog* is the Welsh word) with the boys. I was soon part of the family . . . part of the workings of the shop, too, coming inside in the evening tired and a bit smoky and smudged, just like Har. I could not have been happier.

At Har's house, I was learning three things: how to work metal, how to speak a bit of Welsh, and how to be an utter bad-ass with power tools and sheer brute force while also being a really good mother. She was nothing if not a contradiction – at least according to the gender norms I knew – and it eased my mind simply to watch her live her life. She was tough *and* she was tender. She was sometimes filthy, sometimes in a frock. This I understood. I had both halves in me, too, only I never understood how to make them work as effortlessly as she did. She was just unapologetically herself – all the time, in every scenario.

Blaen Cammarch

It was the worst winter in thirty years, they said. On New Year's Day, Jack and I walked in the Radnor Hills atop banks of deep, drifted snow, striding right over the tops of five-bar gates. It looked like another planet altogether. Only the presence of Jack and sheep reminded me that I was still in Wales.

The snow kept coming. The roads became impassable within days, but work, too, would be impossible – even if we could get to it. The stones would be frozen to the ground and each other, the ground treacherously slippery with ice and tightly packed snow underfoot. We stayed close to home, mostly working on the next year's firewood supply. With three pairs of socks on under my wellies, I could be sweating everywhere else and still have numb feet. My gloveless hands ached (gloves were not allowed for axe work since they can affect your grip and cost you a foot) until my heart rate and core temperature finally increased enough to warm them from the inside out. The cold was brutal, and – coming from a more temperate part of the world – it was the first time I'd ever had to live with it.

Stuck at home for days on end, we finally became desperate enough one night to walk down for a pint or two of middling beer in a pub we knew we didn't like. Jack told me stories as we sat amidst the 1980s decor of an almost empty bar, and he soon had me laughing so hard I couldn't control my volume any longer no matter how quiet the pub was. There were tales from the Army, from being a driving instructor, from teaching . . . He could always find humour in both the absurd and the painfully human. As my laughter subsided, I began to reflect on what a strange stretch of days this was. I had learned a lot about timber and snow and even driving off-road in winter conditions, but I was reflecting on my life and myself, too.

What a snob I had been about working people, blue-collar folks, rednecks – whatever you want to call them. For the first time in my life I was beginning to understand how satisfying it is to work with one's hands as we chopped wood and worked on chainsaws, or as I built walls and toiled in the blacksmith shop. I had always assumed in my comfortable, intellectual life that the people who had those kinds of jobs – dirty jobs – hadn't done as well in school as I had, perhaps hadn't had a choice. It had never occurred to me that perhaps they chose their occupations because they found them interesting or satisfying – or that I might. Or that the work of life – keeping up the woodpile, for instance – could bring such contentedness.

A few days later, as we hunkered down by the wood stove against a blustery night only just kept at bay by his draughty old windows, Jack said to me, 'I hope this trip hasn't unsettled you too much. I feel terribly guilty.' I had probably been moaning again about graduate school and my dead-in-the-water thesis, or perhaps wondering how on earth I had lived twenty-six years of my life without wood stoves and country-side, chainsaws and walling hammers.

We'd been out coppicing hazel and hawthorn that afternoon before yet another snowstorm blew in, and when it finally got too wild outside to continue working, we came in to light the fire and pour a drink to warm us. Port for him, whisky for me. We were chilled to the bone by then. Between the weather and the work, it had been a punishing day – I could feel the windburn on my cheeks still, and my damp hair smelled of chainsaw exhaust – but there was something wonderful about it, too. How deeply rewarding to have the contrast of that cold, bitter work and to come in to the warmth of its result.

It was a peaceful moment by the fire, but I could see ominous clouds gathering on my own horizon. I worried aloud to Jack for a long time that night about how I would get on back in the 'real world' without these things in my life every day, and he worried about me in return. 'It just seems like this is how it's supposed to be,' I said, shaking my head in frustration as I stared into the glow of the fire. Hard work and countryside life now seemed part of my natural rhythm, and I felt bewildered at the very thought of their loss. I was going back instead to central heating, a laptop, near neighbours and traffic noise.

'I hope you will be all right when you get home,' he said, responding to the look on my face as much as the words I'd spoken.

'I don't know,' I said weakly, trying not to let my frustration turn into self-pitying tears.

He knew intuitively, having watched me out on the hill during those few months, that I was a wild animal soon to be taken into captivity, and it made him sad. He had been there himself years ago, and he knew what that was like.

This man, who had opened his home to me, taught me his ancient craft, and generously shown me an entire secret, sacred world that existed on the other side of the fence, felt like he had done me some sort of harm. I seemed unable to find any words to reassure him that this had been a good thing – a magnanimous and incomparable gift. Jack felt that he was responsible for derailing me. He wasn't . . . at least not in a negative sense. He was, however, responsible for bringing me to life – for giving me the things I suddenly felt I couldn't live without. It had been an extraordinary and transformative few months, and I felt profoundly grateful even as I knew that I probably wouldn't be OK. I think both of us knew that we had opened a sort of Pandora's box in my life. In a sense, there was no going back. I couldn't shove the lid back on the box, and frankly, I didn't want to, no matter how big a mess I might have made. Wales, I knew, would haunt me.

I had been longing to feel relevant, to find satisfaction at the end of my workday, and to feel grounded. I found all these things for the first time while I was away in Wales. Graduate school had given me nothing of the sort. The Smithsonian was better, but still it was often roundabout fulfilment: I took pride in being part of something much bigger than myself – something I felt was a wonderful service to the people. In Wales, it was the opposite: I took comfort in the fact that I could step back at the end of the day and *see* what I'd done, feel it bodily. My work was concrete and substantial, my relevance obvious.

After so many years working at a computer, I took comfort in the ancient lineage of the work, in the age and heft of the stones, the ring of the hammer, the true privilege of being in

54

touch with nature and my own physical being. I relished every glimpse of the precious sun as it peeked through the clouds for a moment, every sore muscle, every chance to stand atop a piece of wall we'd just finished, feeling – if only for a moment – like the strongest woman alive. Even days laced with fatigue or frustration were good days by quitting time. I finally understood what I needed work to be.

Jack had shown me a way of life out in the hills that I couldn't have imagined, and it felt like my second skin. I had really bonded with Angharad and her family as I lived with them and worked at her side in the shop during my last two months in Wales. I'd survived blisters, bruises, back injuries, burns, homesickness and the biggest blizzard in Britain since the winter of 1962–3. I had learned volumes during my time away – about myself, work, art and life – but there was so much more I needed and *wanted* to know. I was terrified to go back to a comfortable, tidy suburban life with no need for physical labour of any sort, and I didn't know when I might see these friends again.

What was I supposed to do with all of this? I felt powerless.

I dreaded my return to America for that reason. In some ways, it did feel like time to return to my home country – I had been gone a long time, and my mother had undergone a heart procedure on New Year's Eve while I was snowed in and helpless to get home even if I'd had to – but at that moment, the suburbs seemed about as welcoming to me as the frigid wind howling outside the panes. It's not that it was a bad life I'd been living at home, but I simply wasn't going back the same person. Wales had changed me in fundamental ways, and all that I'd fallen in love with there made no sense with the life I'd left behind me in America. The two pieces did not fit each other. There would be friction when they met. How would I manage now, different as I felt?

To make matters worse, I knew no one would understand what had happened to me while I was away. I wasn't sure that I did yet, truth be told, but I knew it was big. I was aware that I would soon be faced with everyone's questions and expectations even as I was struggling to process it myself. People would ask about my trip, but I knew I couldn't really explain. What I had been through was an experience that didn't fit so well into words. Wales was the first place that ever made any sense to me. It was the first place that I ever made any sense to myself, and I loved what I had discovered. I didn't know how to tell people that everything I'd been working towards all those years now didn't mean so much to me. I didn't know how best to say that I might look and sound the same, but in fact I *wasn't* – to announce that I did not fit my own life.

I flew west in a heartbroken daze, prepared to dutifully stifle a new vitality in myself I had come to relish, but what I found in Wales had stirred up a sea change in me that eventually I could not fight.

Durham, North Carolina

Unsurprisingly, when I returned from Wales in February I was a bit lost. For one thing, I was stuck inside now. I took a job at a hip little bakery in Durham, North Carolina, as I finally tried in earnest to write my Master's thesis. I'd begun to understand while I was away in Wales why so many of history's great thinkers and writers have not been people who've laboured in the fields or blacksmith shops all the day long only to come home and be brilliant at night. Most days, I had nothing left by nightfall, and my thesis fell by the wayside once again. I couldn't put it off any longer now. I would cook by day and write by night.

It jarred me to go straight from the wilds of Mid Wales to work under fluorescent lights in a professional kitchen that didn't boast a single window to the outside world. I was grateful that I was still working with my hands in some way and to be learning something every single day from my chef, who truly was brilliant, but there was no mountain air, no birdsong, no breeze, no wood to split, and absolutely no solitude. 'Stifled' doesn't begin to approach what I felt. The bakery was exciting – a little twenty-four-seat joint that cooked seasonally and did a banging farmers' market business as well – but I walked around in a daze most of the time, dividing my time between a job that punished my body and an arduous task that punished my mind, and the latter didn't pay.

I had to push on, though I did so on autopilot. I was still working towards my original goals because a life in craft just didn't seem possible at that point. It looked like a long-term position as a historical researcher on a landmark exhibition would soon materialise for me in Washington if I could get my thesis finished. I was supposed to want that, and I kept telling myself that I still did. The thing is, I hadn't come back from Wales the same person, and it showed. I'd been granted committee approval the year before for a thesis project on local food communities, but now all I wanted to write about was craft revivals and hands-on, creative work. I thought I could squeak by with this, writing mostly about the young farmers and chefs in my community who'd chosen their back-breaking work because they felt passionately about it and wanted to do physical, creative jobs no matter how much education they'd attained. I was writing about myself, of course, and it was only thinly veiled. My committee were not pleased with the delays in my progress or the shifts in my focus.

By August, the Smithsonian job offer was indeed before me, but I simply couldn't muster any excitement for the very thing I had worked and networked for seven years to get. The Smithsonian is the big league for folklorists and historians. Job openings there are as rare as hens' teeth, and highly competitive. Miraculously, I was being handed one. I was grateful, but balked. Suddenly, I simply couldn't stomach the idea of Washington – the commute, the business clothes, the days spent at a computer, the meetings. Wracked with guilt over what my gut was shouting, I talked to innumerable loved ones and mentors about my fate. All but two said, 'Go! It's a wonderful opportunity! It's what you've been waiting for! Congratulations!' Jack was one of the two who understood my hesitation. Even my boss, who really couldn't spare me at that point, told me to go.

I cried for days as I tried to get up the courage to say no. 'No' was the only answer I had in my heart no matter what anyone else said or what made sense on paper. I knew by then that the only women I had ever really identified with were a blacksmith and a baker. I understood them as workers (artists, really), as mothers, as friends, and as members of their communities. Angharad and my chef had both inspired me to think outside the box and consider less traditionally 'successful' career paths. I was no longer after prestige – just excellence and satisfaction, and maybe in dirty clothes.

I had grown to love my job in the kitchen, and I knew how much I could learn from my boss if I stayed. She was an amazing talent, and everyone knew it. It was mesmerising to watch her make pastry, and at the stove she was inventive without pretension or fluff. She encouraged me and gave me all the little pointers and lessons she could. What's more, I was part of a vibrant, thriving food community: chefs and farmers, brewers and coffee roasters, wine merchants and cheesemongers, and the journalists, academics and cookbook writers who put it all down on paper. It was beautifully interconnected, and there was always something exciting going on. I had strong ties here. Why would I leave all of that for a desk job in the city?

Though I was stepping into the unknown where my career trajectory was concerned, I said no to what was probably going to be a very good job in DC. Even I couldn't believe what I was doing, but I knew it was what had to happen. I had suddenly stopped pretending to be perfect – to have perfect ambition and behaviour and good sense – and it scared me to death because I didn't know how else to be. It scared a few others, too, by which I mean anyone who had any sort of vested interest in my ever attaining full financial independence and a semblance of long-term security. Walking away from something so prestigious, so secure – particularly to stay in a kitchen making ten dollars an hour – was, to put it mildly, not encouraged in my family. It was risk I was programmed from an early age not to take.

Having reached my big decision at last, I made the dreaded phone call to Washington with a shaking voice one morning on a day off work. It was voicemail I reached, thank God. I followed it up with an email to be sure my message was received (while thanking God again that I was choosing a world where people did not use phrases like 'follow it up with an email'). Afterwards I got ready to head out for a long bike ride to clear my mind and settle my nerves. I would come back and work on my thesis in an hour or two. Just before I walked out of the door I checked my email one more time.

It's possible that the timing was just coincidental – especially since the draft I'd recently sent my committee was absolute crap – but that very same day a member of my committee (who also happened to be one of the small team to whom I was saying 'no'), came down on me like a ton of bricks about my recent draft. Had she got word that I'd turned the job down? Was it retaliatory? I'll never know, but it was some of the fiercest and most pointedly personal criticism I have ever endured in my life, and from someone I had really looked up to. With a heavy dose of snark, sarcasm and shaming, she blasted me for having absolutely no understanding of the women's movement, and told me that work of such absurdly poor quality would be rewarded with a pink slip and a swift kick out the door in the real world.

In a full-on, hot-faced, tight-throated, heart-pounding panic I shot off an email to my committee chair to tell her that we had officially commenced my worst nightmare. She had been copied on the offending email, as had the rest of my committee, but she said not to worry – that we would talk by phone that night, and we would get through this. I didn't see how. Reeling, I phoned my parents to warn them through stifled tears that I was afraid I might not graduate.

Choosing to give up the job was frightening enough, but being eviscerated as an intellectual and a human being by someone I trusted and revered had sent every deep fear I ever had about my worthiness as an academic rushing to the fore. It is one thing to choose to leave that world, and quite another to be told you aren't good enough to be there anyway. I was devastated.

I threw myself into my work in the kitchen, clinging to a small but significant shred of hope that I had not just committed career suicide. I *refused* to have regrets. On nights and days off I continued to chip away at my mess of a Master's thesis. I *hated* it by then, but I didn't have a choice if I intended to graduate. Quitting wasn't an option where education was concerned – not in my family – and I had never failed at anything in my entire life. It was a profoundly uncomfortable, wearying time.

Finally, after months of effectively working two jobs as I cooked or wrote in most of my waking hours, I did finish my thesis, and I even felt proud of parts of it, but it was then that my kitchen job became my *whole* life – my sole sense of purpose and satisfaction. It wasn't long before my relationship with my boss became strained. With all my eggs now in one basket, both of us were saddled with an awful lot of pressure to fulfil me.

I was a capable line cook and prep cook by then, and I was never bored. I took a lot of pride in my work and got out of bed excited to go to the kitchen every day, but I was tired, and my ego was fragile after the walloping I got from that committee member in DC. I kept up appearances, but I began to fall apart. I drank too much coffee on the clock and too much booze off it. I ate too much sugar, too little else. I was edgy. Sleep began to slip away, and when it came, it was plagued by vivid nightmares about confrontations with my boss. In my waking hours I obsessed over mistakes and criticisms. As my chef inevitably became more frustrated with me, her criticisms became sharper and her patience wore thin.

I was in a dangerous place personally, and my boss was clearly exhausted from the pressure of running a new restaurant. The shop had been open just over a year, and while it had been a very successful one I knew that she had barely slept in all that time. More and more, we began to find fault with each other, and the tension ratcheted up as the weeks passed. Her criticisms often seemed unjust to me, and I felt she was unfairly retracting any autonomy and responsibility I had earned over the last year. Trouble was, I seemed to have forgotten that she was the boss, so it didn't matter if it was fair. She did try to remind me of this . . .

In the spring, we would fall out for good – oddly, over something that happened away from work that I never quite understood, and just after she had given me a raise. I tried to get to the bottom of things and make amends. I thought we might still recover with time if I just tried hard enough, but it only got worse. No longer the golden child, I became defiant, sarcastic and resentful. I did my job to spite her, really. She was on my ass every chance she got, impossible to please. Things got nasty. It is shocking how horrible women can be to each other when once-close relationships go south. Men would just punch each other and move on, but we tend to keep waging a long, slow war for territory: hurt, embittered and out for blood.

Outside in the alleyway, which was home to all staff ciga-rette-smoking, weeping and fighting, plus the occasional illegal parking and vagrant urination and defecation, she finally broke my heart: 'You're not nearly as important as you think you are. Don't fool yourself: you are absolutely replaceable.' I had been her back-of-house right hand, and she knew this would sting. Then, 'I don't know what you think this is . . . This isn't the festival. I can't be your *friend*.' She nearly spat that last word at me. And yet she had been my friend – very much so.

Still, I didn't quit. Browns don't quit. With naivety border-ing on insanity, I still thought it might eventually get better if I could just hold it together, show her I was willing and prove that I was indispensable.

It never did get better.

By July, I would be forced to resign after my boss announced she was demoting me and cutting my pay, and she would still wind up firing me two days before my scheduled last day because she just couldn't take it any more. Our relationship had become so volatile, so toxic that it was affecting everyone else at work.

She met me in the parking lot the morning before my next-to-last shift. It was Saturday, which meant brunch. I could see as I locked my car door that she had my knife in her hand, wrapped in one of our rented white-and-green kitchen towels, and my last cheque, too. In a calm, quiet voice, she demanded my park-ing pass and my keys to the building, and told me not to come back. I wouldn't even have a chance to say goodbye to anyone.

Stunned and exhausted, with rivers of tears flowing down my face, I phoned my parents as I sat in my car, unable to move. I was coming home, I said. No one had any answers for me when I got there, but for the first time in months, I was not the elephant in the room.

Two days later, I got on a plane to Heathrow.

Blaen Cammarch

All along, the restaurant had been due to close the first week of August to give everyone a vacation, and I had already planned to sprint back to Wales. It would be a quick trip – only about ten days – but I was eager to get back east to visit my friends. I hadn't seen any of them since 2010 – nearly eighteen months before – but I had thought about them every day since. When July rolled around and I realised I was leaving the bakery whether I wanted to or not, I wrote to Jack asking whether I could stay for two months instead of ten days. He was a bit shocked, but said yes.

I arrived at Blaen Cammarch at one of the lowest points of my life. Jack told me that my mother had written weeks ago to say she wouldn't be surprised if I turned up in Wales for a much longer stay. She knew before I did. A mother's intuition, perhaps.

With my nightmares about work beginning to subside, I would sleep that first week as I hadn't slept for ages: deeply, restoratively. Wales was where I would heal. Jack took care of me in the gentlest way. He ran my baths, made my breakfast every day, brought me drinks in the evening by the fire. If we were out walking on the estate and came to a barbed wire fence with no stile, he would simply pick me up and place me on the other side before I even had time to protest. He cleaned my boots when they were dirty, hung the washing out to dry – including my knickers, much to my mortification – and basically tended to my every need. He was rescuing me, almost as if I were a wounded bird, my wings suddenly damaged by a blow I never saw coming. (Never mind that he had plenty of, as he calls them, 'pre-op taxidermy' specimens in his freezer that hadn't survived their injuries.)

We went rambling up through North Wales, where the walls were even more impressive, running straight up the sides of the mountains and often – Jack said – maintained by the farmers themselves. I waded out into the sea below the azaleas and rhododendrons and Italianate architecture of Portmeirion. We camped by magical lakes and hiked to waterfalls hidden deep in the woods, and I ate a mind-blowing flapjack on the side of the road as I gazed up at Snowdon.

Back home, we gazed out over our own hay meadow, mucked about with one old tractor or another, shot his little air rifle at an old kettle hung from a dying apple tree. We ate by candlelight, laughed late into the night.

We were just very, very happy. Even at work we were happy. We were slowly restoring the old carthorse wash at Kate's house, where we'd slogged in the rain and mud two years before. I was delighted to be back in such an interesting place, and in far better weather this time. Kate faithfully brought us coffee, just like before, and her chickens kept us company while we worked, pecking around for any worms we might unearth. She stood chatting with us a while each time she came out with mugs, and I always looked forward to her visits. She was only becoming more intriguing to me as the days passed. A hint of the most benevolent sort of mischief showed itself on the edge of her smile, and though I still couldn't figure out who on earth she was or why this nice English lady was in Wales in the first place, she was so warm and lovely that I just took her as she came. Maybe I'd find out eventually, and in the meantime, I was beginning to feel like we were friends.

As the August days drifted peacefully by, I could see that Jack was in love with me. It was genuine and strong. It didn't ask for much. I let myself lean on him a little, but for the most part, I had no trust left to put in anyone for any reason just then. I was too raw from all that had transpired in the last year. And he was still thirty-three years my senior. Though I knew our connection was a powerful one, I still felt there were rules I needed to obey. I relished him, but danced around the romance bit. I just wasn't ready to go there.

Though I towered over her, Angharad took me back under her own big, strong, older-sister kind of wing. I gave her the rundown of all the drama with my chef. She was horrified. Jack and I were in touch all the time when I was in America, but Har and I often went long stretches without communicating since she was so busy tending to her young kids. That meant our face-to-face catch-ups were long, enthusiastic, and sometimes full of surprises.

'She obviously didn't know what she had. Could she not see your potential?' Har seemed both baffled and offended. 'Bloody hell . . . I can't *believe* she'd treat you that way.' I think she could see how deeply bruised I was, and I was quite happy to have my ego stroked. There wasn't much left of me by the time I got to Wales, and it was time to regroup and grow back into myself.

Har and I spent a lot of time in the workshop together that summer, and I remembered what it was like to be mentored without fear, to take joy in the menial, repetitive tasks that lead to mastery if you see them through. I had taken a night class in welding in Durham while I was still at the bakery, wowing all the men – and they were *all* men – with my plasma-cutting prowess (Har was so proud when I told her this), but I hadn't been at a forge since I left Wales two years before. If I had any anger left, I lost it in the blows of my hammer. Its rhythmic ring against the anvil was a comfort to me as I pounded out 16-mil points and transformed them into leaves that would adorn a set of railings in a nearby village once Har had worked her magic to pull them all together. I was getting my muscle and my confidence back.

My laughter made its way back to me as well. It was good for me to be in the company of silly little boys again. Grown-up problems lose a bit of their weightiness with playful children orbiting around. Barefoot, we kicked a football around in the lush grass, trying not hit Tom's gracefully revolving balance sculptures or Smwj the slightly disabled cat, who, with crossed eyes, didn't have a prayer. Inside, it was the same as ever: Har and I drank wine and alternately gossiped or talked feminism, art and construction as she cooked dinner. Tom and I listened to his vinyl collection – sometimes Nick Drake or Gwilym Morus, sometimes obscure Japanese punk – and thumbed through their Anish Kapoor book when he wasn't off burning the midnight oil on his latest BBC job. I fell into the subtle and soothing rhythms of easy cohabitation.

After a week or so, I drove back north from Har's in a huge rainstorm. As I drove up and out of the clouds on Black Mountain, I looked down to see the storm sitting in the valley below me. When I wasn't fighting through the endless bends and gear changes of that wild road, I admired it all from afar.

I was coming to adore the unpredictable – or predictably inclement – weather in Wales. I loved the sudden rain, the fast-moving masses of clouds and the gusts of wind that drive them. I loved when the sun came out, especially when still-wet roads gleamed below like silver ribbons draped across the hills. I loved to watch the sun and the clouds dance around each other. Perhaps more than anything, I loved the fog and the mist – the drama they added. That all these things were necessary parts of a complete system made them all the more beautiful to me.

The variability of the weather in Wales made me more attuned to the moments of perfection, however fleeting. It made me want to celebrate them. How precious the warmth of the sun after unrelenting gloom and cold and drizzle, the rare, almost sacred evenings of clear skies, crisp sunsets, and bright stars. The subtleties of British skies and light had so much to teach. I suppose I'd begun to view everything metaphorically. My own life had been so stormy until recently.

Back at Jack's, as I lay falling asleep one night in the quietest and most pitch-black place I'd ever known, I did so with a new depth of gratitude. The place I remembered from my first trip was still here. My fond memories had not simply been formed by escapist fantasies or rose-tinted glasses. Wales really *was* wonderful for me, and returning there after the trauma of my kitchen implosion was the perfect thing to do. I found once more the magic I remembered from that first trip, and at a time when I so desperately needed that magic still to be there.

Pendine

As Jack and I worked and played that summer, I met more colourful characters, ventured deeper into Welsh culture and Welsh homes. Some visits were simply passing cups of tea – quick visits with folks I might never see again – but others introduced recurring characters who epitomised the warm hospitality and the cracking sense of humour I'd come to expect. They were all so funny, so enchanting that they helped me forget the pain that I'd left in North Carolina. I relished the chance to laugh and forget myself. I had become too self-conscious, too self-questioning . . . I constantly anticipated being judged harshly, and that is a crippling frame of mind.

Jack took me down to a little village near the coast to see his sister for a couple of days. En route we called in on a fellow I'd long known by name, and whose wife I'd long known by the reputation of her cakes. Dai-It-Is, a friend to Jack because of their shared love of agricultural antiques, was so-called because of the way he spoke on the phone. He'd ring up, and after Jack had said 'Hello' Dai would say, like clockwork, 'Jack! Dai, it is!'

The Welsh system of nicknaming is something in which I take endless delight. Let me explain: there are three million people in Wales and only so many surnames, with staggering numbers of people called Evans, Davies, Jones, Williams, Thomas, Hughes, Morgan, Owen, Rees, Jenkins, Griffiths and Phillips. People tend to be called according to occupation or farm name, or perhaps another quirk, because there are so few surnames to go around. There's Les the Digger, who does excavation. Rob the Mole and Jim the Ferret do pest control. There's Alan Chips, whose father – you guessed it – had a chip shop. There's Huw Dafadfa, who's a Davies, but there are so many of those he's called by his given name and his home farm. Same for William Williams Pantycelyn, composer of 'Guide Me, O, Thou Great Jehovah', also called 'Bread of Heaven' or 'Cwm Rhondda', a favourite hymn in Welsh rugby stadiums. Pantycelyn is called by his farm because he is hardly the only William Williams out there. And Dai-It-Is got his name because there are an awful lot of guys called Dai. It's the shortened form of David or Dafydd. Predictably, his last name is Davies.

I hadn't met him yet, but I was very fond of his answerphone messages. He had a big, enthusiastic voice. I would soon learn that he had a heart and a set of hands to match.

We arrived at Great House, Dai and Nelda's home since retiring from pub life at the Green Bridge some years before. Nelda, of course, was called Nelda Green Bridge after her pub, and probably in local circles that was Dai's nickname-surname, too.

Dai-It-Is had a beautiful, full head of white hair and *huge*, handsomely weathered hands that told the tale of his time as a blacksmith. He greeted us warmly outside the house as we stepped out of the car. Nelda, whom we found inside, was a stocky woman with a husky voice full of character and piss and vinegar that covered a wonderful, tucked-away sweetness and reflected a lifetime of cigarettes and smoky pubs. She presided over the greatest spread of cakes and pies, shortbreads and sandwiches I had ever seen or indeed will ever see. Everything was delicious, but we couldn't have eaten it all if we had stayed for three days, and I felt as if I would give myself instantaneous diabetes in my attempts to be polite.

Nelda was still a bit intimidating to me, but that's partly because of the other part of her reputation that preceded her. It wasn't a cakewalk being a pub landlady, and rumour had it she'd pulled a decorative piece of antique cast iron off the wall of the Green Bridge to whack a customer on the head after she'd asked him nicely to mind his language . . . and he didn't. Nelda meant business, and though she and Dai-It-Is clearly loved each other very much even into their seventies, she didn't cut him any slack. Needling her beloved husband, Nelda instigated the best set of storytelling I think I had ever heard. They were mostly stories about Dai getting injured at work, and Nelda – playfully, exasperatedly long-suffering – having to deal with that.

There was the tractor tyre that exploded while he was inflating it, nearly blowing off his hand. There was the time he nailed his hand to the wall while trying to fix something on the house. *Then* there was the time they went to London and came back to the hotel, tipsy after a big night out.

'We were on the Special Brew then,' said Nelda, looking at me with a knowing nod. (I had no idea what this meant, but Jack later clarified that this was a high-gravity beer only suitable for professional drinkers.)

71

It was late, and they were too hot because of the infernal radiators in their room, so Dai, ever a fixer, climbed up to try to open these huge, old sash windows, one of which then came crashing down unexpectedly and crushed his hands. Nelda described the swearing and the blood in colourful detail.

'*Ohhhh!*' Dai said, the pain of remembrance in his voice, 'It was *terrible*.' (Even the English-speaking Welsh slightly soften and trill the r's in 'terrible' in the most distinctive way.)

By the time Dai got to the story about the classmate from blacksmithing school who nailed a pony's foot to his ankle, I was laughing so hard I could scarcely see straight, let alone remember a little bakery somewhere across the ocean. The Welsh have a wicked sense of humour, with a particular taste for bad puns, lovable quirks, and tales of egos humbled. Welsh men seem to have a special talent for telling embarrassing stories about themselves, and their wives are happy to pitch in with embarrassing husband stories where they can. I was still so shy then that I just listened, taking refuge in laughter as people regaled me at every turn.

Dai disappeared for minute and returned to the kitchen with a hardback world atlas. He asked me to show them exactly where I came from. They were just as curious about me as I was about them. What was it like at home? Was it hot? How far was it to New York? To Florida? To California? The scale of my country fascinated them, the sounds of its names, too. Wales could sometimes be a surprisingly connected place with far-reaching international links, but for most, the thought of someone like me appearing on their doorstep wasn't even within the realm of the possible. Jack always told me that many older, rural Welsh I encountered might never have met an American before, and certainly not in their own homes. A few might have been to America on holiday (I knew one farmer's wife who'd been golfing in Charleston in my home state, for instance), and if they were *really* old they might have met American soldiers and airmen as children during the war, but I was an oddity for most of them, out rambling the countryside in search of stone and stories. They made the most of me while they had me.

Two years prior, long before we'd ever met, Dai sent me an old walling hammer he had lying about. Tools were an excellent way to win my affection, little did he know.

Blacksmiths of the traditional sort have stockpiles of old horseshoes, hammer heads, tractor parts . . . just old, slightly rusty metal bits that might be needed for something, if only perhaps to scrap for cash one day. He pulled this piece of steel from his stacks, cleaned it with a grinder, fitted it with a new handle, oiled it, and sent it to me through Jack to help encourage my interest in the craft. Old tools, we all knew, were sometimes the best tools. I'd proudly taken it home, feeling grateful for this man I'd never met who nevertheless seemed to understand me in ways nobody at home did. It was an unforgettable gesture of friendship.

Dai was a man you knew could make or fix anything, who simply understood intuitively how it all worked. He had a head for horseshoes *and* engines, and a great enthusiasm for me, this strange, young American thing who finally turned up with Jack. His stockpiles of old metal – 'my retirement', he had called them – and his big blacksmithing shop were gone by then, but he was still making small things for fun. Just before Jack and I left, he disappeared from the kitchen one more time, reappearing with a smile and placing into the palm of my hand a tiny brass anvil.

'Don't lose it,' he said, looking into my eyes. He closed his big hand around mine, clutching the anvil safe.

'I won't lose it,' I promised, smiling back.

I would fly home not too much later to face unemployment, and as I wondered what on earth to do with myself (and if perhaps I had ruined my life by giving up that Smithsonian job even though I *still* couldn't stomach the thought of working at a desk in Washington), I would look down at this little anvil on my keyring and see a reminder of the people who believed in craft and my place within that world. I wasn't alone in that. I hadn't imagined it.

Durham, North Carolina

Heartbreak, as I was learning, could cross oceans, or simply sit and wait for you 'til you came home. I had only hit pause while I was away. I could not outrun my pain.

I got home to North Carolina with no job, no health insurance, and – as I gradually figured out – a partially torn rotator cuff (slightly too enthusiastic a finish to my blacksmith work). I was thinking of farming in the spring – moving to the outdoor portion of the food chain instead of returning to the pressure cooker of the professional kitchen – but I didn't know what I would do until then, so I finally filed for unemployment benefits and hoped that my weakened shoulder would heal on its own in the meantime.

Within days, I got a letter in the mail informing me that my old chef had disputed my claim to unemployment benefits. Seriously? I was already ashamed to be filing for them. Browns aren't unemployed! We don't take handouts! She *had* run me off, and this was my legal right, as I reminded myself, but something in my DNA still made me feel guilty. I would have to face a phone hearing in November, which meant listening to her rip into me all over again. My heart sank with dread, and every old wound reopened.

I had felt strong in Wales that summer. I loved the woman I was when I was over there – confident, curious, optimistic and busy – and I was so frustrated that she had disappeared again just because I was back in America. I was beginning to realise a nagging escapist streak in myself, and it worried me. I longed to run away – back to a place where life felt easier. Out on the wall with Jack and back at the forge with Angharad, I thrived. At home, I was broke and bewildered.

I didn't know what I wanted apart from the same kind of life I had there. I wanted space and foliage, sunshine and rain, wellies, good beer and wine, and walls filled with books. I wanted the love and respect of my friends and family, the chance to be honestly and productively tired at the end of the day, and to be proud of myself. It didn't seem like so much to ask, really. But what did that mean for jobs? I still couldn't figure out how to be a blacksmith or a waller in America. There wasn't an obvious way forward, and all I could think about was how to pay the bills and not be completely miserable. I tried to reassure myself that something would come up. I hadn't yet realised that I'd have to sort that part out myself.

The evening before I'd flown home, Jack and I put the Land Rover into four-wheel drive, forded the Cammarch and climbed up into the hills above, distracting ourselves from yet another uncertain goodbye. I stood atop the trig point on Garn Wen, arms outstretched, eyes closed, almost reclining onto the strong, chilly south-westerlies behind me.

Back in America, I tried to remember what it felt like for the wind to hold me. I felt like I was in free fall.

Adrift

One thing I was learning as I dived deeper into manual labour and craft is that I don't fare very well when I'm unoccupied for long periods of time. I need the physical expenditure of manual toil, the mental space created by working with one's hands instead of one's critical intellect. It is a meditative space, the only way I stay sane.

All I can say is that I *survived* the months I had to wait until I would begin farming in March. Unemployment was not for me. I won my benefit hearing against my old boss, although all that money covered was my rent, and that was about it. But money wasn't the point, really. I needed something to *do*. I wanted to work – I was going crazy without it – but I couldn't find anything in the job listings that made any sense for me, and most people don't want to hire you for a stopgap position anyway.

I had little choice but to be idle. The job listings were shit. My shoulder wasn't good, and I didn't have the money to see a doctor, but also I was back in the suburbs. I could hardly sneak out onto the hill and go gapping on neglected field walls, and there was no need to cut firewood with the electric central heating system in my place. I couldn't even *volunteer* for hard work, which felt a bit cruel.

That winter felt interminably long and poor and murky. I drifted between the houses of friends and family up and down the East Coast, trying to distract myself from my misery. I managed to forget it all for a few days in New Orleans, drinking and dancing in the streets to brass bands, surrounded by friends old and new, but when the Bloody Marys and liquor slushies wore off and we drove back east in an exhausted daze, the same old stuff was still there.

Cedar Grove, North Carolina

In late February, I packed up my Durham apartment and headed west to the farm at last. I was relieved to leave the city, especially one where I still had so much emotional baggage.

It was with great delight that I settled into my tiny cabin overlooking the pond. It was crammed full of bare necessities, and relics from Wales filled the few empty spaces I had left. The change I felt upon landing in Cedar Grove was immediate. It was a world away from everything I'd known in the six years since I first moved to North Carolina.

I spent my days with my hands in the dirt, cultivating vegetables with two other women, in touch with every season, every rainstorm and breeze and passing cloud, every hour of pounding sun. In the evenings I stayed on my porch alone for as long as I could, watching the lightning bugs come up out of the grass, or listening to the roaring chorus of spring peepers after a big rain. Some nights I visited my neighbours Mimi and Pete for long, raucous, boozy dinners, and we always ate by candlelight out under the sky. Other nights, I anxiously watched the radar app on my iPhone in case a tornado might be imminent in the hurly-burly of the latest ground-shaking thunderstorm rolling over. If it was, I might have to run at any moment for the walk-in cooler, built of concrete block and far more durable than the converted 3-by-6-metre wooden shed I inhabited under a different sort of radar: county building inspectors.

I enjoyed an elemental existence that summer, when I had views and food to suit royalty, but absolutely no money. I think I made $800 a month? But I had no rent to pay, and I mostly bought stuff like cheese and coffee and chocolate and beer when I did go to town to the grocery store. I had plenty to eat, and I was content. Alone on 40 beautiful acres was the life for me. Sometimes I'd find an especially impressive green tobacco horned worm in the fields and keep it for a day or two as a pet, but mostly, it was just me.

On the farm, I found a privacy under the stars and before the dawn that I had never had before. I had led a quiet life in Wales – stars and all – but it had never been just me, and I certainly never greeted the dawn. Many nights and most mornings in Wales it was too cold to linger outside because I wasn't there in the right months, and without question, I wanted to be in bed, safe under my duvet. It was different in Cedar Grove. Some nights I would come home from town – in to visit my friends or maybe find some internet access, home again to sleep – lulled into a state of wonder by driving the country lanes with the windows down to the gorgeous throb of the thick summer air, alive with tree frogs and cicadas and crickets. Sometimes the beauty of the stars caught me so off guard that I simply could not go inside no matter how tired I was. I stood in the little mowed patch around my cabin, neck cocked all the way back, just staring up in love with no sense of time. And I was always relieved to be home, no matter how much fun I might have had at whatever hip bar or dinner party I'd just been to in town. It was far more beautiful out here . . . though not always more comfortable. In the hottest months I slept with the front door open, leaving only the screen door between me and whatever was happening *outside* that might want to come *inside*: bugs, snakes, dogs, lizards, intruders, blowing rain, oppressive heat. Nature was never far away.

In the mornings I rose at first light, and I always walked outside while I waited for the kettle to boil. I unlatched the simple hook and eye, made of flimsy alloy, and stepped out into the dewy grass in my bathrobe and garden clogs to gaze east and await the sun, which came up behind Angharad's tree, now back in a setting more befitting. I marvelled at the difference in colour from minute to minute, day to day. I looked towards Wales, knowing their day was already well under way, and wondered what they were all up to. In high summer I looked wistfully east around the time I knew Jack would be sitting down to elevenses out on a hill somewhere. He had some sort of biscuit or doughnut, and was drinking coffee from his blue plastic coffee cup with its fading red letters. Har would be in her workshop, layered up in spark-bitten clothes, welding helmet flipped up, Earl Grey in hand and Radio 2 on in the background. I loved to think of them going about their days. Something about it was comforting to me. I relished where I was, but I thought of them every day, without fail.

Jack and I wrote often. I fantasised in my letters about having a bonfire on top of the hill behind the house, of sleeping out under the stars under piles of blankets. It was so hot and sedate where I was that I longed for something else . . . For

81

wild, chilly nights, for the need to huddle round the flames and bundle myself in the thickest of woollens. Could we, when I returned? He promised, often on stationery depicting stone walls or bright red Massey Ferguson tractors, which by then I had declared my favourites. I read his letters as I sipped my morning coffee out of a mug he'd given me. 'I'd Rather Be Dry-Stone Walling', it declared, almost mockingly.

Washington, DC

Iwas so happy that summer that I had begun trying to figure out how I could start farming on my own. I could see it now: a ramshackle old house I'd eventually fix up, a vintage tractor, heritage breed livestock . . . I'd learn to butcher, sell at a local market, make lots of handsome farmer friends . . . I'd have a chainsaw and an axe. Trouble was, I had no land and no capital. In fact, I had $17,000 in student loan debt, which didn't exactly feel encouraging. I didn't feel I had a lot of options, and I was getting nervous.

I began, much to the shock of any friends to whom I was brave enough to confess it, to think about joining the military for a few years to save some cash. I was feeling unsettled again, wavering in my earlier confidence that things would eventually work themselves out. I began to worry about The Rules. I felt like my life was out of bounds. Was I straying too far? Asking for trouble with all this self-indulgence? I wasn't sure, and I began to grope for security.

In July, as the Folklife Festival was in full swing once more, I drove up to DC to be with my old colleagues for the weekend. There was a staff reunion planned for the Saturday, and it would be a relief to drink some beer and reminisce with my friends, but mostly, I'd come to see Parker.

Parker was the retired director of the Folklife Festival and one of the few people I trusted when life seemed unruly and confusing. A big-picture kind of woman, she was intuitively aware of the details, but never one to get bogged down in them. She was sharp, discreet and full of stories, and though soft-spoken, commanded a room and indeed an entire festival site with ease. We'd had a special relationship from the start.

I had written to her beforehand to tell her we'd need to sneak off at some point to talk alone – that I was wrestling some big questions. Ever gracious, she was happy to grant me that time. Looking out over the festival site, three years on from the summer when Jack and his walls were there, we talked once more over the direction of my life.

I gave her the rundown of my situation – that I loved farming and wanted to stick with it, but didn't really know how. My gig was up in October. I didn't have any money saved. I didn't really know what to do next. Then, I steeled my nerves and introduced The Military Option. 'I've been thinking about it for a while,' I said, almost apologetically. 'Military service is something we do in our family.' I mentioned that Jack had done it, too, and that I'd recently become good friends with a female Air Force pilot who made it all seem a little more approachable.

But more than anything, I explained rather weakly, I felt it was time to earn some money, to stop indulging myself with what were obviously dead-end careers. Though I couldn't have articulated it exactly at the time, I felt I'd been dodging responsibility by cooking and farming and building, as if those weren't legitimate careers. Maybe if they'd paid more I wouldn't have questioned my choices so much.

I'd begun to cry by then.

Gesturing to the village of tents in front of me, I told her in between stifled sobs that I didn't want to feel I was turning my back on this world . . . a world built on creativity and art and cultural exchange. She listened quietly, intently, nodding and chewing her trademark Nicorette gum.

She thought for a bit. Then, she started to talk.

Parker asked me some very wise questions that day. Importantly, she passed no judgement. The one thing she made me promise was that I would thoroughly investigate what my experience in the military would be like as a woman, and to be sure that I was ready to accept it. 'There are no "good" or "bad" decisions. There are just "decisions",' she said. 'Most of them are reversible, but this one isn't.'

Thinking back, I had a lot of 'almosts' in my twenties. In hindsight most of them were absolutely absurd. I recognise my pattern now: I come to a break in action where I feel financial and thus career pressure; convince myself that I 'want' to do something that seems very logical and reasonable at the time; struggle for weeks or months, often with tears streaming down my face; look within myself – usually with the help of clever, clear-eyed others – only to realise I can't pull the trigger because it isn't who I am, no matter how financially beneficial it might be to do 'X'. Law school, the Smithsonian job, military officer training . . . I have often had very unconventional goals, but attempted to shoehorn myself into very conventional paths to achieve them, and that's just not how it works. I have bumbled my way through and fought at first against every 'brave' decision I have ever made.

When I was finishing university with a liberal arts degree, I hadn't a clue as to what I was qualified to do or even where

85

to look. *Obviously*, I should go to law school. It is what all terrified, well-meaning liberal arts graduates think of doing. Only one person had the nerve to tell me she thought it might not be the best fit for me, but luckily my LSAT scores were mediocre enough that the choice was effectively made for me. Tulane University in New Orleans offered me a place with no financial aid, which meant about $150,000 in loans. Even before the student loan crisis of 2008 onwards, I knew that was a lethal amount of debt for me. It's a house and a half where I come from. I let the offer pass me by, and made the very responsible, lower-middle-class decision to look for a proper job . . . Something vaguely professional with office-y clothes and a retirement plan and health insurance – something befitting a woman with my *summa cum laude* degree in – essentially – very good analytical reading and writing and not much else (a.k.a. American Studies). And I would hate that job, but I would learn a lot, and then I would go on to graduate school and to the festival, where I belonged. I agonised over law school, and in retrospect it is amazing how quickly it began to seem ridiculous once I'd given up the idea.

Parker and I talked more about my time in Wales, my love of craft – something that, at that point, she had more faith in than I did. I told her I still couldn't see a way forward, and that I felt in so many ways that my heart was across the ocean. I was – I heard myself explaining – scared.

Any time I talked to someone in my life at home about what I was coming to want for myself, it felt like tenuous ground – a sort of coming out . . . about work and craft, about Jack . . . I was so shy about it, so unsure that I was allowed to want what I wanted . . . always waiting for some-one to tell me I was being selfish and ridiculous.

Parker knew I loved Jack even if I still wasn't sure what to do about it, and I think she knew before I could get my own head around it that we were not just having a conversation about careers. It was bigger than that – it was about what I wanted for my whole life. She asked what my hesitation was with him. She prodded me – always gently – to perhaps reconsider my assumptions about how life works and what I am capable of. 'If you can't trust yourself yet, trust me,' she said.

As we got back to the question at hand, she reminded me that her career unfolded the way it did – utterly full of magic and meaningful relationships that span continents, cultures and generations – partly because she'd been lucky, but also because she'd always made decisions based on what she'd like to be doing next week rather than in five years. This struck a chord. And I knew good and well that I was lucky, too.

Back when she was still my boss, Parker would appear almost out of the blue when you least expected her and most needed her – how she always knew, I could never figure out – often to advise on situations that were technically far beneath the level that should have concerned her as director, or perhaps to facilitate a bit of what we liked to call Festival Magic. Some things, I thought to myself, never change.

'Thank you,' I sniffled.

'You are one of my children,' she said.

It couldn't have been felt more deeply on either side.

I didn't have the answers by the time I left that bench, but I did feel clearer by the end of the day. I emailed her a few days later to thank her for hearing me out, helping me think.

'The thing about you is,' she replied, 'if I keep you talking long enough, you answer yourself.'

Back on the farm that week, I was on my knees in a jungle of overgrown cherry tomato plants, scouring the lowest branches for fruit, and the dam suddenly broke. One has these intense conversations with one's self out in the field, or on a wall, when the brain has time to process and wonder passively. All of a sudden, with spindly branches resting atop my head, I realised that I didn't need to be a naval officer, and I wept with relief. I had wrestled with it for so long that I can't begin to explain the release I felt at letting it go. The whole scene was absurd, but at least I had my privacy.

I realised that I had no right to turn my back on craft. Not after all I'd been through and put others through those last three years. Or maybe I had the right, but it would have been dumb. I also began to take into account the fact that literally *dozens* of people I love and respect were shocked and thought I was crazy, but not in the way I expected. I *expected* them to think it was nuts because they were anti-military. In fact, they thought I was nuts because they loved the journey I had been on, and they *all* had faith in me. People knew I could do whatever the hell I wanted to do. I was the one who'd forgotten.

A thunderstorm broke open above me. I simply turned my face up to the sky and let the drops wash it all away.

Falls Church, Virginia

My going-away party that fall was epic – a review of my entire life in North Carolina, which saw me transition from business to academia to a kitchen and then a farm. My people came from far and wide, and we laughed and ate and drank until long after the stars had come out. They were a testament to the life I'd made for myself there during my twenties, and as I stood there watching them all interact – sometimes for the first time – I knew I had done well. It was so charming that I nearly cancelled the move. But as I pulled off the farm for the last time a few days later, my old Volvo almost dragging the ground under the weight of my most precious possessions, I knew I was doing the right thing. It was time to go.

Moving home to South Carolina that autumn left me free of rent and other people's spaces for the first time since I left for university about ten years before. I didn't have much money, but that didn't matter. What I had once spent on housing, I now began to spend on plane tickets, but before I left for Wales this time I had a wall to build in America.

While I had been in DC that summer, my friends Kim and Eric took me to the edge of their slate patio and wondered whether I could build them a low seating wall once I finished on the farm. Kim had worked at that fateful festival alongside me, and so not only did she understand the magic of it, but she also remembered a lot of the people who had begun to shape my life in significant ways. In fact, back in 2009 Kim was one of the few who told me, 'Go!'

This would be my first solo, income-earning wall. Could I do it? I felt I could, but what I could achieve – structurally and artistically – remained to be seen. Kim and Eric were the first to give me a chance . . . and to pay me. I felt even more pressure to perform as money entered the equation. I felt slightly nervous at first, but I was pleasantly surprised at how quickly it all came back to me: excavating for the foundation; sorting for curves and corners and hearting; fitting those first few stones together . . . I was away.

What therapy from digging with a mattock and a shovel for foundations!

How I *loved* the feel of my array of hammers and the various clunks and cracks they made as they broke stones in the way I wished!

It was good work, and I was grateful for it. I was also grateful to be on my own schedule again for the first time in six months. If farming had taught me anything, it was that I was truly meant to be a solitary creature during much of the work day – if I wasn't at Jack's side.

As I neared the top line, I found in one of my jacket pockets a piece of stone that I'd brought back from the hilltop above Jack's the year before. I decided to use it as hearting to give this wall a real, physical connection to my journey. There, in the suburbs of DC, my Welsh connections resonated with particular clarity in that moment. I was bringing it full circle. It meant a great deal to me to build for people who were so appreciative of the skill, the end product *and* the story. Kim and Eric were supportive from the get-go.

I struggled for a while that last afternoon to give my wall a nice, stable, heavy-yet-clean-looking top with the mix of fieldstone we had. What you can easily get away with on a farm wall looks like crap next to a lovely, composed patio. I felt pretty sure I'd finished the wall that day, but when I looked at it through the window the next morning as I ate my breakfast, it nagged me. It wasn't right. I put on my work clothes and went outside.

I pulled off the entire top course, reselected and reconfigured my stone. My task was a puzzle, but with giant 25kg pieces. I stepped back and looked carefully for bumps or dips. I squatted alongside my wall, staring down the top line like the barrel of a gun, looking for any inconsistencies. Finally, there were none. Four hours had passed. Satisfied at last, I stepped up and walked my copes to check they were solid. Nothing budged.

Kim and Eric were thrilled with their new wall, and by the end, I was as well. It became what we all wanted: something not too perfect-looking, but strong and interesting and at the ideal height to be extra party seating or a platform for a wine glass or platter. This was functional art, suburban as well as stockproof.

Before I left, we had a wall christening party that drew family, neighbours, friends and a few favourite Folklife Festival vets – including Parker – who fawned over it as if I had given birth. Wine disappeared with semi-alarming speed. A sweet soundtrack danced in the background. There was a much-needed and appreciated bonfire. Good cheeses, magic rosemary crackers, jambalaya, apple pie and the messiest toasted marshmallows. Best of all, people sat on the wall just like they were supposed to, and they did so naturally. It drew them in. It was the first time I'd ever really watched other people interacting with something I'd built – usually it was just me and Jack and sheep – and it was pretty touching. I had fun answering their questions about its construction and telling the story of how I learned and just generally listening to people tell me how beautiful it was. I felt like the belle of the ball.

As one period slips away, another begins.

The Heart of Wales

Ialways found it slightly unbelievable that I could get into an appropriately fuelled tube of metal and arrive eight hours later in a different land. Jack did, too. For the first three days, in response to my regular and enthusiastic exclaiming, 'I'm here!', he'd echo cheerily, 'You're here!' I was living well below the Federal government's poverty line and spending an obscene percentage of my income on plane tickets, but I was happy.

Above a little place called Aberedw, we pulled over on a grassy spot alongside the road. With lunch in our rucksacks, Jack and I headed out across the common, following in the tracks of sheep, who somehow always know the best way up.

The hills were brown and red, with only scattered splashes of green remaining as autumn faded into winter. We climbed up eventually to an escarpment that we deemed an appropriate roost for lunch. I sat with one gaitered leg extended before me and the other cocked to hold me still on the slope. My tea steeped and steamed on a tuft of grass by my hip, cooling. The sky was silvery grey. I leaned my back against a huge stone and gazed down over a moorland fell below, covered in bracken and peat bogs. I held my breath, and I heard *nothing*.

Cedar Grove had been rural, but even on the quietest days there was always jet noise – always. Sometimes there were low-flying military helicopters, too. Or the neighbour's penned-up hound dogs, excited by something they could not reach, someone target-shooting a mile away, the noise of big trucks rumbling up and down NC 86. But Radnorshire had oases of true quiet. These places in the hills felt mystical to me, desolate and deserted in the best possible sense, but with a calm, clear energy of peace and safety and freedom. Throughout my scorching summer, I dreamt of this.

I sometimes find it difficult to explain why I kept going back across the ocean even in the days before we were openly in love with each other, but that afternoon was kind of it: these moments on hilltops or by fires. It was the peace of the countryside I was after, the work, and perhaps the fact that I felt by then Jack was the only person who really understood me. I didn't have an agenda when I went back except to be there in the hills with him. We loved to listen side by side to the nothingness and the wind.

As we moved into December, daylight was weak, and gone in a flash each day. Time came almost to a standstill. Everything seemed to move slowly on the surface, like a river clogged with the slush of ice. It was a period of little work and low metabolism – all but hibernation. We spent as little energy and money as possible, staying close to home apart from the occasional trip to the pub for curry 'half-and-half' (half chips, half rice, and very, very Welsh). There'd been one wild night of drinking and singing and storytelling at a pub down in Llanfallteg, but mostly it was a quieter time, one for getting to know things intimately.

My two previous trips had been very social ones: up and down to Cardiff and Brynaman to see old festival friends, trips with Jack to explore here, there and everywhere. This time, we mostly stayed home together, poor but content. What I remember most is being bundled against the cold in an absurd number of layers (so many that I lost track of the shape of my body), lingering in bed to avoid the cold, and huddling by the fire. (It was *really* cold.) But I grew to love the work of staying warm, and with fewer distractions, we enjoyed each other more. It left me feeling more rooted at Blaen Cammarch. I was learning how lovely it could be to stay home with the right person.

I saw less of Angharad in those days. (I saw less of *everybody* in those days.) Jack and I weren't open with anybody about our relationship, and as it intensified, we withdrew into each other. I saw Kate more than anyone else, and though I was longing to open up to her about it, I wasn't quite ready. At home, I didn't talk much about my relationship with Jack even to my closest friends, and I definitely didn't talk about it in Wales. He was worried about being judged harshly, and I wasn't quite sure what it was apart from intense. Even if I had discussed it outside our tiny, private world, what would I call it? Can you have a sixty-two-year-old 'boyfriend'? And I had always hated the word 'partner'. 'Lover' felt too glamorous a word for me. I didn't know what he was – only that I loved him and didn't want to be without him.

That winter we burned the hawthorn I had cut and stacked during the blizzard two years before while we were snowed in. It was ready now, burning hottest of all the wood we had on hand. Jack read me poetry aloud by the fire many nights . . . Sometimes his own, sometimes the great World War I poets, sometimes British classics such as Wordsworth. I fell asleep under blankets in the toasty, dim lounge as words on life and death and nature and love swirled around me. Never had I been so sleepy in my whole life as I was that dreamy, soporific December.

The world was frozen hard when Jack drove me to Heathrow on the morning of 16 December. This was my third goodbye in the UK, and I had grown to hate them. We both had stinking colds – Jack had been ill for weeks, and my head was so heavy I could barely breathe. I had a hacking cough – perfect for air travel. I pitied whatever seat mate I might have. I clearly had a sort of pestilence and shouldn't be allowed out, but it was time to go.

When I cried – which I had done often in those final days, feeling sorry for myself as usual but multiplied tenfold because of the cold – it made it even harder to breathe. Jack, for his part, was simply exhausted. His had gone to his chest, and he'd been given antibiotics.

In short, we were both a mess. He would be left alone to be a mess in our space, and I would have to go home to be a mess and surrounded by people I couldn't tell about particularly *why* I was such a mess. The cold, in that sense, was a good disguise. I wouldn't need to be cheerful or energetic, and I had every excuse to stay in bed.

That winter was the moment when Jack and I finally gave in to what had been there all along, and I was now deeply, if secretly, in love with a man I couldn't be with most of the year. Inevitably, I began to think on things like happiness and duty and their relationship to each other. I had just left the comfort of Wales for the confines of my overstuffed childhood bedroom and the reality of my pitiful excuse of a bank account. There was a life on the eastern side of the Atlantic that was just out of reach most of the time, but it seemed

98

perfect. *Was* it out of reach, or was I not brave enough to stretch for it?

I didn't know where to put my energy or my faith. Did I try to make a life out of my love for Jack, or should I take this opportunity to try to find a new, age-appropriate life here in South Carolina? Should I try to get past this very complicated, half-formed love affair once and for all?

Greenville, South Carolina

I didn't question myself in Wales. I did so endlessly at home. Coming back to America nine days before Christmas left me jobless over the holidays. In those quiet days when so much of real life slows down – and mine was already pretty slow by then – I was left with an excess of time to worry yet again over the course of my life. I still had a lot to figure out.

Just after New Year, I finally convinced myself that I had nothing to lose by putting together a simple website for a stone business I didn't actually have yet. I had no tools, no truck, no clients ... but why not? The domain would only cost $15 a year, and the hideous-but-good-enough-for-a-poor-person web design templates were free. I had done enough projects solo and with Jack to net me a sufficiently convincing number of photos that I could post as evidence of my authenticity and prowess. And I had proved to myself back in October at Kim and Eric's that I could plan and execute an entire, beautiful, sturdy wall all on my own. I figured I could probably do the work, but could I get the clients? It was so hard to take the first step. I knew I risked failure. I risked finding out the truth.

So I made a pathetic little website, hit publish, and assumed that was probably the end of it. At least no one could accuse me of not trying. A little.

In late January, my cousin found me part-time work as a construction labourer with a general contractor. Jim was kind enough to hire me to hurl a sledgehammer at the remains of an old brick house foundation, clean the bricks of their old mortar, and then move and stack them for salvage. I was making $8 an hour doing mindless work, and the well-off, well-coiffed, Lulu Lemon-clad shoppers in Whole Foods looked at me like I had a very contagious and horrifying disease if I turned up in my construction clothes to grab a coffee or a sixer of craft beer in what they felt was their world. I wanted to shout at them that I had a Master's degree and this was a *choice*.

I had the weight of the world on my shoulders in those days. I felt so alienated and adrift in my own life. I still wasn't sure if I was allowed to have or even want all of the things that I so desperately *did* want for myself. I had been through the exact same thing last winter, and it was getting old. Meanwhile, I began to wonder in earnest if my parents had yet noticed what a directionless loser I had become.

As I stacked bricks or sat alone in my bedroom with beer I couldn't technically afford, I thought of Jack, and I pined for the privacy and quiet of the hills. I felt I was just filling the gaps until I could go back. My life in America felt pathetic and empty. I was sad to admit that – even privately to myself – but it was true.

I tried to remind myself that I had great potential to make a place for myself in Greenville. It seemed like the logical thing to do. Maybe I was working a grim construction job, and maybe I missed Jack all the time, and maybe the big-name blacksmith in town wasn't at all friendly when I introduced myself at an open studio one night, but there were loads of hip, inspiring little art galleries cropping up in the mill village my family came from. I'd found a couple of cool new coffee shops and a bar that felt like my local. I was reading and writing a lot – doing my best to feel hopeful and trying to find some personal grounding for who I was to be when I wasn't in Wales.

I decided I needed to at least *try* to make some sort of life for myself here. I'd made my stupid website, and now I would make the first concerted effort in my entire life to 'put myself out there' and date a bit, hoping I might find someone to help me feel less like I wanted to run away. I wondered if I could *not* want Jack if I just tried a little harder.

In almost no time, the dating website I'd been mortified to sign up for coughed up a guy I really liked. Matt. I did that thing that women do, suddenly and almost unintentionally envisioning the entirety of the rest of our lives together as soon as I took a liking to him, which I think was about an hour and maybe two beers into the first date. In a classic Millennial move, I joined his kickball team, which was equal parts drinking and sport, and met some of his friends as they gathered to make homebrew.

We had easy fun when we did see each other, but it soon became clear that Matt was even more commitment-phobic than I was – even to the next date – and though I found him incredibly attractive and clever, I quickly became disenchanted with the casual, texting-based world of thirty-something men. I couldn't read these guys – especially not from a screen – and I really didn't feel cool and clever enough to hang. It all felt unnatural, but this was – on paper, at least

– where I was supposed to match and mate. I told myself I should just be patient and at least see where it went.

But I knew good and well that I was in love with Jack. I just felt tortured because I believed for a hundred reasons I couldn't and shouldn't be with him . . . age, distance, potential parental disapproval, the sheer, subconscious terror that my biological clock might finally become audible despite *years* of complete radio silence. Matt was just a lovely distraction from all the big things I could not know, could not decide: men, work, where to live apart from this bedroom . . .

In the meantime, I had pretty regular work with Jim so would just plod along with that for now. I was content enough to let someone else do the thinking and planning for a while. I wasn't particularly ambitious at the time because I felt I couldn't be. Instead, I simply focused on getting my bearings again in my hometown after eleven years away and learning as much as I could every day at work.

I got to do a bit of carpentry (though I did a lot more caulking and painting and staining). I learned to use chop saws and circular saws and Sawzalls, builder's squares, various nail guns. I started to understand sixteen-on-centre framing, soffit and fascia, tongue-and-groove panelling, and even tile. I installed batts of itchy fibreglass insulation. I handed lots of tools to Jim while he was up ladders, and once I even had the privilege of cleaning up his mortar mess with muriatic acid after he got pissed off at our brick mason and tried to point up himself . . . using his fingers.

Construction was OK. There was always more to learn if you were paying attention and had an inner compulsion towards excellence, mastery and creative problem-solving. I was figuring out that I had that very compulsion, and that actually it was a need. Jim was patient with me when I was slow or a little clumsy, and I forgave him almost daily for making me get his breakfast at McDonald's on my way in to work. If nothing else, we laughed a lot.

Things got interesting in March. I had a few email queries from customers who'd found my dinky little website and (gasp) wanted some stonework soon. Those wouldn't be until June or so, but I would have to tell Jim soon that I'd be needing some time off in the summer. I needed to stay in his good graces since it was unlikely I'd have consistent enough business to keep myself afloat. I assumed there would just be a project here and there throughout the year – a week or two at a time – and I liked the idea of continuing to learn general construction. The more skills I had, the better. When I finally told him, Jim was excited for me – even gave me a bit of advice when I went out to give my first estimates – and he seemed happy to let me come and go as my work required in the coming months. This might work out perfectly, I thought. I was starting to feel the tiniest bit of excitement.

One sunny day not long after, I was high up a ladder and painting newly installed siding on a house when a text message dinged in my chest pocket. One shouldn't really be rifling through one's overalls to locate one's iPhone while up a ladder and covered in oozing, gunky, carcinogenic-in-the-State-of-California caulk – it is rather taking one's life in one's hands – but I was bored, frankly, and I wondered who in the outside world was thinking of me in that instant.

It was Angharad. There was a picture of a baby in a onesie, lying peacefully in the natural cradle formed by the thighs of a mother in repose. Eluned was here at last, having just missed a St David's Day arrival. Har had given birth at home in her little white farmhouse – again. She'd had my respect from day one, but this was another reminder of just how amazing she is. She is certainly the only woman I know who pounds hot steel *and* gives birth naturally at home.

Jack rang up to ask if I'd got the news. To my shock, he offered to fly me over to surprise Kate at her big seventieth birthday party later in April, saying I could meet the baby then, too. It was an offer I couldn't refuse. I couldn't think of anything cheerier: a chance to celebrate the woman I had quietly come to think of as my fairy godmother and to meet the mighty Angharad's tiny new daughter. I asked Jim if he could possibly spare me for a week. He made a big, silly production of it, laughing that I was abandoning him in a time of crisis, but of course he said yes.

At that point, I was going to fly to Wales no matter what he said, but of course I preferred to go knowing that I'd have work when I came home. I liked Jim, but working for him could be frustrating. He was not the most organised guy in the world, and I never knew 'til the morning-of whether I was even going to work that day. Sometimes I felt I was learning how *not* to do certain things, especially after the huge, arduous concrete pour we'd just botched. Luckily, he let me go without too much hassle – but what choice did he have? It was rare to find a construction helper who would show up when requested, and not call to say I was in jail after a weekend arrest for drunken fighting or unpaid child support, and I didn't steal from him or have any drug problems to speak of. I was worth my weight in gold.

So I found a bottle of Pierre Moncuit – the champagne my friend Mimi called 'liquid diamonds' – and wrapped it in a hundred different layers in my duffel bag so that it might have a prayer of getting to Kate intact, and I hopped on a plane to Manchester.

Blaen Cammarch

Powerful storms had battered Wales throughout that winter and early spring, and a late blizzard had trapped and killed many lambs in snow drifts across the country, but when I arrived in April the sun was shining, and young lambs bleated and gambolled *everywhere*. Gone was the frozen, silent land I'd left in tears in December, and the predictable euphoria of both spring and returning quickly took me over. Jack and I chatted and laughed happily all morning as we drove south from Manchester, wiggling back and forth across a seemingly arbitrary English border. It was as easy and close as if we'd seen each other just yesterday. Any daydreaming about Matt evaporated instantly, and everything else about life at home felt just as it was: an ocean away.

By the time we reached the Wye Valley on my favourite, starkly beautiful stretch of the A470, I could barely contain my excitement. I'd landed at a godforsaken hour and hadn't slept a wink on the plane, but it didn't matter. I was a woman on a mission: I had heroes to celebrate, babies to meet, and stone to shift. All sorts of delights awaited at the end of the road.

Kate's house was on our way home, so we stopped by just before lunch so that I could surprise her properly before the big party on the weekend. Jack went in first to say hello and scope out the scene, finding her in the kitchen. I hung back, hiding quietly in the hallway amidst all the jackets and wellies, and listening through the door for my cue.

'Close your eyes,' he said to her. 'I have a birthday present for you.'

It was then that I stepped from around the corner and wrapped her in a huge hug. Confused, she pulled back and opened her eyes. 'Whit, it's you! I can't believe it! Darling, how wonderful!' The look on her face was priceless. She dived back in for a proper hug. I was absolutely delighted with myself.

When Jack and I got home that afternoon I bathed and kipped like always. When I woke a few hours later, groggy but happy, we headed up round the back into the fields. Jack knew a spin on my most favourite of machines would nicely round out my first day back, so off we went to fire up a tractor. At the sound of the diesel engine, lambs and ewes came running from every direction, associating that noise with the dispensing of food. Thus my homecoming was heralded by low-RPM engine chugging, loud, chaotic bleating, and Jack's laughter at my joy. I hopped off the tractor to walk amongst the slightly skittish crowd of sheep I had summoned. I dashed about trying to catch the cutest of the spotted lambs, knowing I wouldn't, but having fun trying anyway. It was a pastoral feast for the senses: shit, diesel fumes, wildflowers, the golden light of sunset on the hills above, and a chorus of expectant ruminants.

107

The next morning the tree boys came to take down the huge, old ashes by the front gate since ash dieback disease meant their days were numbered now anyway. The chainsaws stopped for a moment as I emerged from the house dressed incongruously in a green silk strapless number, a huge fleece, full make-up . . . and wellies. The boys had never seen me in anything but filthy dungarees until then. Blaen Cammarch, though majestic in its own right, is not a place for finery – at least not if one wishes it to remain fine. I picked my way carefully through the mud, spiky heels in hand, thinking gleefully all the while about the day that I would eventually get to split this entire pile of wood.

When Richard opened the front door to welcome us to the party, he let his jaw drop comically before exclaiming: 'Oh, my God! You've got *legs*!' Apparently, people really had got used to me as a ragamuffin.

The weekend was filled with stark but lovely contrast: lambs by the hundreds, cantankerous old tractors, chamber music in a barn, cocktail dresses with strappy heels (my 'very un-Radnorshire shoes', as Kate would laugh with delight), posh Cambridge folks and farmers, coronation chicken and game pie on a buffet in the study, and all with plenty of wine.

It was at Kate's party that I began to see for the first time what a community I had here. Amongst many unfamiliar, out-of-town faces, there were plenty that I *did* know, and it was the first time I had seen so many of them in one place. We were all together, moving happily through Kate's beautiful old house, and they just treated me like one of the gang . . . As if I'd never left. It was a cosmopolitan crowd, local church folk here, bohemians and creatives there. Anything went – so long as it did so with nice manners.

The timing could not have been better. I was sort of in between a lot of things – confused as to whether I was more suited to dungarees or silk, and whether they were mutually exclusive. In that moment I found myself surrounded by a crowd of people – mostly women I thought the world of – who were not only delighted to *see* me, but *by* me.

All older than me, all extremely elegant and well-read and brilliant, all a little bit untameable, I found a cache of women in Wales who were half glamorous, half wild and perfectly content in the middle ground of the two. They made contradiction look so wearable to me, whereas I had always carried it awkwardly. These were the kind of women who were equally at home at the stove or the piano, in a barn or on a stage, on a blowing hillside or in a gallery. Cover them in mud or cashmere or both – they didn't mind. They were unapologetic about what they loved, about what might seem incompatible on the surface.

And here they were in one place for Kate's birthday, fawning over me, welcoming me back, excited to hear what I was up to, loving my scruff and my polish all at once. I can't tell you how much I needed that. I was looking at thirty in the next month, and I knew what I loved, but I wasn't sure who I was . . . They had every confidence in what I was doing with my life, which was funny, really, given how little they knew me and how uncertain I was myself, but I trusted them. They seemed to understand parts of me that I hadn't yet got my own head around, and it was in the midst of their affection that I began to see myself clearly. For the first time in my life, I felt beautiful and strong rather than tomboyish and awkward. I felt – as I had with Angharad – not weird, but cherished and kindred.

Most women where I grew up just didn't get me. They never had. They tolerated me, perhaps thought of me as quirky and entertaining, but others were outright judgemental and critical, or just blanked me if I talked openly about what was important to me. I collected some wonderful, hilarious friends back in America once I moved away from home, but even they didn't get my obsession with axes and wood stoves and opera, for instance. At that point, I simply didn't have this sort of deep female kinship on my side of the ocean – a shared spirit of adventure, obsessing about the same sorts of beauty, accepting of big, wild emotion and a need for an equivalent physical space – and finding it at last was one of the greatest gifts of my life. Kate's own warmth and universal acceptance of me were a start, but she also became over the years a nexus for all sorts of lovely people who made sense to me and who shared my love of a certain way of being. They aligned with the sort of life I was beginning to envision for myself – full of beauty and adventure and contradiction. Plus champagne.

I began to realise that year in the company of these remarkable women that I was no less a woman because of my job or my mannerisms or the fact that I didn't do fucking beauty pageants. I had always felt I needed to apologise for being too womanly in construction, or not womanly enough in other arenas. What did it mean to be a woman? What a huge question, and what a stupid one, too.

As I spent time with them I was finding validation for all sorts of things I'd been puzzling over in my life – validation for the person I already was. I realised that I neither needed to resolve nor apologise for all the conflicting, contradictory, disjointed parts of myself. I didn't need reconciliation or explanation, but acceptance, and that had to start with me. None of them had tried to stuff me into the boxes I was trying to fit myself into for some reason, and they weren't aware of any particular roles that I was predestined to play out. This was the moment when I really started to make my own rules about my life, to permit myself to want what I wanted, and to trust that my instincts would not lead me astray.

At the party that weekend, I met a woman who felt like someone I had always known. Rose was young and enthusiastic, and she'd spent a lot of time in America for work. Between her age, her travels and her warm, generous spirit, she seemed to understand me in a different way from anyone else I'd met in Wales. We hit it off quickly. As we moved through the crowded party arm in arm, another guest asked us if we'd come from America together, which made me laugh. We'd literally met that morning. We just had an instant affinity for one another.

I offered to drive Rose back to the train on Monday. She'd only come out from London for the weekend. As we made our way up the A470 to the station, we gossiped about all the guests at the party. In a lull between laughs, I heard myself blurt out a confession of my love for Jack. Fumbling a bit, I told her that I wasn't sure what to do about it. It was there, and it was powerful, yet it was *beyond* illogical to pursue.

It was the first time I'd talked openly about it with anyone. As much as I liked her already, it wasn't terribly likely I'd run into Rose again, so I guess I felt safe about opening up. And she had known Jack a while already, so I knew she understood how special he was. Car journeys seemed to make it easier for me to talk . . . I didn't have to look at anything but the road as I spoke. If someone made a horrible face at anything I said, at least I didn't have to see it.

Lovely Rose, she didn't bat an eye. 'I can tell you that what you and Jack have is rare,' she said softly. We were parked by the station then, and I turned to see her smiling lovingly at me and nodding. 'You should enjoy it.' We hugged a tight goodbye on the platform, and I waved her off as the train pulled away to Birmingham. Driving south to the sounds of Radio 3, I reflected on how nice it was to say it out loud and to feel understood for once. . . and exceedingly glamorous, a word I would never have applied to myself, but one that Rose did repeatedly in the forty-eight hours I'd known her. She was wearing Versace specs. I thought she probably knew about these things.

A few days later, in ragged dungarees once more, Jack and I were at work pitching cobbles at a Radnor Wildlife Trust site not far from Rhayader. The sun was still shining brightly. I was learning a new skill, and I had a Cornish pasty waiting for lunch. This was a perfect day as far as I was concerned.

A cuckoo called just up the valley. I couldn't believe my ears. Excitedly, as this was the first live, wild one I'd ever heard in my life, I said, 'It sounds *just* like the clock!' Jack erupted into a huge belly laugh: 'That is *so* American!' It took him ages to stop cackling at me.

Amused, but also slightly annoyed at being thought so stupid, I said, 'What I *mean* is it's remarkable how realistic the clockmakers have managed to make cuckoo clocks *sound* – not that the bird follows the clock, you plonker.' He just kept laughing. We were both so drunk on sunshine that it really didn't matter.

By the time we got to Kate's for dinner that night, I was exhausted, and my elbow ached, and my ears were ringing from the *thwack, thwack, thwack* of my hammer on the wood that drove the cobbles into the earth. She sent me straight to the bath, where I sank into her giant tub with utter delight. All six feet of me could stretch out flat beneath the water with only a slightly tilted neck. With an irrepressible smile on my face, and knowing that champagne awaited me downstairs when I felt ready to emerge, clean and perfumed, I thought to myself that I couldn't be happier anywhere else on earth in that moment. I was right where I needed to be: somewhere between dirt and champagne. I was with my people in beautiful spaces doing work that I loved, and that, as I was discovering and affirming all the time, was what I needed to be happy.

Garth

With Kate's festivities beautifully wrapped up and the sun still miraculously shining, Jack and I headed south to Garth to see some of his favourite customers. We had worked on Jenny's mountain walls before, but this time it was one of the more formal estate walls that needed our attention – closer to the house, originally lime-mortared and with nicely dressed stone. Part of it took a tumble sometime earlier that year. When Jenny phoned, she said, 'Save it until Whitney comes if you like.' And so he did.

Jenny always greeted us with legions of fresh Welsh cakes when we arrived, enough to last even the hungriest wallers several days. Good thing – we could see pretty quickly that this job was bigger than Jack had first thought. We had to take down a lot more than the original collapse, as a long stretch of wall was leaning perilously. There was no point rebuilding on top of a slipped foundation. Though it was built with lime mortar, the stone was so beautiful we would rebuild it dry in the exact same style – with a bit of 'cream filling', as Jack described the uniform course of thick stones at its middle.

It was the first time I had ever stayed at Jenny's. To stay in a house where someone has such long family memories across generations was a real treat for someone like me, who grew up in a 1968 ranch house, which – though lovely and home – did not hold the same wonder within its walls. Jenny's Penderel ancestors had come to this hill and indeed this house just a few generations after sheltering a king on the run from Cromwell's army following the Battle of Worcester (that would be the eventual King Charles II, and the oak tree in which he hid in Shropshire is sometimes called by their name). Jenny presides over something very special, with layer upon layer of lives and stories built up over successive generations. Naturally, that comes with great expense to upkeep, not to mention the burden of preserving and passing down all the stories and antiques and the general spirit of the place, and she bears that responsibility beautifully.

Jenny, characteristically direct, asked me how I slept when I came into the kitchen for breakfast the next morning.

'Great – like the dead!' I replied.

'Good,' she said warmly, adding, 'I was born in that bed, you know. And my father died in it . . . But it's a new mattress!'

Jack was already there on the little settee in the corner, and he nearly fell off it laughing. Little cracks him up more than Jenny, who despite being wonderfully good-natured and intentionally humorous, often makes us laugh in ways she doesn't intend.

I felt like an offensive mess sitting at their lovely breakfast table in my filthy dungarees, but they insisted it was absolutely fine. Filthy dungarees, big waller elbows, cloth napkins with silver rings, and a white tablecloth Jenny's mother painstakingly embroidered decades ago . . .

I began to realise during that trip just how poor my manners were, not because I was a thoughtless ogre, but because my friends routinely demonstrated such overwhelmingly *beautiful* manners. It wasn't like this at home. We were a family around the dinner table. It was rare we ever had an outsider – even a close friend – let alone a stranger from a strange land whom we were only just getting to know. And there would never have been wine – never. We were Baptists and even Christ's blood was Welch's absolutely unfermented grape juice. This was a whole new world for me, and I loved it. Every meal felt luxurious, but they were always full of laughs, too. No one in that house took themselves too seriously, so you could never be uncomfortable even if you – like me – hadn't grown up around things like langoustines and kir and fine art.

Johnny and Jenny were the perfect example of how exquisite manners can and *should* make people feel welcome, loved and cared for. They taught me what a luxury it is to be truly and generously hosted.

There was something about Jenny that reminded me of the best kind of Welsh Mountain Pony: magnificent and high-spirited, but rugged and determined, too – undeterred by anything or anybody. She was bossy in the most loving way, always gracious, and with excellent taste in art and food and design. She was empathetic in the extreme, which sometimes got her roped into all sorts of bizarre scenarios, but she loved to laugh, most especially at herself and all the little human dramas playing out around her. Laughter was how you kept going.

Johnny, for his part, was no less a character. Well into his eighties, he was still devastatingly good-looking . . . Dashing, with a big smile, quick gait and even quicker wit. He was a retired coal merchant, determinedly honest and forever outraged with crooked businessmen, crooked church officials

115

and crooked governments, among others. He had an admirable and indefatigable sense of justice and fairness, but he was equally passionate about poetry, too, and an excellent piano player . . . So excellent, in fact, that the first time I heard him playing the baby grand on the other end of the house, it took me a while to realise it *wasn't* Radio 3. He ran the wine service at his table as seamlessly as I had ever experienced in my life. No pretence about it, just always kept your glass full with something gorgeous, and usually overjoyed to tell you just how cheap it was!

Johnny and Jenny had the kind of marriage we'd all want, and I loved to listen to their banter, forever teasing each other in mock annoyance. They were wonderful, and they embodied so much of what I was coming to value.

Jack and I finished the first section of restoration in a couple of days. The remainder he would return to do alone in June. From there, we headed just up the road to Angharad's house for my final big surprise of the trip.

She was gobsmacked when I walked up to the kitchen window. I had texted her from Jack's phone to make sure she was home, so she was expecting just the big guy – not me. After a notorious childhood of blown surprises and leaked Christmas gifts, I was finally getting good at this subterfuge stuff.

I did not understand until I met Angharad's child how much I could love a stranger. It was in this moment I realised that the infant children of people you love are possessed of some sort of magic powers – or at least this one was for me. All my life I had disliked babies – vehemently, vocally – but this one melted me in an instant. I have a photo of us from that day, both looking slightly in love with each other, with baby vomit all down the front of my shirt. Ellie was *heaven*.

We sat out in the sun with Har, and Jack held the baby for a while. It looked good on him. I thought how much I loved this whole scene: the sun, the blacksmith in a slightly softer state, the man, the new little friend . . . I felt even sorrier that it was almost time to go back to America.

The last few days of the trip we mostly spent out roaming the countryside. We picnicked along the river in Abergwesyn. I took off my shoes, rolled up my trousers, and explored the rock formations, tea in hand. Jack snoozed in the grass. I watched him sleep and thought about how lucky I was. I didn't know what would happen with us, but we had just had a run of spectacularly sunny days, working a bit, but wandering the hills, side by side, even more. It seemed better to have our time together in bursts like this with predictable suffering or incompleteness in between than not to have it at all.

Kate and I strolled across one of her fields my last Sunday in Wales. With all the hullaballoo of parties and guests, she hadn't realised I was leaving so soon. When I told her I had to go in two days, she hugged into my side and touched her cheek to mine. 'And then you'll be thirty,' she said. 'Just a smidge.' It would have been impossible not to love her.

Inside, we cracked into a bottle of fizz and all pitched in with supper. Kate sent me out of the kitchen to do some little chore for her, and when I returned she and Jack had put three candles into the mashed potatoes for me. 'One for each decade,' she said. 'I didn't have thirty in my little cupboard!'

We stood on her doorstep together that evening after supper, looking out over the valley beyond. I could feel her turn her gaze to me. She stepped closer, threading her arm around my waist. I draped an arm around her shoulders. 'You're so beautiful, Whit,' she said, looking up at me. She spoke so softly I wasn't sure I'd heard her right, so I smiled and shook my head, laughing it off, still staring out across the lawn as I tried to paint that view into my memory forever. Whatever it was, she'd repeat it if it was important.

'You are,' she insisted.

Kate and I really didn't know each other all that well, and though we were both a bit shy about some things, I knew by then that we were very fond of each other. Something in her spirit spoke to mine. We seemed early on in our friendship to have an understanding of each other that didn't rely so much on words.

After Jack and I drove away down the front drive, waving to our friends on their doorstep, we went across the valley to walk the hills above and catch the sunset. I was probably a little bit drunk that night, but definitely drunk on love.

And so I went home to turn thirty.

It is difficult now to describe the magic of this particular trip – this entire year, really – without sounding ridiculous and a bit saccharine. It was almost as if someone had cast a spell on me, so radically different did I feel after those two weeks away. Filled with a sort of optimism and confidence I had never had before, I flew home from Wales for the first time without tears. This was the moment when everything in my life that had felt disjointed and chaotic those last four years finally began to come together in a way that made sense. Once that happened, there was no turning back. I was on my way.

Greenville, South Carolina

Thirty seemed like an age when you were supposed to have your shit together a bit. On the surface, I didn't. I didn't have any money, and I wasn't doing the things that were 'normal' for where I come from, like marrying, having children, holding down a steady office job, buying property, saving for retirement, or even living independent of my folks. Hell, I couldn't even cope with a pet or a houseplant.

I knew this wasn't a particularly glamorous moment in the arc of my life story, but I had come home from Wales feeling like the world was suddenly waiting for me to decide what I wanted from it. I had my first couple of clients on the calendar, and apart from the logistics of the projects that awaited me now, I wasn't worried about anything. I think I sort of knew by then that I would be OK, even if I couldn't quite see how just yet. I was very aware that I wasn't miserable, and by then that was enough.

I couldn't face going back to Jim, and after I got home, I never did. I saw him once to pick up my last cheque, feeling sheepish and guilty, but he seemed to understand that I was destined for other things, not least because I hadn't shown particular promise as a carpenter.

Matt and I broke up in text message. Sort of. Had we even been together? I never was sure about these things. I didn't understand dating. (Still don't.) Whatever it had been, it was his decision not to have any more of it, and though I was insulted by the medium (and of course slightly annoyed that he didn't seem to find me as amazing and irresistible as did all the friends I'd just left in Wales) I didn't particularly mind. He was no Jack – in fairness to him, no one was.

More importantly, work would require my full attention and energies in the coming days. I had a lot to figure out, and there would be no space in my life for anything else for a while.

I prepared to begin my first project for a stranger, someone who'd found me on the web and believed me to be some sort of professional. I understood when I made my website that this might happen, but it was still somehow shocking to realise I was about to test the waters as a professional waller in America. I still felt like the world's biggest poser.

This was new territory in so many ways: self-employment, running a business, walling independently of my mentor . . . and charging money for it. For all that I had tried, I had never tried being in charge of myself, and I had never once had an interest in becoming a businesswoman. I don't particularly like numbers, for starters, or offices. And though I do come from hardworking folk, I am not from entrepreneurial stock. We always let other people take the risk of running the business itself. I didn't have that luxury if I were to make space for walling in America, and I didn't have the luxury of waiting 'til I felt I was ready. It was time to dive in and just see what happened. Sink or swim.

This required me to be willing to fail (the last few years had prepared me well for that). It wasn't just a question of failure, though, but facing my deep-seated discomfort with imperfection as I grew, and that was *much* more difficult for me. Walling was the one thing I wasn't instantly brilliant at that I still wanted desperately to persist in, and that took a lot of courage. Ditto for stepping out into the world of business, where I had not a clue how to begin. Was there some sort of *Small Business for Idiots Who Actually Aren't All that Interested* book I could pick up somewhere? I felt so vulnerable, and mistakes in business risked not only shame, but financial losses and even legal repercussions. Does some alarm go off when you are making a grave mistake on your business taxes?

As I took my first tentative, fumbling steps on my own that spring and summer, I was wincing at myself all the time, but I kept going.

Money was so frightening, so meagre in those days. In one sense, my career as a waller was shaped not just by love – by going back and forth to be with Jack – but also by the fact that I never had enough money for a metal workshop or for land to farm ... Walling was a portable skill and required few tools. I had never had much interest in money. I had always had enough-ish, and I'd never once had any credit-card debt (to do so was a cardinal sin in my family), but now I would have to start paying a bit of attention.

I remember so vividly how my stomach dropped the first time I flashed my credit card to order stone, realising I had no contract with my client, no money in the bank to cover the cost when the bill came in a month, and no money to get a lawyer on the case if things went south unexpectedly. As I bought my first tools, I stood in the aisle of the hardware store for ages trying to make a choice between two $30 shovels of different shapes. I needed both – square-nose and pointed – but I couldn't afford *two* shovels. Once I had those tools, I moved them in my Volvo sedan with its back seats folded down, and I borrowed my father's truck at the beginning and end of a project to move my wheelbarrow to and from the job site. A pick-up truck of my own was out of the question, so I made do.

My first jobs were in my hometown. They were just small projects – garden walls, usually built with lovely curves – to accent my clients' existing landscaping, or to define a space and provide a framework against which they might plant in the future.

At first, I was flabbergasted by my clients' relief at finding me. Apparently, it wasn't easy to locate someone who did traditional stonework. There were guys around who had been building chimneys and walkways their whole lives, but no one was building actual dry-stone walls in the old way like I could. Everyone said they'd been searching for ages before they found me.

Perhaps I shouldn't have been so surprised given the amount of terrible manufactured faux-stone veneer ('lick and stick', we call it) cropping up everywhere around town, but I suppose that had just convinced me that most people couldn't tell difference between the fake stuff and what I could do. The people who *could* were the ones who called me.

I do not come from a world of dry-stone walls and matching stone cottages, so folks at home can be forgiven for not having the keenest eyes for detail, and I found that many of my clients had travelled to or even hailed from enchanting places where stone dominates the built environment. Some people, though, simply gravitate towards stone naturally . . .

Something about it speaks to them, just like it does to me.

The question of what to charge these excited people (once they found me) was a tricky one, and I agonised over my estimates. I wanted the work, so I didn't want to be too expensive, and I didn't feel terribly confident about my skill level yet, so I was careful of asking more than I was worth. And would I get my stone quantities right on the first try? That was the big – and potentially very expensive – question. Stone was not cheap, and miscalculations could easily run into three or four digits. I had to be ready to flop, but equally, I knew I might pleasantly surprise myself. Time would tell, and I was aware that I was charming enough to make sufficient apologies to my clients if necessary. If I had to, I would sacrifice the additional stone cost out of my own pay if I screwed up. Determined always to be fair and honest, and notoriously stubborn to boot, I would make this work no matter *what* I had to do.

Greenville, South Carolina

People have often asked me where on earth I came from if I am not from a family of crazy, rule-breaking people. I am a bit of a black sheep, it's true. I have often wondered how I got to be as I am – so different from my roots – but like a magpie, I have picked up bits of people and culture as I've gone along. I have a natural curiosity, a hunger to know what delights are out there in the world. Moreover, my parents encouraged me to travel and to learn, and that I have done. It is perhaps the greatest gift they have given me after a stable and loving childhood.

Jack admitted to me once that various clients and friends in Wales had carefully nosed around over the years, asking him leading questions to try to figure out who I was and how I got there, assuming that I must come from money if I were able to bounce back and forth across the ocean and earn so little. I was shocked ... slightly offended, too. It wasn't even a possibility in my head that I would be funded to do something of this sort—some sort of youthful exploration not necessarily tied to prosperity. That isn't a thing where I come from.

I do not come from that sort of privilege. I am white – possibly the biggest privilege in the current world order – and I had the luxury of a good state-school education and a home in a comparatively stable and free democratic nation – but there is no inheritance, no trust fund. It was not upper-class folly or ritualistic rich-kid play. It was a conscious and potentially dangerous decision to walk away from the upward trajectory of a family that not too long ago was thoroughly blue collar (or no collar), partially illiterate, and sometimes hungry.

Some thought I was stumbling off the edge of a very scary cliff. Actually, I leapt. It was the only way I could ever have been happy. But what my family wanted for me – and what I was taught to want for myself – was to get as much education as I could, take as normal and responsible a job as I could, and be *safe*. I was supposed to enjoy a kind of prosperity and security that so many generations of my family did not have.

My grandmother Ilene is the eldest girl of ten children, raised on a string of tenant cotton farms in Upstate South Carolina in the twenties and thirties. When she was a child her father, Luther, had her standing in the field waiting on the sun to come up so that they could start hoeing cotton as early as possible on land they did not own in hopes of a profit they'd never really achieve. They moved to a different farm almost every year as Luther tried in vain to improve his lot, but nobody got ahead sharecropping cotton. It was a losing game. Most years you wound up owing your landlord any profit you might have eked out since he'd usually been the one who'd sold you on credit the seed, the fertiliser and the use of the land. The game was rigged, and in the meantime the children kept coming. Birth control just wasn't part of their world. I'm not surprised Luther drank a bit, leaving poor, frustrated Leila no choice but to dispatch their children into the woods now and again to find him wherever he'd passed out. It was a hard life.

My grandmother was not able to finish high school because her mother needed her help in caring for the younger children. Her only hope for a better life was to move to the city, maybe get a manufacturing job and a decent husband. Her father never really got ahead until he picked up and moved to Florida, and even then he never had much. He did manage to get his family a little house of their own in a place called Apopka. He worked at the packing houses for the orange groves, eventually as a security guard. Leila, a tiny woman, found a bit of work in the greenhouses, sometimes with her unmarried daughters at her side.

Leila never learned to read and write. She couldn't drive either, but she loved to ride, I'm told. She had married my great-grandfather when she was fourteen in order to get away from a horrible stepmother. Her own mother had died young. Luther used to joke, 'I married her young so I could raise her myself!' But it couldn't have been an easy life. Still, they made it work, and they stayed together until death. My grandmother once said to me, looking off into the distance as we sat on her screened porch talking through layers of family history, 'I know my mama's in heaven, 'cause she sure had hell on this earth.' She was quiet then, shaking her head, her brow furrowed. Her mind had drifted to a sorrowful place that I could only imagine.

As a young woman, my grandmother moved into the city as soon as she could, marrying my grandfather around the time he got out of the Army after World War II and went to work in the textile mills. (My hometown once called itself the Textile Capital of the World, so jobs were abundant if not especially lucrative, and anything paid better than sharecropping.) My grandmother eventually went to work in the factories, too. Days were long and wages remained low. Working conditions could be difficult. There was lint *everywhere* in the mills, and lung ailments were common. My grandfather suffered with tuberculosis from time to time,[*] once sent away by his doctor to a sanatorium and requiring special sets of dishes and cutlery when he finally came home again. Making ends meet was a struggle each week, and my mother told me recently that she remembers women from a local church bringing them food while my grandfather was away. This would have been the fifties – hardly the time of Dickens.

In another episode, my schoolgirl mother had to choose between getting a bicycle, which she desperately wanted, or accompanying her beloved aunt Carrie Lou on the train to Washington, DC, where she was to receive treatment for ovarian cancer at Walter Reed Army Hospital. Carrie Lou's mother was working, and so was her brother. Her husband was away in the Air Force, and her father – another family drunk – was estranged. My mother, aged eleven, was the only one available. So it was the bicycle or the train ticket for Mom – there just wasn't enough money for both. My mother, ever tenderhearted and selfless, chose the ticket. Her aunt would die not long after, aged thirty-one.

Though my grandmother never had much for herself or her children, she still did better than the generation before her, even if that only meant scrubbing the laundry on a rub-board *inside* the house instead of boiling it in the yard. My own mother, too, did a little better than her mother. She went further in her education (and could have done well at

---

[*] My mother is a carrier to this day due to childhood exposure, though she has never developed the disease.

129

university if her parents had had the money to send her or the knowledge about how to get scholarships), got a steady job with the county school district that came with a pension, and found a husband with a good job, a kind heart and wider worldview than the family she'd come from. They bought homes, breaking the pattern of moving year after year in search of a better situation. My parents travelled for *pleasure* rather than in search of work, and my mother could have most of the things she wanted even if she felt a bit guilty spending the money after growing up with so much less. She finally got a bicycle.

And then there was me, first-generation college graduate, and with lots of bicycles over the course of her childhood. My father said to me just after I'd returned home with my newly minted diploma, 'You know, Boogie, this has been the end of a dream for me. I always wanted you and Taylor to finish college, and you did.' He had tears in his eyes. And he had worked bloody hard to make that happen for us at a job that I wouldn't necessarily call his 'passion'. My father should have been a coach, but he spent his career in engineering firms because he's good at maths, and that's a responsible job. There were parts of it he really liked, but it has always seemed to me that what he really loved was football and moulding young people to do the right thing and be responsible citizens.

Everyone in my family – even my community – was proud of me after each degree. No one quite understood what it was I'd studied – American Studies? Folklore? – but they knew I'd done well. This was less about their worldliness than my habit of picking odd things to study rather than practical ones like engineering or teaching. (I remember a fellow folk-lorist from Kentucky once told me a story about someone at home thinking she was a 'forklift driver', having slightly

130

misheard and then translated into something more easily recognisable.) And the time I spent working at the Smithsonian meant something to people even if the specifics of my jobs remained a bit unclear. Everyone knows that place.

It makes sense, then, that my grandmother had mixed feelings about my decision to work in the dirt like a peasant when I'd just finished a Master's degree and moved out to a small organic vegetable farm when I could have been in a fancy museum. We talked happily about her childhood on the farm, but she also said to me that she worked so hard to get away from that life and couldn't understand why I was going back to it when I had an education. It's hard to say to someone who grew up in the Great Depression, 'Because I'm not happy in an office in town,' but that was my answer.

Not everyone I've talked to about this understands the class issues bound up in these sorts of generational divides, the set of expectations – articulated or not – placed on the younger generations. Jack understood what I was up against because he, too, had experienced it. Like me, he was the first generation of his own family to go to university and enter the professional class, and there was tremendous pressure to make the most of his opportunities to move up in the world. (He had degrees in Economics, Education and History, to name a few, and he had worked plenty of 'real' jobs with proper pensions before becoming a full-time waller around the age of forty.)

I had a very hard time at home feeling as if I had any right to try a different sort of job that might make me happy. I felt guilty, ungrateful. I also had a hard time believing that I might succeed if I did try. In Britain, no one seemed to think it was strange or selfish at all that I wanted to stack rocks for a living, and no one seemed to feel the bottom was about to fall out for me. Why was it so different across the ocean?

131

When I got to Wales, aged twenty-six, the whole world looked different. *I* looked different. Friendlier, more beautiful, more open-minded and filled with possibility. It was tantalising. From the start, my British friends were more accepting of me, more enthusiastic, more optimistic – and thank God for that or I might never have been brave enough to make some of the choices I have. I have become increasingly aware that your limits in life are in very large part shaped by what you believe is possible, and these friends somehow seemed to believe that absolutely *anything* was possible.

They delighted in apparent eccentrics like me, which has spurred me on in ways I'll be grateful for until the day I die, but I can't help thinking their delight is made easier by long-standing financial security in the family line – good property to inherit at the very least, and probably a very nice education, too. (Plus the National Health Service. The financial burden I carry for health insurance is a big one – for years I couldn't afford it at all – and Angharad said quite plainly that not having to worry about the cost of her family's healthcare is one of the things that has made self-employment possible for her.) Along with that education, and the education and careers of their forebears, comes a whole web of beneficial social connections, but more importantly, a special kind of confidence about one's place in the world. I don't begrudge my friends for what they have (none of us can help what we are born to, high, middle or low), but the circumstances of one's upbringing do shape one's perspective on the world . . . on responsibility and – most importantly – on possibility.

They opened my world with their generosity and encouragement . . . and with their shocking lack of scepticism about the relevance of what I was doing. It was worth doing if it offered meaning and expressivity and contentment; money

132

was beside the point. They took me seriously long before I did, showing deep respect for the work and using words like 'artist' to describe me. It was all very strange, but also wonderfully refreshing and emboldening. They possessed a kind of confidence I never saw where I grew up, and I have been trying to figure out ever since *why*.

Careers in the arts, for instance, are thought irresponsible where I come from, unlikely at best. It's just not done. Neither was craft revered on a large scale. My friends in Britain are committed to art and music and literature, and that carries on through generations, but my people were lint-heads and sharecroppers who could never have afforded pianos, let alone learned to play them.

Most people I went to high school with didn't go to university afterwards, and they certainly wouldn't have been stupid enough to major in something as irrelevant and unmarketable as English Literature or Music if they did. (As a child, I remember hearing a snarky, 'Want fries with that?' any time someone mentioned that kind of major.) One is supposed to get as skilled and reliable and professional a job as one can. Anything else is reckless – higher education was a privilege made possible only through the very conscious, calculated sacrifices of others.

A friend in Wales once said to me that your art chooses you, and you must open yourself to it almost as a duty – a notion which struck me as both beautiful and true. But where I grew up, they'd just be asking who was going to pay the light bill. That remains my inner contradiction. I have been programmed to believe that the bottom will fall out – that I should have saved more money, and that would have been easier with a 'real' job. A creative, individual path is a risk.

I remind myself regularly: some of my grandparents didn't have enough to *eat* growing up. *My great-grandmother never learned to read or write.* It was not so long ago, or so far removed from me, that people's basic needs went unmet. These struggles are so dire that they bear repeating, not least because most Americans take food and literacy for granted these days. We get annoyed if the line is too long at Starbucks or if we don't have 4G LTE signal (or any Gs at all in much of Wales, thank you very much) to send an iMessage. I have sometimes been guilty of the same, but I stop and remind myself often that I am being a total brat. What *actual* problems do you have? How would you look in your grandparents' eyes right now, Whitney Brown? I like to think I would for the most part appear quite grateful and self-aware. And I like to think they would want me to be happy – that was what made their struggle to survive and improve worth it. It's hard to know what they would think. My great-grandmother Leila and I couldn't have much in common, could we? Would we understand each other at all?

My father's father, Pop – the grandparent I believe would be most interested in what I'm doing now, and with whom I most wish I could have a conversation about it – was the poorest of them all. Although he always worked at least two real jobs and side jobs to boot, he was also the one who turned down the supervisory position he'd earned with the telephone company precisely because he wanted to keep working with his hands in the outdoors. It might have sat him in a comfortable chair in a suit and given him a higher salary, but my grandfather was a man who knew himself, and he knew what he needed to survive. He needed to stay hands-on, physically engaged, in touch with the beautiful parts of northern Pickens and Greenville counties where he often worked. And so that's what he did. He would retire an overqualified, well-respected lineman (who needed knee and shoulder replacements eventually). Maybe he could have had more

134

money or a more sophisticated title, but that wasn't the point. He was happy as he was. I'm sure he wouldn't have phrased it as such, but he followed his passion.

Pop was a man who knew duty, who executed it. Part of his motivation was that he had known hunger and shame as a boy. When he was old enough, he joined President Franklin Roosevelt's Civilian Conservation Corps (CCC) and left home. His father was an alcoholic, and my grandfather was not the favourite son. As a child, he often lingered at friends' houses close to dinnertime, hoping that he might be offered some food. Many nights he went to bed hungry. The CCC, he would later tell us, was the first time he had ever had enough to eat in his entire life, and he didn't mind that a lot of his pay cheque went home to his mother. (That was the deal for the boys who joined up. It made their families more willing to send them.) It was there he got his start with hard, physical work, fighting forest fires outside Gilroy, California, among other things. From there, he joined the US Marine Corps in 1942. He passed drill sergeant school as an Army Reservist in his forties – a rare achievement that was recognised with a beautiful silver sword I coveted as a child – and he served until he reached the Army's mandatory retirement age in his sixties. When he left the Marine Corps after the war, he joined Bell Telephone and worked there for the rest of his career. When he retired from Southern Bell and the Army Reserve, he kept busy through loyal service to his church and charitable causes. He tinkered endlessly on lawnmowers and as a handyman in those days, too.

I wouldn't call it a selfish decision *per se* that he kept his job as a lineman for the telephone company all those years ago instead of moving up to a higher status and higher salary, but I'll just say that I don't think he made a lot of decisions that were in any way mindful of his own happiness. He missed my father's high-school graduation, for instance, because he was working that day. He just *worked*. It was survival, stability, duty. And to know that he loved work so much *and* was so committed to continuing to use his body for it in the outdoors means something to me. A man who never did anything selfish just *had* – like me – to find a way to stay outside, to use his hands. The difference is that he started there and didn't have much formal education. I had to consciously make the decision to step out the door and into the overalls.

Would we understand each other at all? We just might.

Meadows of Dan, Virginia

When I met Diane Flynt at a dinner in Mississippi a few months after I got canned from my kitchen job, I was at a low point in my life. The last thing I wanted to do was talk to someone new about who I was.

On the best of days I dreaded these getting-to-know-you conversations. Since graduating from high school, I'd never once had an easy explanation for myself. I had always studied something odd, or taken a job that was difficult to describe. Now, I didn't even *have* a job. I didn't really know what to say about myself. I could talk about my recent trip to Wales, I guess, but who in the States had really heard of dry-stone walling anyway? As we started to talk, I prepared myself for a blank stare and a polite 'Oh, how interesting.'

But Diane was cheerful and genuinely curious. I remember she had a warm smile and very well-designed glasses, both of which endeared her to me instantly. She was a cidermaker, she said, and that perked me right up. I realised Diane probably had to explain herself a lot, too. We connected initially over the dry ciders of the West Country. I told her I'd just had my first – and fallen in love with them – that summer when Jack took me to the Great Dorset Steam Fair. She had gone to cider school in Somerset some years before, she said, and she asked me why I'd been in the UK. That led me to walling.

To my shock, Diane was a rare American creature who knew what dry-stone walls were, and she was the first American to greet my revelation of this skill as something other than a cute quirk of personality or a curiosity. She made me feel interesting instead of strange. A keen gardener, she was fond of walls and told me that she had plenty of stone at her place in Virginia.

Though I didn't have a clue at the time, Diane would eventually lead me to the biggest break of my career.

I certainly didn't expect that anything would come of our conversation that evening, but Diane is a woman who makes things happen. She has a head for business and marketing, and she knows the importance of networking. Though she hadn't seen any of my work, she believed in something about me, and she made good on her promise to help connect me with potential clients in Virginia.

In the intervening months while I was off farming in North Carolina and building in Wales, Diane emailed a small group of her friends. These were successful businesspeople, civil servants, journalists and artists, all of whom were keen gardeners with pockets deep enough to employ somebody like me. In her message (which made me sound much more established than I actually was) she offered me like some lucky find that she wanted to share with the worthy. Might they like to add some stone to their gardens? Some sent kind emails in response, saying how wonderful and hello. No one took the bait at first. Then, a man named Jim wrote to me, wondering if I might build a low seating wall around his existing patio. Finally. This was exactly the kind of thing I wanted to build: 20 metres of pure, curving dry-stack, looking out over the mountains beyond.

Immediately, I wondered whether I might be in over my head, but I put on a brave face and drove north to meet Jim and his wife Silvie and do the estimate. When I went to see Diane afterwards, I told her that I knew I could do the building, but I didn't know *what* to charge or where to buy stone or even where I'd sleep if I were working in Virginia. She said she could help with all of that, and with the confidence that she was behind me, I arranged a tentative start date with Jim and Silvie, pending completion of an ongoing Greenville project plagued by thunderstorms.

A few weeks later Diane welcomed me back to the mountains. We sat out on her big stone terrace swilling rosé as dusk descended along the ridge and the fireflies made their way up out of the grass. It had been a stressful push to finish the Greenville job, and I had raced to pack and get up the road for this one. I was frazzled when I arrived, but that evening dosed me instantly with the peace and magic of the Blue Ridge. It was the most beautiful thing I'd experienced since I left Wales in May. There was something very special about this place.

If my clients found it anything other than charming when I turned up the next day in a Volvo sedan stuffed full of tools, they never let on. Jim and I went down with his truck and trailer to buy the stone at a place called B&B Produce which, curiously, was mostly a roadside fruit and veg stand but also sold a bit of landscaping stone. I remember how surprised the staff were to discover that it was the woman – not the man – stepping out of the truck who was the mason (as they'd refer to me; despite how literal it is, 'waller' is a meaningless term in America – and indeed most places). They didn't give me any shit about it, though. They were as nice as they could be, curious more than anything, and they looked on enthusiastically as Jim and I picked out some lovely pallets of grey, mossy fieldstone. The skid steer loaded up our trailer, and away we went.

Jim showed me where the beer fridge and the bathroom were, and then he left me to it. I set about digging in the hot June sun, using a borrowed barrow to haul away the turf and soil. I cut open my pallets and began sorting my stone to see what we'd bought. I got my foundations in just fine, and the wall began to creep up. I seemed to spend huge amounts of time, though, just moving stone from the pallet to the yard. And it was lovely stone, but I struggled to get enough quoins for the four cheek-ends I had to construct. (The wall had an opening in its middle that aligned with the doors of the house, so really, was two freestanding walls.) It wasn't long before I ran into a problem, and it wasn't a small one.

I somehow grossly miscalculated the amount of stone I needed, likely due to this type's high density as much as my own figuring, and things were generally going slower than I had hoped. Luckily, my clients were gracious about both issues. Jim went up and down to B&B a few more times to get stone, never batting an eye at the additional expense or time. But I was still so annoyed at myself, and I tried not to want to punch something . . . Usually, some sledgehammer work took care of this urge, but alas, there were no huge stones to make into little stones. Comically, I couldn't spare the stone to relieve myself of the frustration of not having enough stone, and I tried to take it all as another lesson in patience (something I was not born with an abundance of).

Every night I went home filthy and exhausted, covered in that particular grime made by sweat, sunscreen, dust and stone chips all mixed together. I was often dispirited by the weather, my disappointing building speed, or my poor estimating skills. Powerful thunderstorms were an almost daily affair, sometimes raining me off completely or sending me cowering for shelter from the danger of lightning strikes so high on the mountain. But there was something about Virginia. It had a bit of magic about it even on the aggravating days, and the beauty of it all made it difficult to stay frustrated for long.

With all that rain coming and going and blowing and howling, dramatic clouds lingered on the ridge tops, and thick fog and mist sometimes descended even in summer. As I drove into Floyd one evening along the Blue Ridge Parkway for beer and food, I was quickly overwhelmed by the beauty of the scene in which I found myself. This drive was gorgeous on the most mundane of days, but this was dreamlike. The storm had cleared the air of the oppressive humidity it had held all day, leaving the mountains feeling clean and fresh. In silvery light with flashes of brilliant gold, old trees stood stately and sculptural along the winding two-lane road. As low clouds rolled through, sometimes hiding them, sometimes revealing them, it seemed a sort of surrealist animation. If I could not be in Wales, this was pretty damn good. I pulled my car onto a verge near Rocky Knob to watch it play out and simply laughed aloud at my luck.

It was a great feeling to finally be throwing stone around in America. I never thought it would be possible. It had its frustrating moments, but most of that was because I was young and impatient, perhaps didn't quite have all the skills yet that I needed, though working and thinking and struggling would be the only way to get them.

Jack and I worked easily together most of the time. Jobs went faster. I had to think less about logistics when he was in charge, and he was *always* in charge. In America, everything was harder because I had all the responsibility, but I was aware that I would also get all the glory, and my clients so far seemed to be much more vocal and excited about my work than our farmers in Wales. Their praise and enthusiasm were a wonderful thing to have in my ear as I bumbled my way along, questioning and reconsidering almost every move I made.

There was a festival staff reunion coming up on Independence Day, so I took a few days off work and headed north to see my old friends. It was about a million degrees outside in DC, and we kept the beer flowing fast that afternoon. I found Parker, and we sat talking intently. How different my life felt now from a year ago. We laughed together over the change, and she seemed relieved to see me at ease this time instead of weeping. We both knew that I was where I needed to be. I thanked her again for talking me off the ledge where military service was concerned. 'Think of all I'd have missed already,' I said.

'I knew you'd figure it out,' she said with a shrug. I knew that I wouldn't have without her, but I didn't press it.

'How is Jack?' she asked.

'Oh, he's fine. Sassy as ever,' I said, shaking my head. 'I'm heading back over next month.'

'When are you going to marry him?' she asked, smiling like a Cheshire cat. Her face said she knew she'd asked the million-dollar question, and she was very pleased with herself.

'God, *I* don't know! It feels *sooo* complicated.' I laughed, rolling my eyes at my ongoing predicament.

'Why?' she asked. I was never allowed to make blanket statements.

We talked about age once more.

'Twenty good years is twenty good years,' she said, convincingly. 'And there is always Act Two.'

I could never win an argument with Parker. She was far too practical, and always three steps ahead of me.

After a couple of scorching days in the city, I brought Jim and Silvie's job to happy completion. They took me along to a big dinner party where future work immediately cropped up. The crowd I met that night were mostly not from the mountains where they now lived, but had all built second homes there or moved there in retirement. Missing their highly social city lives, they have networked sufficiently to form a giant dinner club of successful, curious, friendly and fun-loving people. High Altitude, Low Society, they'd christened themselves.

If you've been vetted by one of the members, an entire world opens to you. Tales of a lady stone mason preceded her, for many had heard of me before getting the chance to shake my hand that night. The boys at B&B Produce in Cana were talking about me in front of Jim when he went to pick up more stone, at which time he learned that he had the 'best-looking stone mason in Virginia'. This entertained the crowd. As Diane and her husband Chuck aptly pointed out, there wasn't an awful lot of competition.

It was fascinating and mildly embarrassing to me to be the centre of such intrigue at a big party, but I survived because everyone was so overwhelmingly kind. By the end of the night I had invitations to come see a few potential projects, as well as to spend time on a narrowboat in the UK and meander down through Baton Rouge and Cajun country with expert hosts. I wondered whether I was somehow extra lucky? Extra charming? Extra weird and fascinating? A pity case? I didn't know, but I didn't mind.

I wouldn't realise until a little later that these were basically the kinds of people I'd found in Wales, too: those who value creativity, beauty and the land around them, and who move through the world with open, curious hearts. Only they sounded like me and knew what cornbread was, and it was hotter here, and there were poisonous snakes and bears and fire ants and ticks and the like. Always in the South something is waiting to bite you, sting you, eat you, feed you, or at the very least pass moral judgement on you. It can be kind of intense. Not to mention heat, humidity, violent thunderstorms and sunburn. But the thrumming of the night air, the smell of honeysuckle, the genuinely friendly customer service and the men holding the door open for me (like I expect everywhere but almost never get) ... These things still charmed me endlessly, as did these new people. America, I reminded myself, wasn't all bad.

Wye Valley

With another cheque safely in the bank (where it never stayed long), I had come right back to Wales. That's how it went in those days: I did just enough work to cover a few routine expenses and my next plane ticket, and off I'd go again for as long as Jack would have me or until a major holiday called me home. Finally I had managed to stop worrying that some great voice would come down from the sky to stop me. I began to stand behind my choices unapologetically for the first time in my life, but the funny thing was, for all the bravery that took me, no one ever turned up to challenge me. I steeled myself for a fight that never came. Perhaps it was only ever with myself. In some sense, I would always be on the run from the stifling, abstemious Evangelical culture in which I grew up, but mostly, I was just a waller going where the walls were.

I never told my parents that Jack was something more than a friend. I was tempted every now again – usually in moments with my mother when we were just sitting together in the sunshine talking about the world – but I never could bring myself to do it. I felt so private about the whole thing. I suppose I still didn't want to risk their disapproval (especially remembering my father's reservations about my going to Wales in the first place). I knew I was terrible for being so secretive, but I also knew it was my right, and they had always respected my privacy. Perhaps they knew even then, but I wasn't going to bring it up, and they weren't either.

What they did know was that I had fallen in love with Wales in a very powerful way, and that wasn't going away any time soon.

One Saturday night not long after I arrived, Jack and I rendezvoused with Johnny and Jenny to see an outdoor performance of *As You Like It* by a young theatre company out from London. It had rained all day. We almost got stuffed into a barn, but as we were collecting our tickets and buying drinks, the clouds parted. Blue sky appeared. Theatre volunteers hustled to towel off our seats and we would watch the performance in the cosy, lush outdoor space after all. I was thrilled. It was much better, I thought, if the Forest of Arden could be outside, with living trees all around us. As the play unfolded, we could hear sheep and geese going about their evenings in the nearby fields, wind rushing through the leaves of the willow trees . . . It was magical – the perfect merging of art and nature. I laughed so hard in some scenes that I cried – who doesn't love a cross-dressing love story? – and a beautiful summer night in the company of friends was a wonderful thing in itself . . . even with midges.

I discovered a world of riches in Wales when, for the first time in my life, I was amongst people who took classical art and music and theatre not only as routine, but also a crucial, instinctive part of life . . . Something as normal as breathing.

148

It's not that I had personally grown up impoverished, but the legacy of the South's (and my family's) poverty showed itself quite clearly.

These were people who *were* artists, came from artists, and not knowing any better, they took me in as one of their own. These were people who painted and sculpted, who played the piano – very well – as a hobby, who loved their gardens, who put on plays, whose shelves and tables were covered in books, whose beautiful voices rang out in song down the hallways of their homes. Seeing how beauty was so intricately woven into their daily lives helped me understand not only what was possible, but also to spot a need that had gone unfulfilled my whole life. I hadn't even known it was there.

When I came back to Wales, I was coming back to a world that felt timeless and beautiful, not quite so driven by shiny new consumerism and Evangelical Christianity. It suited me better. And then there were the hammers and axes, the wildness of the hills. I led a simple, lovely, peaceful life in Wales. I beamed like an idiot half the time I was there. It all seemed too good to be true, and yet it wasn't. It had been here waiting for me all along, and it felt like it would be here long after I was gone.

I thought more and more seriously about the notion of enduring, timeless beauty and the patina – hard-won through age – of both people and objects. I studied it all around me, and it felt far more present for me in Britain. Shakespeare, Tallis, nature, middle-aged women and the grandest, most radiant old women, seasons and the flowers and foods and rituals that match them all; hedgerow medicine; worn-out rugs that only became *more* beautiful in their faded, thin state; beat-to-hell Barbour jackets; treasured old woollens; legions of lovely, mismatched old china; a special pot for mint tea that had already been glued back together once.

149

It was the same for our walls. The stone on a rebuild always looked funny until it weathered a bit, got its mosses back, suffered in the wind a little.

I felt greatest affection for objects that bore the marks of being well loved and regularly used, handed down across generations or carefully selected off a second-hand shelf. I was most drawn to people with great stories and a few wrinkles. I could see that ageing improved the things that survived it.

These things spoke of a certain quality of life, of endurance and sentimentality, of a keen ear and a particular sort of discerning eye. These were the things I had come to love in Wales.

Caerneddau

Jack and I were wandering up Caerneddau, just another in the dozens of hills we've walked up together. I was angry about something . . . Something I'd taken too seriously, as I do, or something he'd been too rude about, as he does. I walked a few metres behind on purpose, paying no mind to the quaint observations he was making about the birds he spotted through his field glasses, which was his way of paying no mind to my mood. He would not engage. I was spoiling for a fight. Together, we were ruining this hill, which was otherwise full of sheep and rare, glorious sunshine. It was a sublime August afternoon.

I don't remember who broke first. Did I finally get him to answer me when I spoke to him? (He ignores me for sport when he knows it will anger me *even more*, and he always shied from confrontations of the emotional sort anyway.) Did he finally just walk up to me and wrap his arms around me while I was still fussing at him about something, again ignoring my words? Or did he just yank me down to the ground in a comical wrestling take-down move that meant 'shut up and get over yourself'?

I don't remember. But before I knew it I was laughing, and then crying, and then laughing again. We were lying flat on our sides on top of this grassy, tufted hill, holding on as tightly as possible to each other. Tears rolled sideways over the bridge of my nose and down to the earth, a purge of all the enormous, contradictory, pent-up emotion I'd been carrying. His arms and the sunshine were by then all I could feel.

We were alone, and in a place no one ever goes. This has been the story of our time together. This is where it works, and when we fight, it is almost always about something or somebody from the outside world.

I had been angry with him about something ... I don't remember, and I may never have understood exactly what it was in the first place. I have always been angry at him in a way ... Mostly because he is thirty-three years older than I am, which isn't something he can help. And yet I *was* angry. I fought the attraction from the beginning, knowing it was 'inappropriate', and wondering in the back of my mind if this was one of those 'dirty-old-man' scenarios. No, in fact, it was something real and bigger than either of us ever could have expected. I think we would have run had we known, but we eventually found ourselves in the midst of a tortured, star-crossed, *ridiculous* and often wonderful love story – one I wouldn't have traded for anything. But in a way, I had mourned its end since before its beginning.

I loved him, and I raged at him. That was the way it went. In those days it was a non-stop volley between the purest happiness I had ever known and a deep sadness that churned constantly below the surface. It was so good that I wanted to see it through. There was no reason to push it away or leave it

152

behind me. It had the gravitas of a life-changing, life-spanning relationship, but I knew that it wouldn't work forever.

There were no dreams of growing old together. He was always the first to point out that he was already there: old. No couples are guaranteed any part of their future, but certain parts he and I were guaranteed *not* to get – at least not together. When we did find ourselves in the same geographical place, our time was always pre-stamped with an expiry date: my return flight, visa expiration dates, sudden death, something. Unease loomed in my heart for one reason or another, though there were plenty of moments sparkling and magical enough to make me forget for a bit.

Despite any of my early hesitations prompted by wrinkles and baldness on his part – the physical manifestations of age – I eventually discovered that people can still be very, very alive at sixty and beyond, and they tell much better stories. I realised at some point along the way that I was having fun despite the initial protestations of my eyes. So I learned to see differently: the heart does not see age.

Once, on a long drive with Kate, she said, 'Tell me the story of your life, Whit.'

I bumbled my way through the nuts and bolts of schools and jobs, and as my tale arrived awkwardly and inconclusively in the present day, I laughed to her that I had just told her a good story very badly.

Not yet satisfied with the picture I painted of my life, she said, 'Tell me more, Whit. Who's the first boy you loved?'

I had to tell her that there hadn't really been anybody. I had been in love – or so I thought – with a boy named Will in high school, but he didn't love me back. I used to get stoned and watch him – also stoned – playing bass over in the corner, and I sort of twisted his arm into going to the prom with me at the last minute, but that was it. It was young, a bit silly, totally awkward and completely unrequited. Not remotely romantic.

A scant handful of men passed through my life after that, but no one who amounted to anything. I had a bit of fun here and there, especially with Danny, who picked me up – literally and metaphorically – on the handlebars of his bicycle and zoomed me down the DC streets late one summer night. And then there was Matt for a minute in the spring. But I had never really had a steady man in my life until Jack. Everyone else had either been unbearably boring, unavailable, or too afraid to approach at all, though I didn't realise the latter until I hit my thirties. Apparently I can be a little intimidating, but actually I'm just terribly shy.

It was Jack, really. Jack was my first 'boy'.

'I think you two should hitch up,' she said. 'You make a good team.'

We talked about age differences, parents and their expectations, immigration concerns, children with an older man, death . . . all the things I found daunting, we talked out as we moved east along the motorway. Kate and I had never before talked much about Jack in that context. 'I had wondered from time to time, Whit, but I never liked to ask.' Embarrassed, but also eager to talk, I think I told her sheepishly, 'Well, it's cold in Wales. Of *course* we sleep together.' Immediately, she affirmed, 'Of course you do! It *is* cold.' Naturally empathetic and extraordinarily kind, she would not let me feel awkward if she could help it – not in that moment, not ever. I had talked to Rose about the relationship for a few minutes back in the spring on our drive to the train station, but really, Kate was the first person apart from Parker I opened up to about Jack.

In the time we'd known each other, Kate had shown me that she was eager to humanise people rather than judge them and set them apart. Her perspective on things always felt fair and loving, envisioning the best and most hopeful in any scenario. She was a woman who seemed to be governed by a mix of deeply felt intuition and beautiful manners that never failed her, and I trusted her to be both honest and fair.

Jack was a scholar, a poet, a warrior. He was both gallant and gentle, sophisticated and practical. He didn't need much luxury, but he loved it when it came his way. He was confident of his abilities, but never cocky. Strong and resilient, he had not an inkling of self-pity, a trait that weepy old me envied very much. With a vast range of experience, an amazing sense of humour, and a real knack for storytelling, he kept me entertained without any trouble at all. He was brilliant and challenging and hilarious, and his wide-ranging skills and interests impressed me.

'Who,' I asked Kate rhetorically, 'at my age has a prayer of stacking up to that?'

Beyond the roll call of virtues, I just loved to be with him, and that was all I cared about. Kate agreed that this was all that mattered. I struggled over the appropriateness and practicality of it for years before eventually just throwing up my hands, crying 'Fuck it!' and deciding to just go with it and be happy. I told her I knew that no one mattered in that decision-making process but Jack and me, knowing that I was trying my best to convince myself of the truth of this statement. 'Exactly, Whit. And people who love you will understand that . . . Eventually.'

In fairness, endless older women in my life had tried to tell me this over the years: Parker, Kate, Rose – the ones to whom I poured out my heart in those years of figuring out who I was and what I wanted.

At some point in this period, I realised I could 'what if' my entire life away. Joy could slip right through my fingers if I expected it to be perfect or simple or to look a certain way. All my life I had been daunted by the risk of vulnerability, pain, rejection and failure. Whatever my big, charming exterior advertised, I had often let fear govern my life. Like trying my hand at walling on my own back in America, opening myself to love, too, meant risking shame, embarrassment and judgement. It also offered the potential for huge rewards, but I wouldn't know unless I tried. It took so many years for me to get up the courage to do that. I simply had to do it in my own time.

I was slow to do a lot of things as a child, hesitant to accept reality or to try something until I knew I could get it right. I was easily frustrated and embarrassed – a proper perfectionist – with an amazing ability to deny various necessities. Physically, I might have grown fast, and I was always quick to share my displeasure in a given situation, but I was slow to tie my shoes, slow to potty train, slow to speak for myself in restaurants or anywhere else in public, because I was comfortable right where I was and didn't see any need to move on in anyone's time but my own. And I was fiercely independent ... when I wasn't being utterly dependent upon my mother and hiding behind her legs, that is. What a challenge I must have been: a headstrong but painfully shy child.

And then one day, for no obvious reason, I would finally decide to get on with whatever it was that had been waiting on me. In the case of Jack, it occurred to me that I was not living life to the full no matter how much I might be travelling and adventuring if I was denying the love that was privately consuming me. I was playing it safe.

Did you ever think you would fall in love with someone your parents' age? Of course you didn't. *I* certainly didn't think that. No one imagines they will be enraptured with wrinkles and bald heads and arthritic joints. But let's get something straight: it happens. When you become a person who moves through the world without preconceptions – or when you at least become someone who is willing to challenge her preconceptions on an ongoing basis – rules vanish. (It helps enormously to purge judgemental people from your life – or at least from your most intimate negotiations. Run with the hopeful, romantic bohemians if you can.) You move by feel alone, and sometimes, you fumble your way to surprising caches of happiness.

Finally, sometime in the hot months of 2013, I simply gave in to what felt right. I was too tired of fighting it. And finally, I was beginning to feel a little bit brave.

Brecon Beacons National Park

I was about to find out whether I could pass the Initial/Level 1 certification exam for the Dry Stone Walling Association of Great Britain. That meant four days of practice on a piece of wall near the Brecon Beacons with instructors supervising, followed by a rather gruelling seven-hour take-down and rebuild on test day with examiners hovering nearby, making marks and comments about my technique. I had to get it mostly right, and I *had* to finish. If I didn't finish in seven hours, I automatically failed.

I'd been building well, but I had never walled against the clock before, and that is a very different way to work. It is valuable to be aware of how you spend your time – how long things take, and how you use your body – but it does take some of the peace out of the job. I knew I had the skills, but I wasn't sure about speed. In fact, I was borderline terrified. I found it extremely unnerving and uncomfortable to be forced to build as quickly as I could at the expense of technical perfection and visual cohesion. For this very reason, it was good for me.

The thing I have to remember in walling is the natural imperfection – or perhaps inconsistency – of my materials. Stone is an imperfect medium. With a few exceptions, a stone is shaped how it is shaped. As a waller, you can chip off an awkward corner, or dress a face a bit, or even whack off a complicating bulge on the top or bottom, but you aren't going to make stone into uniform bricks. The hammer is only for minor adjustments for a tighter fit. My job is not to be a stonecutter; rather, it is to craft something strong and lasting out of stone left in a mostly natural state. My job is to make imperfect materials cohesive, which requires me to comprehend and command an endless array of shapes.

What exactly did this test mean? Practically, it meant nothing, but I still felt tremendous pressure to perform well. No one I knew in America had even heard of the Dry Stone Walling Association of Great Britain, let alone its certification process, so whether I passed or failed wouldn't make an ounce of difference at home. But I suppose I looked at it as a chance to validate a decision that had led me down a path that had been equally fascinating and challenging. Maybe it was the moment of truth: had I given up my Smithsonian job foolishly? Did I have any actual ability at this craft I'd chosen?

I know, too, that I wanted to make Jack proud. He had invested an awful lot of time and energy in me. How would I stack up in the eyes of professional wallers who weren't invested in me personally?

And I needed to be proud of myself. I wish I could tell you that I was such a rogue by then that I wouldn't have cared a bit about my results, but I'd be lying. The straight-A, valedictorian, *summa cum laude* student in me still wanted to ace the test.

159

It was a muddy mess on the mountain that day thanks to heavy rains and lots of repetitive steps in a small section of ground. Mud slows down building – not at all what you want on test day – but we all slogged on as best we could. I stripped out my piece of wall expertly and quickly, already pulling ahead of my fellow test-takers. To a degree my speed was dependent on theirs since our pieces of wall would have to interlock with each other all the way to the top. I could only get so far ahead. I looked nervously and frequently at my watch, which only fuelled my anxiety. I kept an eye, too, on the instructors so that I knew when I was under surveillance. They would come round every half-hour or so, watching, but also walking on the course we'd just laid down to check it for stability, or tugging on stones further down the wall to make sure they wouldn't budge. I felt dizzyingly frantic all day, never able to allow myself to believe I'd make it by the end.

Relieved and a bit shocked, I finished on time, jogging back and forth to heave up my copes towards the end. A few onlookers had gathered. One asked if I'd grown up on a farm because he was so impressed with how strong I was. It didn't stop him trying to help me lift up the heaviest cope stones, but I shooed him off as gently as I could. It was a point of pride for me to do it myself.

I beat the clock, but I wasn't sure how I'd fared in my technical scores. Standing back, it looked like a pretty decent piece of wall, and the instructors hadn't said anything terrible to me during the day as they'd made their rounds . . . The examiners called us into a tent one by one to learn our results. Sean Adcock, a waller from North Wales who teaches all over the world, called my building ability 'exceptional'. Will Noble, a Yorkshire legend (and father of the aforementioned Lydia), agreed in his lovely, loping accent.

Afterwards I sat on a wall, celebratory bottle of beer in hand, looking out over a landscape turned golden in the late-day sun. The rains had gone now. I was surrounded by my fellow test-takers, some triumphant, some not, but all relieved to be done for the day. Jack arrived to pick me up, and I watched him relish the good news and drink in the examiners' praise for his protégé.

I fell asleep in the bath that night, and by the fire Jack would say to me with rare sincerity in his voice that he was proud of me. There had been no qualifiers or playful insults to accompany his words. It was almost embarrassing, but I couldn't have been happier to hear it. I had made it: I was a waller by anyone's standards.

It was a *huge* moment for me, not least because it wasn't always clear that I had done the right thing. And it wasn't ever quite clear that it was going to work out in the long run. The moments when I thought, 'Oh, here's the obvious next step' or 'This is *definitely* right and I have *not* messed up my life' were few and far between.

All those years when it looked even to me like I was adrift, I had been slowly laying track to this moment. Every time I reached a stopping point in my life – the end of yet another job, or the completion of another big project – I scraped together the money to fly across the ocean one more time so that I could dive back into piles of stone and mud. Some people thought me escapist or perhaps slightly lost, I know, but I simply kept returning to the things that made me want to get out of bed in the morning. I kept going back to the walls.

Some of us have to stumble into our careers, bumping into them as we chase after something else. I was chasing sanity and love and wonder out in the hills. In moments, I found them all.

The Red Lion

The next Wednesday, Jack and I headed up to the The Red Lion, allegedly the oldest pub in the county, to celebrate. We had two locals we were fond of – the Neuadd, down in Llanwrtyd, with the Heart of Wales Brewery and the two shaggy dogs in the bar, and there was this one, which sits a few miles up the road from Beulah on the way to Kate's. The food is pretty good for what appears to be the middle of nowhere.

Pubs were funny. They could be joyous places, full of singing and joking late into the night. Or they could be places where despair went to sit and console itself, pint after pint of cheap lager, consumed by men sitting shoulder to shoulder but perhaps still alone. The occasional 'All right, bud?' grumbled at familiar incomers as they came to join in the silence. Our locals were more the latter, but they were still somehow charming in their way. The Lion was cosy, the barman friendly, and on Wednesdays they did Steak Night, always with cuts of local Welsh Black rump.

People had begun to recognise me by then – this was my fifth trip, after all – and Jack and I were so tall that we did attract a bit of notice, even if no one ever said anything to make us feel we stood out. We just knew. It probably didn't help that I was young and American, and he was much older and Welsh and not properly local to the area. I hardly passed for his daughter as I might have if we shared an accent. People talked about us rather than to us for the most part. But whatever they thought, the locals began to accept me as a fixture in their pub tableau even if we didn't necessarily interact much. It didn't matter – for the most part, I was content just to listen and observe, just as I knew they were doing to me. And at that moment I didn't care what anybody thought of me: I'd just passed my exam, and I was on top of the world. I was strutting through life.

As Jack and I stood up to leave our table that night, he realised he'd left his jacket on the back of his chair, so he ducked under the low doorway back to the dining room. As I stood waiting for him, just beside the ancient doorway – a good four inches shorter than my natural height – I heard from across the bar, 'Ooo, that's a big girl, isn't it?'

I stifled my laughter and looked over slyly, not wanting whoever it was to feel embarrassed. I was amused, not insulted. I saw two farmers – both shorter than I – leaning against the wall with their pints, chatting about everything and nothing. They hadn't intended for me to hear them, and they sounded more impressed than anything. I must have looked enormous in juxtaposition to that low doorway. In fact, I *am* enormous compared to most Welsh women and even men, save the rugby international types.

I looked strong, useful . . . Like I could carry children on my back and still shear sheep, or heave big bales. I knew by then that, generally, I amaze Welsh farmers . . . And that's without their having seen me work. Once they've seen that, I've got fans for life.

I was born with a big, powerful body – not like the svelte cheerleaders and fine-boned beauty pageant contestants who had been the prized catches where I grew up in South Carolina. I was an athlete, swinging bats and pulling oars and occasionally serving volleyballs or shooting basketballs. (Really, I was best at playing the heavy, scary positions during the one week a year the girls got to play American football against each other. Centre, Nose Guard, Tackle – the ones that require sheer mass and stubbornness.) I carried a sousaphone in the marching band, too. Mostly, though, I was a scholar, and I had learned to worry about my weight because even at my thinnest, the idiot boys I went to high school with didn't fancy me. I groan and roll my eyes to think of it now . . . That I ever relied upon their judgement, gave them power, wasted my time and energy worrying over anyone else's taste . . . Particularly when any of us with healthy bodies ought not to take them for granted.

I had never been consciously man-pleasing, nor unselfconsciously indulgent (except, perhaps, when drunk at the end of a party and in a kitchen alone with cake), but I did worry far more than I needed to over what and how much I ate. It didn't help that my father had undergone cardiac bypass surgery when he was forty-six and I was eleven, which scared me sufficiently off massive meals and great quantities of fat. Butter? *Never*. I didn't even know what double cream was. Clotted cream was still a mystery. Mince pies had never crossed my lips. Wales brought seismic shifts.

But I always knew there must be *some* reason I grew to be so big and strong. I had simply never found it until I ventured out onto the open hill with Jack. I had always felt too big, too ungainly. I was tall, thick-bodied, wild-haired (with a hint of

164

copper that has always glinted in the sunlight) and freckled (if not utterly pasty or burnt) – a Celt, really – with ugly nails and thighs that touched. I was a Clydesdale among Thoroughbreds. It didn't work for me until I put it to work. In Wales I had always felt I had exactly the right body: a powerful one that could withstand heavy loads, cold and rain, one that could move mountains and transform them into monuments.

In Wales, I wasn't worried about being beautiful, and paradoxically, that is precisely when I began to feel so.

London

Kate and I were sitting in the Café Royal on our first morning together in the city. There, in a gleaming world of golden Siena marble inhabited by well-starched staff, I couldn't help but notice how much my grubby waller hands stuck out. My short nails were always a bit dirty, my cuticles red and irritated. There were by now well-established calluses on my palms and the undersides of my knuckles. I still had scars from burns in the kitchen and one nasty gash on the farm. These were working hands, and suddenly I was in the slick, manicured city.

Setting my white porcelain coffee cup awkwardly back onto its saucer with a bit more clatter than I intended, I spread my fingers before me and inspected them closely, front and back. I laughed aloud to Kate, 'No one's gonna marry me for my hands, I'll tell you that!' She chuckled in surprise, her mind clearly on other things, like which juice to order. 'Someone is going to marry you for your curls and your smile . . . and for the way you talk to people,' she said, quite matter-of-factly. 'You are brilliant, darling.'

I looked up to see her beaming at me across the table.

Everyone deserves her own personal Kate. She was the best possible company for a young woman trying to figure out her place in the world. The entirety of our time in London went something like this – doing fun things together and my being told regularly each day how amazing and beautiful I am, how extraordinary and wonderful the world around us. I loved the way Kate moved through life, always at ease in herself and kind to all she met, always prepared to be delighted by some small wonder along the way. All these years later, that trip is still in the running for the best forty-eight hours of all time. It was a moment that hammered home once and for all the absolute necessity of finding a person forty years older than you that you would love to be in forty years' time. Kate was my person.

Jokes aside, I appreciated my beat-up hands because I appreciated what they said about how I was spending my time. Maybe some women think about the minute details of their appearance throughout their adult lives, but I didn't become acutely aware of my own until around the time I turned thirty . . . I began to inspect and even treasure the lines in my face that say I've been living and enjoying my life rather than shielding myself from it. Sunshine and laughter made those lines, the sea and the walls, a wonderful set of friends and the occasional cigarette. Increasingly, I had gracefully greying temples to match. I did not mind; when you feel like you are using your time well the prospect of ageing does not feel so agonising. It helps enormously to have gorgeous and gloriously fun older women in your life. In every way, Kate was a godsend.

We had come to the city to see *Macbeth* at the Globe, but in London, with no responsibilities outside ourselves for a while, we talked in a way we never had before. They were long, luxurious conversations – the kind that stretch on for days around generous reflective pauses, mundane interruptions, meals and sleep. These were conversations of extended togetherness, unfurling elegantly in thoughtful bursts as we moved about the city on the 94 bus, chatted during the interval of the play, and sat in the big windows of the flat, lingering over late-night fizz or morning coffee.

'You know, if you think about it, Whit, I could be your *grandmother*,' she said one morning, eyebrows raised in a mix of amazement and amusement.

This gave me pause. Over the years I had come to think of her as the perfect balance of proxy mum and pal . . . a sort of magical fairy godmother, unmoored from the constraints of time and age and hangovers. She had never seemed remotely *grandmotherly*. My grandparents, though absolutely lovely, had seemed *prehistoric*, whereas Kate had always seemed . . . well, like me, but with better stories. I looked at her quizzically.

'If your mother were twenty, and I had been twenty . . .' she said. 'But I don't *feel* there's a great age gap between us . . . forty years . . .' She trailed off, still slightly amazed at the numbers.

She was right, but it was strange to think about. Kate had never seemed old to me, but perhaps that was just because she had never lost her youthful curiosity to middle-aged cynicism like so many others do . . . Never had I known a person of any age so happy to be alive each day, so eager to see the magic and possibility of all that lay before her, so able to roll with the punches and even laugh at them.

The more I talked to Kate, the more alike I realised we were, and I was so heartened to see a more developed version of myself – what I *could* be if I kept working at it. I still got so frustrated with myself sometimes, and she seemed a sign

168

that I would be OK. Kate and I shared many traits (most of which we chalked up to be Taurean), but what we didn't share was her beautifully calm reserve, and I prayed that it would come to me with age.

I once reflected aloud to Jack that you can think you are one kind of person when you are young, only to spend a few years in the real world with adults and Big Life Stuff and subsequently realise that you are *nothing* like the person you thought you were. I was *convinced* that I was a laid-back creature when I was in my early twenties.

Stifled amusement crept across his face. 'Darling,' he said, buttering me up for a dose of truth, 'you are one of the most highly strung, opinionated women I have ever known. I'm not saying that's a bad thing, but you are unusual.'

Jack of course got the raw, difficult parts of me as well as the lovely ones. We agreed with a laugh that I might not be to everyone's taste.

I had learned a lot about myself in the last few years, as I finally got up the guts to grab life by the horns and really begin to wrestle, but there had been casualties along the way. Mistakes were made.

My reaction when challenged was to get angry – usually out of embarrassment or self-righteous exasperation at having been questioned – and I certainly didn't like to have my motivation, integrity or loyalty disputed. I hated being misunderstood or thought less-than-capable. I was thorny when it came to my ego. *Some* might have thought me prideful. Actually, I was just insecure.

This was where Kate stepped in. She could see me. She got it. And while she said a few things to nudge me in the right direction, mostly, she just showed me how I *could* be.

She had an understated sort of strength, an unshakable inner resolve. She was self-assured, but in a graceful way that was never abrasive. She was the kind of woman who naturally brought out the best in everyone around her ... A quiet force of nature, gently pushing you along like the tide.

Before Kate, I had mostly known women who were so soft that they were passive, or women who were too hard. Too many things had happened to the latter in their personal and professional lives (not infrequently because of men), and they had gone too far in the other direction to compensate. I couldn't relate to either. In Kate I saw something that made sense to me. She was an incredibly powerful woman, but restrained. Always gentle, always kind. Her warmth was her trademark. I wanted to be more like her, at ease in the world and herself – and not just in forty years, but now.

I had some work to do, but Kate had always believed in me. She was not the first, but I think she was the first I really listened to, and at the age of thirty, I was finally learning to accept a compliment.

As we parted in Shepherd's Bush that last morning, she headed to Paddington to catch a westbound train, and I hustled across the common with an extra spring in my step. I was on my way to meet Rose.

Much to my surprise, we'd kept up a scattered but enthusiastic email correspondence since we first met back in April, so I let her know I was coming to London. She happened to have an extra ticket for a play that afternoon, so off I went to Southwark to find her.

I waited a while in the appointed place. No Rose. Finally, a text: 'I'm inside! Come in through the bar, and tell the girl on the door you're coming to meet me. She'll be expecting you.'

There she was, crouched on a step, looking incredibly glamorous from head to toe, and wolfing down a sandwich out of a packet. I laughed. She could be disarmingly incongruous. It was one of her most endearing attributes.

We moved quickly inside the theatre – the bell was ringing – and as we settled down on the wooden benches of the Globe's lower gallery to watch a show that I would never make much sense of, Rose leaned her head on my shoulder. It was chilly that October afternoon. Something about her felt weary. I wrapped my arm around her waist, and there we sat in the comfort of each other as the surrealist pageant unfolded before us. All I remember is Billie Holiday, an astronaut, an enormous piece of fake meat and a lot of gold lamé hot pants.

After the show, we wandered off to a mediocre coffee shop for some peppermint tea and a proper chat along the river. As we looked out over the murky water and the grey skies, bridges and domes above it, we cut straight to the chase: love, careers, ageing parents, hypothetical children and a bi-continental search for the place and the people that felt most like home, all in the span of half an hour. I never struggled to explain myself to Rose – my love of Jack, my feeling torn between two countries, my work coming at me in intense waves with great, scary silences in between . . . We seemed to understand each other intuitively, which I think was a relief to us both.

I talked with Rose about many of the same things Kate and I pondered together, and the more I talked, the more comfortable I got with what I was saying. It felt good to hear the confidence growing in my own voice as I talked about what I loved and what I wanted, to see it echoed in Rose's face as she listened.

Rose was welcoming of honesty, complexity and raw emotion in a way I'd never had with a friend while sober. I could say without worry what I needed to say. I was allowed to be vulnerable – deepest fears, wildest dreams, white-hot anger. Nothing scared her (notable exception of spiders), and little eluded her, and whatever came out of my mouth she greeted with the utmost empathy and enthusiasm. We were thinking about similar things in our lives, and I think it felt good to share both the worries and the hopes of it all.

Her appearance in my life felt slightly surreal, a stroke of cosmic luck. She was a lot like Kate, but where Kate had that gorgeous, clear-headed peace and gentleness, Rose had a sort of provocative fire. She was born, I felt sure, under some dancing star, and though we sat talking and joking familiarly, I was quietly in awe of her. She possessed a wisdom and strength that seemed beyond her years, a rare sophistication balanced with a sort of lingering, irrepressible wildness, and she kept me on my toes. (Actually, she scared the shit out of me sometimes, but in productive ways. She pushed me to face my fears, but always with love.) She was the most powerful and magnetic woman I had ever met, and what I saw in her, I knew I had in myself, only less bold and more fledgling. Simply knowing that she existed in the world made me braver, less apologetic, less awkward and lonely.

We hugged a long goodbye in the street and, not knowing when I would see her again, I stood to watch her go.

Rose on the streets of central London was something like a wild deer . . . shy and hoping not to be noticed, but so magnificent that she really couldn't help but attract attention. Earlier that day, as I waited for her along the river – I sensed she wasn't known for her punctuality, but was so charming you didn't care – every tall, dark-haired woman who approached caught my eye, but none had her magic or her grace. It was the same as I watched her walk away that evening, back to whatever wood she had come from.

Greenville, South Carolina

It was surreal to be in my childhood bedroom with the windows open to 70 degrees and crickets and tree frogs. The night sounds of the south were so evocative – one of the few things I had missed, along with Mexican food and sincere customer service. It was in the forties when I left Wales, and grey, and no night noises but fires and rivers and owls. It was always surreal to come back to South Carolina – lovely and comforting because it felt instantly like I never left, but also disappointing precisely *because* it felt like I never left. The feeling of adventure subsides too rapidly. I have to think really hard to remember where I just was – what that place felt like, smelled like, sounded like. And when you miss people – so much a part of place for me – that is particularly what you want to remember: their perfumes and colognes, the sounds of their laughter, the feel of a signature piece of clothing that you might have hugged a lot, and the contours of their shoulders under it . . . Details.

Awake ghastly early with jet lag, I stood out under the moon. My mind drifted to a night the month before when Kate drove us back in darkness from Pembrokeshire after a long two days of sailing. A huge harvest moon rose before us, directly over our road home. 'How beautiful,' she said. 'How lucky that she's there in front of us where we can see her – not behind us, or hidden by a hedge.' And then she did that wonderful thing that Kate can do: recited the perfect poem for the moment with not an ounce of irony or self-consciousness. This time, T.E. Hulme's 'Autumn':

> *A touch of cold in the Autumn night –*
> *I walked abroad,*
> *And saw the ruddy moon lean over a hedge*
> *Like a red-faced farmer.*
> *I did not stop to speak, but nodded,*
> *And round about were the wistful stars*
> *With white faces like town children.*

Smiling, I would go inside to write as I awaited the dawn, a cup of tea steaming away at my side. It was only about three weeks since I'd left Wales – since I last hugged my friends – but my double life was a time warp. It felt an eternity since I'd been gone, whereas it just felt like everything in America had been on pause.

At home, it wasn't just the work I missed or Jack or the hills, but the texture of Wales, too – the whole of it. All of the things that delighted me in the beginning had become normal by now: bone-handled knives, Agas, lapsang tea, Welsh cakes, British manners, hot water bottles for bed, hot flasks for the road, baths, Radio 3 *and* Radio 4, the Proms, village shows, nettle tea, tractors, arnica, ancient family homes, cask ales, opera (even if simulcasted!), theatre in the round, artists in the flesh, bracken, gorse, heather, sheep, sailing, rugby, smoked salmon, singing in pubs and sincere discussions of astrology. None of these things were part of my life in America, but I had become accustomed to them. They felt like part of me now. And so to go home without them was to go home without a part of myself.

It's a strange thing when you feel you don't fit your own life. I knew I wasn't alone in that, but it didn't make me any less unhappy about it, and I wanted to figure out how to make it better. I didn't like feeling *so* odd and out of place and secretive when I came home. Was it so wrong to want to wield an axe? Never watch television? Swan about in silk dressing gowns and use the best china all the time? Be a little bit cold inside?

I wanted to figure out how to make a whole life out of building and thinking and writing and travelling. Deadly earnest, holding both my hands across the table in London, Rose told me how important it was to say out loud the things we wanted – to be clear about it.

'I don't see why I can't be a dry-stone waller and a globe-trotting public intellectual with posh sunglasses,' I said.

'Exactly!'

I would spend the winter scheming for just that.

Meadows of Dan, Virginia

Early in 2014, with the winter still upon us, a set of blue-prints arrived by post. In the spring I would take on my most challenging project yet. I came highly recommended by word of mouth by then, but privately I wondered if I was up to the job. This project was a bit like a hydra, with many scary moving parts that were an awful lot to keep up with, even for someone more experienced than I was at the time. It was 125 linear feet of nothing but curves, changing widths and height variations across rolling terrain. It was not a dry-stone project because its design defied the physics of stone. Gravity would not be enough to hold it together. Mortar would be necessary. To make it even more terrifying, I'd be working for a wealthy client and his well-known landscape architect . . . and I'd never had blueprints before . . . what if I couldn't read them properly?!

My job was to figure out an appropriate balance of beauty and technicality, and never before had I been forced to juggle so many variables at one time on a wall. There were no straight lines, no consistent heights or widths, no level ground. A waller did not design this project, that was clear, but it would be beautiful if I could just figure out how to pull it off. It was a fascinating process (though at the time I mostly wanted to pull out my hair or melt into tears with stress).

I went with my client and his wife down over the border into North Carolina to shop for stone. I knew from introductions made by our mutual friends that Walter and Sally had both been journalists, and they asked me more about my history as we made our way along the mountain roads down to Greensboro. I always half-dreaded that conversation with new people because my story has so often solicited blank stares and silence. The reception was different this time.

'Your résumé must be amazing!' Sally said enthusiastically, turning to smile at me from the front seat.

'I'd always thought of my résumé as a liability until I realised I never wanted to work for anyone else ever again if I didn't have to . . . and even if I did, the type of person who'd be put off by it is probably not the kind of person I need to be working for anyway.' I realised the latter as the words came out of my mouth. From the driver's seat, Walter heartily agreed. I could see his eyes smiling in the rearview mirror.

It was nice to feel confident and unapologetic about my path for a moment, but I had plenty of nerves left over how much stone we would need to order. I had agonised over the numbers for days, knowing all the while that even my best calculations didn't change the fact that every type of stone builds differently, and every quarry packs its pallets in a slightly different manner. Each type of stone has a different volume per ton, too. What you see on the yard is not necessarily what you get when it arrives at home and you cut open the wire mesh. There might be a whole lot of crap in the middle that just isn't usable. Walter didn't seem at all bothered about the 15 tons I said I needed. I remember the calm with which he made the purchase. I almost felt sick, but Walter's casual confidence reassured me.

Heavy rains commenced within days. This was a mortared job, so there was no toughing it out in Gore-Tex and wellies like I might do on a dry-stack project. I needed to speed through it all to catch my next flight to London – I seemed always to have a looming flight by that time – but I simply had to surrender to nature, just like a sailor stuck in port with no wind to speed him on his way. There is only so much we can control, and the best thing is to accept the situation and wait with humility and patience.

Defeated, I hunkered down in the old farmhouse which had become the guesthouse when my clients built their asymmetrical modern wonder just up the hill. I built myself a fire, snuggled down with a book. Black tea by day, red wine by night as the wind roared like a jet engine just outside the house. Rain lashed the windows all through the night and pounded the metal roof. I expected at any point I might suddenly hear the thunderous crashing and cracking of trees uprooted from the soft, soaked ground, great limbs breaking under their own weight.

I went through a lot of ups and downs during those weeks at Walter's. When the weather broke I finally got to work, and I was regularly overwhelmed by just how much I had to do. It was a time that tested my patience, my back, my intellect, my diplomatic skills and my determination. I was daily discovering new levels and varieties of exhaustion. I woke most mornings feeling as if I had been cast in concrete, unsure whether I could will myself out of bed one more time.

Barrowing stone uphill again and again across the lawn one afternoon under a blazing sun, I was beginning to feel sorry for myself. I felt like Sisyphus. I was bone-tired from weeks of heavy work coupled with the stress of my own expectations and self-imposed deadlines and the sleeplessness that came along with both. I'd already needed to change my flight to London once, and I still hadn't constructed the technical, swooping bench-back, nor the fiddly field stone veneer under the sculpture platform, nor had I cut and laid the heavy, precise bluestone slabs for the step treads and platform surface. And I was fed up with mixing mortar . . . how many tons of sand had I gone through?

It was a perfect day of mountain spring for anyone who wasn't at work. My clients, I happened to notice, had their windows open, so it was probably best if I didn't continue my usual string of mindless profanity – the essentially innocuous workplace chatter of construction. As I passed nearer the house on my way towards my mixer, I heard music coming from inside. It stopped me in my tracks for a moment as I strained my ears, trying to catch enough to cue my memory. Definitely twentieth-century. I walked on down to the enormous gas-powered paddle mixer, put on my ear defenders and fired her up. I could hear nothing but muffled engine sounds as I methodically shovelled sand and cement. Sitting down on the cool concrete steps of the greenhouse, I checked my email as I waited on my mud to mix. Sometimes in those moments I found a cheery note from Jack or Kate or Rose, urging me on, saying they couldn't wait to have me back with them soon. 'Gin, hugs, and dancing,' Kate promised.

On the way back up the hill with a fresh barrow of mortar I was met with the rousing, swelling, *grateful* tones of the apex of Aaron Copeland's *Appalachian Spring*. Finally. I dropped the handles of the wheelbarrow, coming to a standstill. I nearly collapsed with something I can only label as bewildered relief. The surprise arrival of such beauty in the

179

middle of such a grind is startling, and it takes a moment to understand that it is not a figment of one's imagination.

I found out later that evening over a steak dinner that this was Walter's annual spring ritual for a day when the sun and its warmth first returned to the mountains. 'It seemed like a good day for it,' he said.

Moments of unexpected sweetness continued to find me, but I began nevertheless to run low on both patience and energy. As the weeks passed and I moved towards the most difficult part of the job, I found myself slightly furious with a man in Greensboro who was remotely managing the installation of the project. I needed to try to bite my tongue. This was my first big job, after all, and my client was paying this firm a good fee, but I found my liaison both unhelpful and insulting by turns. He didn't mean any harm, but he was oblivious to the fact that he was more a thorn in my side than an aid.

This fellow had sent me blueprints that in some ways were perfectly clear – if there's one thing I understand, it's shapes and lines – and in other ways totally baffling as they showed little respect for the physics and practicalities of natural stone, or the lie of the land in relation to it. They had highly specific measurements: the wall was supposed to change in height and width by an inch every linear foot, but this was sort of irrelevant in my obviously less sophisticated waller brain.

In the course of questioning him over various things so that I could figure out how much stone I needed to order, I somehow managed to convince him that I was an idiot. I believed him myself for a bit, but then I realised that he was a drawing and calculation man, and I was firmly fixed there on the ground with the actual objects and shapes and grades.

Later, he had the nerve to bring out a full-scale drawing of the bench-back I was supposed to erect. It was the *pièce de résistance* of the entire structure, save the sculpture that had sparked the design of the whole project. I could not believe that this guy was driving two hours north to bring me yet another drawing. 'Think of it as a template,' he kept saying cheerfully. He was convinced that this life-size drawing was a gift to me, something to make life easier for my tiny little brain.

For starters, the damned thing kept blowing away as he tried to tape it all together on top of a windy mountain in springtime. Next he intended to stick the thing onto pieces of hard foam insulation board so that it would stand upright behind the bench like a giant science-fair display. I didn't have the heart to tell him that his true to scale, 6-metre-long picture with its precise measurements was basically useless to me because I'd had to change the measurements of the *entire* wall since none of his numbers gave him the actual rise and fall lines they wanted when you stuck it on an undulating hillside. There were certain fixed values in the form of the ground and the concrete that was poured, and the wall had to be relative to those. I *could* build it the height he specified, yes, but it would look completely out of place. But he would stick his drawing together, and I would humour him, and then he would go back to the city and leave me to build in peace. It was easier to pick my battles and win the war.

In deference to my client and to the designer himself (not his minion who had come north), I used this outsize, mansplaining drawing for about a day before I got fed up with its very existence, not to mention its tendency to be blown over or simply fall of its own accord about every twenty minutes, and then I hid it in the garage. Walter just laughed. He never questioned me, always trusting me to do what I'd come to do.

The bench-back looks exactly like it's supposed to, thank you very much.

Towards the end of the job, I found myself stopping in my tracks and smiling at this wall because it turned out to be so striking and elegant. There were places where I could spot imperfections straightaway – probably noticeable only to the specialist – but other parts are stunningly beautiful, like the top lines of the bench and the squiggly, dramatic, tapering curve down the hill. Some parts were so good I had a hard time believing I actually built them. Standing back on the last morning and looking from afar at what I had just completed, I was reminded once again that walls are more than the sum of their parts. By the end, when the hammers are finally put down, if the job is done well, a wall is something bigger, more impressive, more lyrical. Imperfections fade into cohesion. I had made this happen with my hands and my eyes. Maybe I was pretty good at this after all.

It is easy to see in retrospect how good it was for me to have to stretch and struggle a bit. The most important thing I learned on that job was that I could trust myself to figure it out, whatever it might be.

I was still terrified about what the invoice ought to read. I agonised for days. Before I had the chance to painstakingly write the thing, Walter sauntered up to me while I was working and casually asked in his lovely Georgia accent what the bill would be.

Shit. This was not how it was supposed to happen. I could almost hear the Fred Flintstone feet scrambling in my head.

I prefaced and prefaced and bumbled, and I finally spat out a number that felt fair to me, apologising the whole way. My incredibly magnanimous client paused.

I was quietly freaking out. I had asked too much! I had offended him! Whitney Brown, you are a greedy idiot! WHAT WERE YOU THINKING?! My heart pounded.

His brow was furrowed. It seemed *eons* before he finally spoke. Quizzically, he asked, 'Are you sure that's enough money?'

If I hadn't already been working on my knees I would have fallen over. Shocked and relieved, I laughed. 'Walter, how much do you think I make in a year?!'

'This is very artistic work,' he said. 'I'm going to come up with a figure that I feel happier with.'

And he did. I've never seen so much money in the bank at one time since, and I would soon treat myself to a week-long sailing course, some new Gore-Tex *and* a new dress, thank you very much. I had lived hand-to-mouth until then, and a decent pay cheque was an almost unbelievable achievement.

It was almost more gratifying to hear Walter call my work 'artistic', and for him to note my work ethic as he watched me picking up every last piece of leftover stone on the lawn despite his protestations on my last morning a few days later when I was utterly exhausted. 'We can take care of that,' he said, waving me away, but Jack taught me never to leave a mess after a job. 'That is what they'll remember,' he used to say. 'You might have built beautifully, but they'll remember that you left a mess.' I reassured Walter that I was happy to do it, and I drove down the mountain a few hours later knowing I had given my all.

Blaen Cammarch

Life became effortlessly beautiful when at last I was able to wake at Blaen Cammarch again and settle back into the other half of myself, an ocean away. I was relieved and euphoric when I arrived, but deeply depleted. Once again, I had come to Wales in need of recovery, only this time it wasn't any sort of drama or heartbreak but just good old-fashioned hard graft that had walloped me. And I had much more of it ahead of me that summer, but I knew intuitively that first I needed baths, lie-ins, fires, the dark mystery of these rivers and the privacy of the hills around them, a few nights in a tent with this man, and some time on the front bench with Kate, just leisurely chatting. We gave ourselves a few days for just that.

Jack was a champion sleeper, and I always slept better when we were together. Something about him made me relax. I felt safe, protected. Still, I struggled to stay in bed when the sun was shining brightly by 5 a.m. As the summer approaches in Wales, the world looks far too alluring at that hour. (I hadn't yet figured out eye masks.)

As Jack slept longer one morning, I dressed and walked alone to take it all in and reacquaint myself with the details of a world I loved so. I didn't see a single soul. It was misty, cool and quiet. Mayflower lined the lanes. Bluebells electrified the fields and woodland floors. The tea-coloured River Cammarch still burbled along, swirling around the rocks under the footbridge at the end of the track. I was so relaxed I almost felt as if I were still asleep, walking slowly through a thick, luscious dream of this place. How I had missed it.

Up on Rhogo a few days later, we finally set about our work. It was a high, rugged place on the road between Howey and Hundred House. There was an open common at the top that stretched out across Gilwern Hill and Castle Bank, and on a sunny day the views were spectacular in every direction. Old, curving walls enclosed fields here and there, rounded at the corners to accommodate the turning of the ox plough and to save the builders the headache of unnecessary junctions. Jack had been on site about a month already, slowly beginning to work his way around one of the beautiful, curving enclosures. It was a big job, one that would take us through the summer and into the autumn as we gradually put back the walls that protected these few acres.

Radnorshire is a strange, ancient, stunning landscape. I can't think of another place that looks quite like it. Ancient sites and abandoned homesteads dot the hills. Jack and I had explored here the year before, rambling through old field systems and up to a huge Iron Age bank-and-ditch fort (now just covered in piles of rock and sheep). My experiences of the Welsh countryside have been enhanced a hundredfold by the man in my life, who happened to be the best guide anyone could have asked for. Jack loved this area, and his enthusiasm paired with its raw, ragged beauty was catching. From the very start, Wales felt special to me in a visceral, instinctual way, but I don't know that I would have come to love it as I do without all the incredible things Jack shared with me over the years. You see a place differently when you understand its ancient history, and I have so many photos of him pointing at something in the distance, fascinated.

Stone walls were the only fences possible in the topography of Mid Wales (and indeed Britain) for much of history. Barbed wire is a new thing, and when it first arrived it was a terribly expensive thing. Wood was usually at a premium, used for heating, cooking, tools, carts, beams in home and barn construction, or off to become boats. Over much of the country stone was not at a premium or even at a distance. It was there in abundance. It often needed to be moved out of the way so that the land could be cultivated. Field walls evolved naturally. Stock had to be kept out of the arable. Fields had to be cleared for arable. That was survival. And the aesthetics evolved over time because people figured out how to build walls better so that they didn't fall down and require even more time and energy. They were designed through experience. Farmers have shaped that landscape, wild though it may look sometimes.

Or the walls were simply thrown up as quickly as possible and left. Gangs of post-Enclosure wallers got paid piecemeal and sped through as best they could. Farmers, if they had a go, did their best and moved on in short order to other essential tasks. The hill farmers I know still do the same today. They are busy people even with all the modern equipment we now have. They haven't got endless amounts of time to devote to unnecessary tasks; there are too many necessary ones waiting.

For a variety of reasons, dry-stone walling as it has existed for centuries in the fields of Britain is an endangered species.

Barbed wire is cheaper and faster, and without grant schemes*, most farmers haven't got the funds or the inclination to keep up the walls on their property. As they fall, they are not repaired but replaced with post and wire, or perhaps temporarily patched with an old gate or hurdle thrown across the gap. I understand why. Profit margins are slim in farming. They are accordingly slim in walling as well, but Jack always says the money is his bonus, for the beauty and freedom of the hillside most days is pay enough for him, but many can't bear the menial wages field walling offers.

This farm had belonged to the Davies family for many generations now, and three were farming together at that time: Gareth, who had the farm; Bruce, his father, who still worked; and Will, Gareth's teenage son who would soon be off to agricultural college. Gareth was a gregarious man with a wonderful

* Thanks to Glastir ('green land'), the most recent agricultural and environmental grant scheme of the Welsh Assembly Government which began in 2012, there was a wave of money available for wall repairs across the countryside for farmers who wish to enter their farms into a broad, multi-faceted land management programme. Farmers can elect to do some bits and not others, depending on the particularities of their farms and the ecosystems in which they exist: fencing, wall repairs, tree and hedge plantings, plant and wildlife conservation, water management and regulation of soil amendments, for example. The options are too numerous to list in their entirety, and the farmers work with Glastir programme officers to plan their goals. The big picture is complex and often controversial, but the bottom line is, if farmers are willing to follow some rules and make some modifications to their practices and infrastructure, they can get government money to finance the changes, which are hopefully good for everyone and everything. Glastir is supposed to be about sustainability. It's never quite that simple, but I think these programmes have an overall positive effect, and they certainly keep the wallers busy. Decades of successive schemes with names like Tir Cymen ('well-crafted landscape') and Tir Gofal ('care of the land') have funded much of Jack's walling career, and many farmers have participated in every iteration of them. They might moan about the rules – farmers aren't a rule-loving bunch, yet must know an awful lot of them – but the numbers in which they continue to sign up seem to indicate that the programmes are helpful in some ways.

laugh, and he stopped by to see us once a week or so, usually with a funny story to tell. I learned an incredible amount about the land, the culture and even modern farming just listening to him and Jack talk. He was deeply interested in history and archaeology, particularly in the area surrounding his place, and it was a point of pride to see his walls restored. He loved to see, too, what we had unearthed in the wall that week: clay pipes, broken china, old bottles, rusty metal bits from derelict farm equipment . . . It told the story of this place.

It was on Rhogo that I really began to come into my own as a field waller. I could talk more about the technical aspects of walling, problem-solve better . . . That had come as a result of my experience at home, where I *had* to figure it out on my own. I had learned to stand back, look, analyse, think things through . . . or simply to get on with it and make the best of the stone I had, trusting that I would pull off something in the perfectly adequate to absolutely stunning range. Radnorshire was a good proving ground in that it forced you to work with difficult shapes, to find a way to make it all work together.

Jack always laughs that wallers from South Wales would never even attempt to make a wall out of some of the stuff we use in Mid Wales. It's like working the most complex jigsaw puzzle imaginable, only without repeated patterns or a picture to go on. The geology of an area determines the style of its walls, from the colour to the coursing to the possible incorporation of additional materials like turf or hedgerow plants.

The Cotswolds and Yorkshire are known for their walls because they have such lovely and abundant stone to work with – even bedding planes, comparatively easily split and dressed. Those places had Jurassic limestone and more pleasing varieties of sandstone. Radnorshire stone is footballs, rugby balls, lamb shoulders, lop-sided backpacks, bags of cement misshapen by rain, dead sheep in rigor mortis, red kites in full spread . . . It is not elegant blocks, and though the result can be far less satisfying to obsessive-compulsive types, it is far more interesting, far more challenging. And sometimes when I pick it up, I really do laugh. What the hell IS this, and what am I supposed to do with it?

Walling is a bit like jazz: constant improvisation within a certain large framework. You've got your foundations and your end goals, but the middle is up for grabs. You build your baseline of skills over the years, and away you go. The stuff Jack pulls off that I can't even approach is kind of amazing. Some of this is due to personality – I feel much safer with order and levelled courses by nature – but simply because of his experience Jack can fly back and forth like a typewriter no matter how jagged a course he's just laid down. It's infuriating and wonderful all at once . . . More on the infuriating side if I have to come along behind him and wish to level up, but it's good for me. I could be too precious sometimes, and precious might be incredibly beautiful, but it is slow.

A lot of Jack's academic research has been on wall typology and reading the fingerprint (for lack of a better descriptor) of individual wallers. Jack and I have very different fingerprints. It's so obvious on our restorations who has done which parts, and at what point we switched off. You might not notice, but we could certainly point it out to you.

As I became more competent, Jack and I often worked on separate sections – sometimes not even close enough to hold a conversation. Most times, I found myself listening to the wind and the sheep, puzzling over the variety of voices amongst them. Sheep could be very comical company sometimes. There is a standard sort of range for their voices, but you'll hear one occasionally that sounds like it's spent its whole life chain-smoking in a pub with a low, growling voice that sounds slightly menacing and embittered. And then there might be a

189

ewe who sounds like she's sucked on a huge helium balloon, squealing out for her lamb, who has wandered off. It makes me laugh out loud every time, and each flock has its outliers.

Just before lunch one day, I heard Jack shouting in what I eventually discerned to be a sort of faux Arabic. I wasn't sure at first if something had stung him or he was having a heart attack, but it was sudden and dramatic and loud. I looked up to find him holding his phone right in front of his mouth – not listening, just shouting, pissed as hell at the person on the other end of the line. Putting his phone away, he finally noticed I was staring at him sceptically. 'Bloody nuisance callers!' he said. 'I'm getting so many lately. I *hate* the fuckers.'

I make Jack sound like a cartoon sometimes, but I felt incredibly privileged to be in beautiful Radnorshire working on these amazing old walls with such a strong, wise and sometimes difficult man. I was keenly aware of it since I was freshly back at his side, and I knew I'd be bored with anyone else. I often looked up from where I was working to see him right on the skyline, a gorgeous panorama of hills behind him. That is how I will remember him always, where he looks best and most at home.

Jack and I sat down on the grass side by side and leaned against the wall to eat our lunch in the sunshine. Ewes strolled by, munching as they went, pausing only occasionally to raise their heads and half-heartedly holler out for their fat lambs. It seemed like they hadn't noticed us. All of us were just mindlessly eating, there together on this beautiful hill.

As May turned to June, life skated on past peacefully. The days were beautiful, balmy and sunny. I worked hard and ate well, and I slept each night in one of the quietest places on the planet. I lingered over bottles of wine, greeted happy hour on gorgeous lawns, stayed up late by fires with whisky and sweet friends. It could stay like this forever as far as I was concerned.

Drygarn Fawr

Sometime while I was in Virginia earlier that spring, cosied down by the fire some rainy afternoon and daydreaming of the gloriously long summer ahead in Wales, I told Jack on the phone that I felt a powerful urge to nest – to make a home, to be back with him and dispense with all these phone calls and emails, to simply be together as we deserved. It was all I had wanted all winter. 'I don't know if men can really understand that – if they ever have that drive in the same way that we do,' I offered, feeling a bit silly for saying something so earnest, so personal – even to him. It startled me to have such strong impulses at all, let alone to admit them to another person.

'You're going to have to trade me in for a newer model, my darling,' he said with a chuckle.

'Oh, I don't know about that . . .'

After a long pause, he asked, 'Does that mean you're going to go around picking up sticks?'

What?'

'Isn't that what birds do when they want to make a nest? Is that what you're going to do?'

It took me a minute, but I finally caught up, at which point we both burst into laughter. All the more reason to be in love with him, I thought.

I never wanted children until I hit thirty. I *actively* disliked every single person under three until Har's daughter was born, and even then I was picky. My brother laughed at this constantly when we were children, especially when I took it upon myself to deface a Christmas ornament bearing my own baby picture, which he'd been waving about with the express purpose of taunting his hot-headed little sister. People assumed women wanted to hold babies. I freaked out when I had to – if someone passed me one without asking. I didn't know what to do, how to hold them, entertain them, make them not scream at first touch. Har's baby the year before had been the first one I hadn't been *completely* allergic to. And diapers and crying in public places? Forget it. And then I turned thirty, and someone flipped a switch. It was a *visceral* desire. Couple that with finding a man you really love, and it becomes overpowering at times. You start picking up sticks.

I had been pondering for ages whether *my* concern about our age difference was the only barrier to my being able to move abroad and live in the country I longed for all the time with the man I missed every second we weren't together . . . whether I was the impediment to my own happiness. Crucially, though I had spent endless hours thinking and writing about this, and even talking about it to people like Kate, Parker and Rose, Jack and I had never discussed it seriously. We knew very early on (and often said aloud, cursing the fates) that if we had been closer in age we would have married and settled down together somewhere hilly and green. But we had never talked in detail about where our relationship was going or whether we could make a go of it together in Wales if I could just get over the age issue. I assumed we could.

I was wrong.

One day that June as we worked on some retaining walls on a farm near Trap, we sat down to lunch together under a stand of beautiful old beech trees. I can't remember how it came up (I hadn't intended to have such a serious conversation over sandwiches and instant coffee) but I think I probably expressed some vague annoyance – by way of saying how happy I was to be back with him and working – at not being able just to move there and have it all the time . . . That we knew we loved each other, and if we both wanted me here all the time it seemed silly *not* to get married.

I had been drumming myself up as the spring wore on, knowing I was deeply in love with Jack, and finally feeling secure in it and in him. I was ready to marry him.

He actually laughed when it came up. Loudly.

'Of course I won't marry you! I could never do that to your parents, and I wouldn't make you a laughing stock.' And just like that, possibility evaporates.

We finished our lunch, finished the workday. It was a bit of a shock, yes, but I thought I was fine.

By nightfall, I began quietly reeling as the enormity of it set upon me, and as we sat in the lounge after supper I began to realise that I would not be able to hold back my tears much longer. My heart was in my throat, my chest heavy with emotion. It was a strange thing, mourning the death of possibility. I didn't know how to say what I was feeling . . . I'm not even sure I knew yet. So I said nothing. I simply announced softly that I was going on up to bed.

He followed not too long after, sensing something wasn't right. And when he got into bed and draped his huge arm over me that was it: I wept, unable to speak sensibly, and he just held me calmly.

I wasn't angry at him, but I did feel foolish and disappointed, and I thought he was a bit of a chicken. The excuses he gave at lunch were ridiculous, and when I could gather my words enough, I told him so. *I* was in charge of me, not my family, and I felt sure they would want my happiness above all else. He finally admitted, disarmed by my tears just as he had always been, that some of it was self-preservation: 'I know you'd leave me and break my heart. I can't be dealing with that. It's a law of the universe that young women leave old men. I can't watch you go off with other men. I can't handle that. I don't want that.'

He added, 'I wouldn't love you any more than I do now. You wouldn't be any more welcome. And you've already got the ring.' He had given me a ring made of Welsh gold on my very first trip, not under these particular pretenses, but the message was clear. Wary of giving my secret life away, I never wore it, but kept it in a wine-coloured velvet box in the drawer of my nightstand at home.

Everything seemed more surreal, more frightening in the darkness. My feelings were changing so fast from moment to moment that I couldn't keep up with them. I felt out of time and space – a bit like a curious onlooker, invested, but powerless. What on earth would happen next?

His arms still around me, I finally slept, exhausted by the work of the day as much as its emotional turmoil. I woke early, rising to write alone with the morning sun streaming in the kitchen windows. I knew that if I were to survive this, I needed to write. It was the only way I ever figured out what I was thinking and feeling. I wasn't sure in that moment if I could even stay, and we weren't yet a month into what was supposed to be a five-month trip. How would I explain this if

I showed up four months early back in America after talking of *nothing* throughout the winter but getting back to Wales? What did it mean if we didn't get married? Did it mean we broke up now? Was this still home? Could a love this intense survive without hope? (Hope, I was learning as this unfolded, apparently meant marriage to me – promising a life together and getting to live it.) I suspected it could not. I had no idea.

I knew it wasn't as simple now as marrying him and moving here and keeping the life I loved in the way I had imagined. Could I ever have, I wondered?

As the idea of marriage vanished – the hope – I felt like such a fool for all the worrying and struggling I'd done the last couple of years, all the self-questioning and self-blame. I'd wasted so much time and emotional energy on the subject, ditto that of my friends. What shocked me most was that his love was not stronger than his sense of convention or his perception that our love for each other was so absurd as to be disallowed.

I knew that morning that I still loved him and didn't want to be without him. But how would I feel in a week? A month? By October? I felt grateful, but also blindsided. I wondered if I would feel so ... *hollow* inside from now on. I had finally opened up completely in the weeks that preceded yesterday's bombshell – gone as deeply into myself and my love as I could. I was glad of it because it showed me what I was capable of at my best, but I knew intuitively that the tenderest parts of me would have to go back into hiding now if I were to survive the morning, let alone the summer and beyond.

I tried to trust that there was some sort of wisdom to what was happening – that it would constitute some sort of growth by its end. Maybe it was about babies ... or some other amazing thing coming up around the bend. Who knew?

I was reeling, but oddly, I was also free ... free to enjoy this moment, but also to explore, to go where I wished. It was very, very strange to console myself with all the possibilities just seconds after I wanted to tie myself to him forever. It was shocking to think suddenly that this really could turn into my last trip to Wales of this sort. Terrifying, actually. I reassured myself that no decisions had to be made any time soon. I needed to sit with this.

Jack was downstairs by then, and he called me to breakfast. I could barely speak. I cried silently into my porridge. My hand trembled. I ate haltingly. I was self-conscious about the state of myself, but unable to do much about it. I remember being astounded at the sheer volume of tears coming out of my eyes. They just kept on and on. My fear was setting in by then, worries that if nothing else he might pull away and be cold now.

When I could gather myself enough, I told him this – that I was scared, unmoored, and suddenly a long way from home. This place didn't feel quite so much like ours as it did twenty-four hours ago . . . Twenty-four hours and a million miles. I wasn't sure where I was or what I needed – in the immediate or in the future. He was patient and quiet; let me talk, but held his ground. I was relieved that the weeping hadn't swayed him. I hadn't intended it to. I hadn't intended it at all.

As the morning wore on, I was still stunned and disorientated, but a strange calm began to come over me. We had planned some time before to hike up Drygarn Fawr that day and spend the night in the hills. As I'd wept in my breakfast, I hadn't felt capable of carrying out our plans. Alone with each other in the hills for thirty-six hours felt a bit ambitious now. I thought instead of phoning Kate to get away for a few days, but by lunchtime I suddenly felt I might be strong enough to go on. I was still nervous about how things might go, but we got the gear together and arranged for a friend to drop us off at the edge of the forestry near Devil's Staircase.

What followed was the most healing thing we could have done.

Once we emerged from the trees onto the open hill, we hit some challenging stretches. There were boggy bits and parts where the seldom-used trail just disappeared, making a map and compass essential. There was a lot of stumbling through difficult, tumpy areas of tall grasses. It was slow going, but we had plenty of time until sunset. The twilight would be generous. It was nearly the solstice.

Whatever the slog, it was worth it when we finally reached our perch at the summit of Drygarn Fawr, the so-called 'Rooftop of Wales'. The 360-degree views extended all the way up to Snowdonia, east into England, out to the sea in the west, and down to the valleys of South Wales. I relished the silence that surrounded us save the cheerful songs of the skylarks. We pitched our camp in the shadow of a massive dome-shaped cairn erected for Queen Victoria's Diamond Jubilee. Here I was in a breathtaking scene, and I had simply walked here with my own two feet, powered by my tear-salted porridge.

The world around us was *heart-swellingly* beautiful that night. We in South Carolina did not have an equivalent to the long and lazy twilight of high summer in the British Isles. It seemed to stretch on to eternity . . . something to be experienced rather than described. Those precious nights around the solstice were mystical, almost otherworldly in moments. The days, too, were so long, so bright, so sweet and mild, and it felt in that endless twilight as if anything were possible (anything but marriage, obviously).

Jack and I had always loved to disappear into nature. Both of us got fed up with the world sometimes, and when those moments came we ditched reality and headed for the hills, seeking the quiet and the distraction of dramatic views. And though I had worried over being alone together in the hills this time – weary from my own emotions and unsure now of our future with each other – this walk was the best medicine for this moment. The teamwork of navigating forced us to work with each other, but in ways that were not *about* each other. And walking was a different way of sharing space . . . It is difficult to describe the paradoxical nearness of walking with someone a dozen yards distant – together and solitary all at once. If you know that person intimately, there is a closeness to it even if there is no eye contact, no exchange of words, no touch. Navigating, walking and then standing atop the hill identifying all the familiar landmarks in sight bound us back together in the familiar – when even as recently as that morning we'd felt miles apart.

We saw no one the entire two days we were out rambling the hills.

Back home the next day we went our separate ways for the afternoon . . . he to a nap and a few errands, me to a bath, my journal, and then to cooking supper. Simple pasta, ample wine. Still feral after our night out with the larks and the stars, it seemed too confining to be indoors at all. We ate out front under the roses, which were in full bloom, and we lingered together over the last of the wine as the sun disappeared. I fetched a jacket from inside, the bourbon, some glasses. A tawny owl hooted across the valley, somewhere down by the river. Jack called to it in return, and when it answered him they began a conversation that was beyond my comprehension.

What I understood was that this man was indeed wild, full of magic. He would not marry me, but these sorts of moments remained. He could talk to owls. I knew that if I never came back here, this was one of the nights I would remember forever.

In the Company of Women

The reprieve of the hills was disappointingly short-lived, and I began to feel muddled in every way. In the last days of June, I reached the angry phase. As my shock and sadness gradually subsided, my feelings transformed to something hotter and more resentful. I needed to get away, get my head straight, get some distance from Jack. Everything about him drove me crazy. It was the moment when all the annoying everyday things about him that I'd begun to overlook as one must in the long-game of love became glaringly obvious to me again. When you think you might spend the next twenty years with someone, you naturally forgive these things as a survival strategy, but now I wanted to kill him for all the toast crumbs on the counter. My blood boiled over the haphazard way he shopped for groceries.

It wasn't about the crumbs, of course, but the anger was powerful and plentiful. It was all too close.

I retreated into the company of women.

My friend Emma – one of the women who'd rallied round me the year before at Kate's party – talked to me about astrology, exploring the finer parts of my birth chart. We talked about what it meant when my stars collided with Jack's . . . communication styles, fears, needs. She took me off to glamorous parties full of writers and artists, where she introduced me like the most dazzling and interesting woman in all of Powys. She brought me back to the Tudor-era farmhouse where she lived with a sailor who was away for long stretches in his old pilot cutter. It was a weathered and beautiful wonderland, lovingly but minimally restored, and filled with only the most carefully chosen objects. I slept – to both my fear and delight – with the sweetest little bats flying around my room as the rain pounded on the roof above. Being with Emma was like living in a really good book that just kept going.

Kate, when she could, sheltered me in her world, welcoming me to sunny hours on her lawn, where I read and wrote and absorbed vitamin D in heavy doses, often with the cat sprawled at my side. Some nights I stayed over, and she sat up late with me talking through all that had transpired with Jack and what it might mean, always going out of her way to put a hopeful spin on things. She took me to the theatre, knowing I was weary of my own drama. On Midsummer's Day, we drove south for an outdoor performance of Shakespeare's *Merry Wives of Windsor*, and I simply lost myself in the magic of the play and its endless one-liners and drunkenness and people hiding in the washing. Afterwards, in the surprisingly balmy darkness, I revelled with actors and audience members around a bonfire in the most picturesque of gardens down towards the English border. We gorged on hog roast, cask ale and Eton Mess, and laughed until it was time to go the long road home.

The next morning, a bit bleary-eyed from my revelry, I made my way to London. Rose and I had planned a short while before to sneak off to Italy for a few days, and the shake-up with Jack made the timing perfect. She had been working her ass off, and I was just overwhelmed with my life, and at the crack of dawn the following day we jetted south as giddy as teenage girls skipping school with nothing packed but their bikinis, sunglasses and a fresh pack of fags to share. It felt deliciously naughty.

As we lay in the sun together, I told Rose the whole saga of recent days.

'He hasn't got a leg to stand on! He is a *fucking* amputee! *WHAT* is he thinking? A beautiful young woman – WHOM, BY THE WAY, HE *CLAIMS* IS THE LOVE OF HIS LIFE – wants to marry him, and he says *NO*?'

Her outrage was exquisite, and it always came packaged in comical phrasing. Rose had the fiery heart of a lion, and she was ferociously protective of me.

'If he won't marry you, I will,' she proclaimed, throwing down the gauntlet. 'I'll show him.' She might have been a bit tipsy after lunch, but she swore she was serious.

Rose and I found mountain lakes to swim in. We rambled arm in arm through sleepy towns and villages. We gobbled up every ounce of local fruit we could get our hands on and enthusiastically foraged for wild herbs and greens around the farmhouse flat we'd rented. We had long lunches with plenty of local wine. We lay in the sun endlessly in the afternoons – sometimes topless, which the budding bohemian in me found novel and delightful precisely because of my latent, lingering Baptist reflexes, though I played it cool, like I always did it this way. With such an elegant creature at my side, I couldn't help feeling a little bit glamorous myself, no matter how bad my tan lines were. I stayed up late, lingering with wine, stars and fireflies, while she read quietly in bed. It was, in a word, heaven.

We found overwhelming joy at every turn and in every gorgeous detail, and in our waking hours we smiled at each other almost constantly over our shared sense of relief from real life. I literally forgot about the rest of the world for four days, which was an easy thing to do in her company. My phone didn't work, and we had no internet or television for the duration, and I was just so happy that I didn't care about anything that wasn't present and immediate. Completely immersed in the moment, I found a peace and stillness that I had lost somewhere along the way.

It was the first time in five years I hadn't wanted to be in Wales, the first time I hadn't missed Jack, perhaps the first time I had been fully present *anywhere* in all that time. It was startling, but a good reminder that there was, in fact, life outside Powys. I couldn't articulate it yet, but I sensed that I had crossed some sort of threshold. Looking back, it was a bit of a forbidden fruit moment, but I couldn't have made myself worry then if I'd had to. It was all just so much fun, so easy and hopeful. Being with Rose was like having a private audience with the sun – the best sort of medicine – and it was hard to give her up when I came home.

That summer I talked with my circle of women about Jack, and they gave me all sorts of perspectives. I was moving into a world I had not anticipated for myself: one filled with the complexities of unusual but no-less-real love. . . Ours wasn't necessarily a polite kind of love, but it was no less legitimate than the young, white, thin, heterosexual, monogamous couples one saw in advertising. The less polite kinds of love – the ones that most didn't speak of – were the only kinds I had known, and I needed to hear about those sorts of relationships and talk about my own. Emma and Kate and Rose gave me the space to do just that, and they shared with me what they could from their own lives. They *never* judged me.

He would not marry me, but Jack was the man who made me say, 'Oh, so *this* is what it's all about.'

And on we went. I was still figuring out what it all meant.

Cwm Elan – Elan Valley

Never did I dream after my first jaw-dropping trip to the Elan Valley in the autumn of 2009 – the day I first met Kate in that horrid rain – that I would eventually have a chance to work there. But of course that's exactly what happened.

There was a dry-stone sheepfold just around the bend from the Pen-y-Garreg dam that needed repair. Brian and Sorcha Lewis and their children use this fold on their farm, where they raise Welsh Mountain sheep, as well as some rarer breeds such as Welsh Mountain Badger Face and Herdwick. It is a beautiful spot overlooking the reservoir. The fold is built to incorporate the natural rock outcroppings of the hillside as part of its walls, saving some labour for its original builders. Over the years, farmers had added races and gates with wood and metal, too – whatever they could cobble together, really. The fold's stone walls were now crumbling, and Brian asked us on our first visit whether one of its walls might move altogether to give him a more functional set-up that would allow him improved control over the sheep and their movements. At the very least, we would get the walls up to the maximum height possible with the stone we had available. Height is the only way to tame Welsh Mountain sheep. They are jumpers and can scale astonishing heights when motivated by their will to escape or to reach a patch of more desirable grass.

Having stockproof pens is a vital necessity for the hill farmer. He must gather and drive his sheep into the fold numerous times in the year, perhaps for shearing, dosing or sorting. You can't handle sheep without having them in a relatively confined space. They are too fast, too fearful. You won't get your hands on them without dogs and pens. There are modern pen systems of steel and aluminium, but the old folds were stone, or perhaps willow hurdles if that's what was available. It all depended on the local materials. In this case, it was stone, and we would bring this beautiful old structure up to a functional standard again for the Lewises.

I knew from our earliest visits to the farm that this would be a special place to work – a dream project, if you will. We would not take a second of it for granted. If nothing else had gone right, the beauty of the surrounding landscape would have been enough. But Jack and I were lucky, too, to have the opportunity to work for such interesting, engaging people as Sorcha and Brian. They ran a productive, picturesque farm with traditional hay meadows and minimal chemical inputs. They were thoughtful, kind, bright people who cared deeply about how they treated their land and their animals, and we liked them very much from the start.

Jack is a great lover of wildlife, and Sorcha a noted expert. She came by every few days, sometimes with the kids in tow after the school run, sometimes alone with her camera. She and Jack would talk for ages about bats and birds, mice and newts, badgers and otters and anything else that flies, crawls, walks or swims in Wales. They both knew their plants, too, though she had an edge over him when it came to botany. I couldn't keep up when faced with such enormous detail, but I listened enthusiastically as I carried on stripping out an unstable section of wall.

Sorcha photographed us as we worked, remarking as I heaved an impossibly large slab, 'You do make dry-stone walling look glamorous, Whitney.' Caught off guard, I think I laughed dismissively that it was just my sunglasses. (I get variously teased and admired for my sunglasses in Wales. '*Sooooo* American,' Jack used to say.)

I did my share of talking when Brian stopped by and we got round to America. I *love* talking to farmers about America. Most Welsh farmers have been to New Zealand before they've been to London, let alone America, though the ones who have been to the land of my birth love to share stories with me about travelling to places like Wisconsin, Texas and Montana. They speak the syllables reverently, but also with an air of name-dropping. Even those who haven't been are deeply curious, especially about what it's like where I come from – even though *no one* knows where North *or* South Carolina is, or even that they are separate states. Most talk of 'Carolina', united as in the colonial days. (I can't fault them for that. Most Americans couldn't find Wales on a map, and plenty don't know that it doesn't have an 'h' in the name, like the animal. Counties? Forget it.)

What do we grow? What is the weather like? I try to explain all this to the best of my ability, but I also have to confess that actually I am from the suburbs and we don't grow much of anything. We used to grow a lot of cotton, but now it is mostly small cattle herds or big, industrial chicken and hog sheds in the two states I have called home. Plus maize (can't say corn, as that's a generic term for grain in Britain) and soybeans. Small family farms on my side of town have all been turned into Wal-Marts, gas stations and ugly-ass strip malls that are probably going to have a lifespan of fifteen to twenty years max before the next new-and-improved spot is built somewhere nearby on virgin land. (I am acutely aware in Wales how much we take our land for granted at home.) I have had this conversation in passing on the road in Beulah, at village shows after the vintage tractor run, out on the hill in both Powys and Carmarthenshire, up on remote farms in North Wales, and even at parties. I know it intimately, and I never tire of it.

Brian, like most Welsh farmers I know, is a soft-spoken fellow in conversation, but sounds like a madman out on the hill, shouting and whistling and effin' and blindin' at his dogs as he works the sheep. You could hear Brian on the wind even when he was so far away you couldn't see him, and that sound of a distant farmer at work is part of the soundtrack of Wales to me. What always astounds me, though, is how rough it sounds for the dogs, but farmers and dogs have their own language. Those relationships are incredibly close, intuitive. They are friends for life, relying on each other every day of the year.

The wall I was working on met its demise partly due to the pressures of time and weather and sheep, but also to the natural deterioration of the stone with which it was built. It was a delicate slate – Ordovician perhaps, though I'm no expert on geology apart from the hands-on qualities of my materials. It had a fine bedding plane – laid down by the sea in sand and mud almost like the layers of butter in a croissant – and as snow and ice had worked on it over the years, it began to slowly fracture and flake. The local stone wasn't suitable for the five dams of the Elan Valley for this very

207

reason: too brittle. Normally, when stripping out a sandstone or limestone wall, it is a fast and furious morning of pitching and throwing and heaving – 'just get it over with' is the *modus operandi*. Those types of stone can handle a walloping, and though taking time to sort and organise is ideal, we usually just throw them into a massive pile, with special stacks for coverbands and copes only. This local slate would not tolerate such forceful handling. Large pieces had to be carefully lifted and gently set upon the ground. Some, if one held them with too wide a grip, would simply buckle in the middle, deteriorating immediately into a pile of chips at and even on top of one's feet. It was a slow, careful process. The smaller the stone, the more time-consuming and tedious the rebuild, so we did our best to preserve the large pieces.

The wall we tackled first on the fold was an interesting stretch for me, not only for the stone type, but because I had to rebuild over orthostats for the first time ever. Orthostats are large stones set upright in the ground. They're not uncommon in Wales, and we treat them the same as if we are building over massive stone outcrops or unmovable boulders. It's not a way that Jack and I would set stone if left to our own devices, but if they are already there and stable, we simply build around them. They give you great jumps in height, which speed you on, but it can be tricky to course around them. They look like great blobs in the bottom of the wall, growing up out of the ground almost like wonky old tombstones.

Next, we would dismantle, move and reassemble a stretch of wall to close a large gap in the fold, as Brian had requested. The two sections we were connecting were not aligned in any way, so Jack laid out a beautiful S-curve. I was delighted to roll up the line and pins and just build freehand. I prefer curves to straight lines, and I'm better at them. They are my walling superpower.

The disintegrating stone was frustrating, but it was an idyllic time in so many ways. Just like the enclosure on Rhogo, Jack had had his eye on this fold for years as he drove through the Elan Valley as a tourist, hoping one day he might have a chance to work on it, and here we were in gorgeous weather and good spirits. We worked hard, but we also spent a lot of time doing other things while we were on that job. We talked to the lovely Lewises whenever they stopped by. We both paused regularly to photograph this wondrous place in moments too good to ignore. (I loved watching Brian drive the sheep down the road just behind us, moving them from one field to another in a great baaing cacophony of wool and shit.) We took time to rest in the shade and ate the fresh, fat raspberries I insisted on bringing up from the greengrocer in Rhayader. Kate and Richard turned up one afternoon in their old Land Rover, canvas top off, to surprise us with a picnic, and we all lounged on blankets in the grass.

The whole of Britain was almost unbelievably sunny that summer. Every day was bright and warm and dry. There was no mud for a while. There was no breeze most of the time, which was rare. It was very hot by British standards . . . not South Carolina hot, but Jack got so overheated some days that he had to go dunk his big bald head in the stream periodically to cool off. It was only the lack of humidity that spared me from heat exhaustion during whole days of work without shade. Perhaps I longed for the romantic allure of a slow and restful foggy morning every now and again, but actually this was the best summer *ever* as far as I was concerned. I was not suffering. We were dusty and sundazzled, but this was mild by comparison to my home territory.

Astonishingly, it hadn't rained proper Welsh rain in months. My friends kept saying it was like the British summer of their youths, which would have been the fifties and sixties . . . but I also kept hearing the word 'drought'. People began to worry about water levels. Looking at the millions and millions of gallons swirling peacefully in the Elan reservoirs, it seemed impossible that anyone could ever run out, but I reminded myself that many farmers simply rely on local springs and cisterns to meet their needs. We did. The vast reserves of water before me were destined to flow down the pipes to people in cities far away. The dams were built specifically for Birmingham, some 73 miles across the border.

After work one day, with the heat steeling my determination, I decided to treat myself to a probably-not-very-legal swim in a tucked-away cove. I had coveted those waters since my first glimpse of them years before. I seemed always to be there on misty November days, when the threat of paralysing cold was too intimidating for a creature from the thirty-fourth parallel. But Jack and I had just worked a long, punishing day, and I felt a drive towards the water that I could no longer ignore. What is the bodily equivalent of thirst where desire to swim is concerned? Does it have a name? Aquaphilia? It was animal, instinctual, compelling me to the water with no choice but to dive in, and at the earliest possible second.

I was hot, dusty, exhausted, and – I noticed as I slipped into my turquoise bikini – brown as a nut on my face and arms, and white as a ghost everywhere else. It was a labourer's tan – a farmer's tan as we'd say at home – and the colour of my skin matched the texture of my hands in what it revealed about my life.

I was nervous of the cold, but also nervous of getting caught. This was a protected watershed after all. Jack would not swim. It was not really his way to cut loose and revel with wild abandon unless he was tipsy and suddenly spinning all 185 pounds of me around a dance floor or even the kitchen if the right sort of jive music came on. But he came with me to the shore below the hay meadow, towels and camera at the ready. I think he thought I was absolutely nuts, but he also saw the delight on my face as I side-stroked my way out through the cool, glassy water. I laughed as I do in the purest of joys: free, unexpected, afloat.

I emerged feeling deliciously clean and renewed. This, I thought, was my kind of baptism.

Jack and I would share an indelible evening in our sheep-fold camp. It was the kind of elemental, rustic perfection in which he and I have always been at our best. The more civilised our environment, the more we tend to get under each other's skin. I think we notice each other's annoying habits more when there is less of the work of life to be done. It is best if we are toting wood and tending fires, pitching tents and fumbling around in the starlight. I adore him in survival mode, but we don't live in that isolated bubble all the time. Those moments are fleeting, precious, necessary for holding onto . . . I cherish them, slow down in them, try to memorise them. They are, as the great and often dour Welsh poet R. S. Thomas wrote, 'the honey the mind feeds on'.

That night, we walked the hills above amongst wild orchids and ruined walls, gilded by the sinking sun. The top dam at Craig Goch, with its elegant arches spanning the spillway, was majestic in the soft light, the waters around it silver and smooth like mercury. All of this was framed in the most vivid, almost fluorescent green of high summer in the hills. As the sun sped away, we meandered back down to camp, nestled neatly inside our walls. We ate a simple supper, and by our bonfire we talked long into the darkness of that surprisingly cold July night.

The marriage conversation felt far away. We were as close as we had ever been – perhaps more so. The pendulum had swung again. I thought back that evening to a wish I'd made in the spring: that I would find clarity in the summer. I had, only it hadn't been in the form I'd expected. (Is it ever?) It was not about whether we would or wouldn't marry, but about realising I loved him enough to carry on, whatever. The pressure was gone and, at last, we could just be.

Neither of us wanted this job to end but, inevitably, it did. We sped through the building of the curve. Both of us were in our best building form, matching pace on opposite sides of the wall, reading each other's needs without much verbal exchange. Usually, he is light years faster than me as a result of his many years of experience, so it is a lucky day when I can keep up. If we talked at all, I think we mostly teased each other, talking shit about how the other was building. I have sometimes experienced the artistic 'flow' state when building on my own, but that day we had a rare synergy, hitting a certain state of flow together, though no one mentioned it. I knew this partly because there were no moments in which I wanted to murder Jack . . . I am unfortunately a bit famous for my temper with him on the job site. (I am not the most patient woman on earth, but in my defence, he knows just which buttons to push when he wants to, and sometimes he pushes them with relish.) Luckily, given the nature of our work, there have always been other heavy things on site to smash and throw, and channelled anger has done me excellent service over the years where my overall productivity is concerned. That is perhaps my other walling superpower, just after curve-building.

We knew we were flying, and it felt great.

One of my favourite things is when Jack and I bet on how long it will take us to finish a job, and we wind up smashing his conservative estimate with our combined speed. He always guesses long; I always go short. At a certain point in any job, a waller suddenly senses the finish line is near. She can almost smell it. She has turned the corner, and a sprint to the finish feels *really* enticing – almost imminent. We hit that very point in the afternoon of what would turn out to be the last day, and I kicked it into overdrive. The burst of energy I get for copes is always a bit astonishing, and I've got the bit between my teeth then. It's 100 per cent adrenaline.

Before we knew it, it was over.

'Well done, Miss Brown! I *never* thought we'd do that in two days!' His tone is completely unique in these moments – it's the only time he ever sounds positively bubbly. 'I told you, silly,' I reply drily and with mock annoyance, though in truth his reaction of giddy surprise brings me *such* pleasure. We both marvel at how much faster two people are than two people . . . two who work well together are more like three.

There is no feeling like the sense of achievement one gets when finishing a piece of wall. It is gratifying in the deepest sense, especially if the farmers are happy with it, and Brian was delighted. This job was one for the ages, we knew, and sad as we were to leave what had effectively been walling paradise, we remembered that other, larger projects waited for us further east towards Hundred House. It was time to go.

As we left, I began to think about the layers of history and human experience particular to the Elan Valley – of those magnificent stone dams and glistening reservoirs as we see them today, of the place as a Victorian construction site, of farms and churches and estates now underwater and the lives that populated them when they weren't. I think of the anachronism of the last remaining farmers there who gather sheep off the hill on horseback even now in the age of the ubiquitous quad bike. I think of Brian and Sorcha's children, who are growing up in such a special place, and I wonder a bit wistfully whether they will stay. I think of the farm woman whose story I was told years ago, who transported her eggs on horse and on foot 20 miles to market back in the nineteenth century, and indeed of the scores of drovers who took the livestock to urban markets from farms in remote hills and valleys all over Wales. I wonder about the Bronze and Iron Age people who must have lived there long before, leaving their mark in cairns and tombs and hill forts, now mostly grown over with thick grass. Cistercian monks came after them, bringing sheep to the hills for the first time, and staying until their monasteries were dissolved in the sixteenth century as Henry VIII assaulted the wealth and power of the Catholic church. The ruins of Strata Florida and Abbey Cwm Hir lie 24 miles apart on a walking path we still call the Monk's Trod, and it passes right through this valley. Percy Shelley stayed a while in the nineteenth century when the manor houses were still on dry land, and must have been inspired by the beauty of it all. The Dambusters flew practice raids here during World War II before heading off to Germany to do their real work. The stories go on and on.

My layers are simply part of this greater fabric. All of us are just passing through. Most of us will not be remembered, but I existed in this place for a time. It has meant something to me. Jack and I were lucky to leave a few physical marks, a privilege of the waller's work. People may come upon our walls years from now, and a few will wonder about those who built them. Most won't. Some later waller may have another grant to restore things a second time, and he or she will definitely think of us, just as we think of those who built before us.

Of course Jack and I like to think our work will never fall down again because we rebuilt it so well that hot summer, but only time will tell.

Llofft-y-Bardd, Beulah

Once the hay is cut and put away for the year, the change is palpable. The days begin to shorten and cool. Moods shift, turning slowly, almost imperceptibly, towards the melancholy . . . filled with some vague sense of loss or dread, perhaps simply for the dark, dreary days that lie ahead. Even in August, you can feel the change. There is something in the air, something about the quality of the light . . . something uneasy and sad. It had been a summer of plentiful sun, but we all knew it could turn its back on us at any moment. We loved it as long as it stayed. The blackberries were still to come, but already we had begun the slow descent to winter. Wood stoves come to life as the nights gradually draw in around us. I left Jack alone on Rhogo for a week, and when I got home he had bad news.

While I had been at sea, learning to manage sails and helm a boat by starlight through the races of Jack Sound, our neighbour Bryn Powell had been killed in a car accident. The coroner said he believed a heart attack had caused Bryn to hit another car and end up in a hedge between Beulah and Llanwrtyd. I was stunned. Jack was heartbroken. We had already lost Nelda that summer. It was the kind of blow that wakes up feuding couples to the frailties of life and, for a time, drives them back together. Death brought an urgency, a vulnerability to those who were left ... or at least it did to me. It shook me.

The rains finally came, and I went to my first proper Welsh funeral wearing a rather undignified pair of green Hunter wellies beneath my navy sundress and waxy brown jacket. In a little chapel on the hillside flanking the Abergwesyn road, we laid old Bryn to rest. Llofft-y-Bardd ('Loft of the Bard'), the farm where he had lived and worked since he moved there as a child, was within view of the churchyard, just across a narrow valley. I shivered in the old church. Though fully, gorgeously bilingual, even the Welsh bits of the funeral service were Baptist enough to be familiar to me from my youth. The sound was the same even if the words were different. It was fascinating to the folklorist in me and moving in every way. Sitting in the hard, wooden pew, I thought about how much I didn't want Jack to die. Ever.

Bryn was a widely beloved character, and would be much missed. His death marked the end of the Welsh language in that valley, as well as the end of anyone in the area who had ever farmed with horses. He was a genuine hill farmer of the old variety, and it was a big loss culturally as well as individually. Hardened old farmers were in tears that day. It was odd enough to see them all cleaned up and in suits, let alone weeping, but their big, rough hands still stuck out familiarly from their dark jackets. I had rarely seen Jack so sad. He almost cried talking about Bryn's tractor, let alone his death. But Bryn was ninety, and had lived his life just as he wished until the very last moment. He was lucky compared to most.

We sang the old hymn 'Calon Lân' for him at the end. I had only ever sung it at rugby matches before, and always in my broken, misunderstanding Welsh, but with no less feeling behind it. It brought us all to tears (though it also gave me the strange feeling that we might break into the Welsh national anthem next). And then out into the open air to shake hands with the ancient but charismatic Baptist minister, to perhaps reach out to Bryn's remaining cousins, to find a friend or two and remember that we were still charged with the task of living. Tom Aberanell and his son Mike were there, Mrs B. (the dowager of the estate), plenty of other farmers I didn't recognise so easily without their hats on, lots of wives I'd never met, and Liz, our photographer friend, who had a particularly special reverence for Bryn and his way of being. And those were just the people I *did* know, but I kept to the margins, mostly. Beulah was a fairly closed community, and the people there had cordially tolerated my presence over the years, but I would always be an outsider in moments like these.

I hadn't known Bryn terribly well, but he had been a regular fixture in my time in Wales. His house was a landmark in the local lexicon, and we talked of him often even if we hadn't seen him in a while. We'd pass him on the road in his little old red Fiesta, or spot him parked in a lay-by near his home, where he sat to take in the view and maybe read the paper or listen to the radio, or simply snooze. Sometimes we'd honk and wave. He'd never see. Other times, we did stop and get out for a chat, and we'd visited him at his farm a few times over the years, too. We had to shout a bit – Bryn was pretty deaf by the time I arrived on the scene in Beulah – but his wits and his humour were intact to the last.

Before long, the Welsh – as they do – started telling stories as they stood around together in the churchyard. They fell back first on warm memories and then on their humour, and I listened with relish.

At home a little while later, Jack and I recounted our own Bryn stories.

We laughed about the time that Jack towed me home behind the Land Rover as I sat steering and braking Bryn's old grey Fergie at the end of a rope. With mere seconds between me and Jack's bumper, I prayed we would not meet a timber lorry or even the postman on the old, winding road down from Llofft-y-Bardd. We got home safely, but I had inhaled so much diesel exhaust I couldn't talk sensibly for the rest of the day.

In another episode, as a thank-you for scaling his barn roof to repair it after a North Atlantic gale had ripped off one of its tin sheets, Bryn gave me one of the strangest things I ever put into my luggage to take back to America. As we stood talking in the farmyard Jack had, for some reason, been bragging to Bryn about my love of a good axe (Jack and I had lots of conversations with people about tools). Bryn, a keen woodworker, disappeared into his shed for a moment, returning with a pristine axe helve, wrapped carefully in newspaper, which he placed into my hands. I marvelled over it, knowing he had picked this out when it was still a living tree and then cut and shaped it with his draw-knife when the time came. He insisted that I take it with me. I was thrilled. I needed this helve, actually.

Already I had taken home an axe head of the particular shape and weight I had grown to love during the blizzard that gripped Wales during my first visit. I'd split my way manically through huge piles of oak, and I grew so enamoured of that particular axe that I also felled an overgrown hedgerow hawthorn with it, even though we had a chainsaw. Jack was so impressed and amused by the time I'd finished that he cut off the jagged stump with the chainsaw and saved it for me as

218

a souvenir. That, too, eventually went home with me. You can imagine the puzzlement of the airport security technicians who must have scanned and then searched the hold luggage belonging to this very strange person with axe parts and stumps swaddled in bubble wrap, wrapped again in sweaters in her duffel bag. Rocks, too, sometimes.

'Have you been in contact with any livestock while you were away? Are you bringing back any fruits and vegetables with you?'

'No, but I'm that fucking weirdo with the axe in her luggage. Is that OK?'

It was always something. Jack and I laughed, reliving that day with Bryn and remembering all the bizarre stuff I had taken home over the years. We raised a glass of whisky to the old boy that night.

I would go with Jack to the empty farmstead a year after Bryn's funeral, just to see the place quietly one more time before it was sold. I longed to have it for myself, but I didn't have £300,000 sitting in the bank, let alone the money to fix it up to what even the most eccentric of us would consider liveable. Peering through Bryn's windows, I saw without his presence there what looked like poverty. I felt shocked. In fairness, the furnishings and personal effects that made it a home had all been taken to auction long ago, but there was no hiding that Bryn lived in a way that, at least materially, most of us would consider impoverished. I don't think he felt poor at all, and in many ways I envied his quiet, simple life, content with his flock and his two-bar fire on his little patch of ground. I dreaded to think who might buy this place and what they might do to it. Bryn's place was not my place, but it felt like yet another piece of Wales slipping through my fingers.

Wye Valley

I was sitting in an armchair in the corner of the kitchen with my second cup of tea. My arms were red with nettle stings and hawthorn pricks from the day before when I'd been out gapping in Kate's fields. The sheep had been out in the road again, having found a weak spot in the top of the wall with greener grass beckoning on the other side.

The house was quiet that morning except for a bit of singing somewhere upstairs, and then I heard footsteps. Kate swung through the kitchen door, radiant, smiling, gloriously perfumed, and full of hugs, just like every other day of the year. I have never figured out quite how she manages this *every single day* without fail – particularly after some of the late nights we'd had together – but I love to be there to see it when she first appears. She lights up the room, changes its energy. Every morning, a minor miracle. You want to embrace her, and luckily that is usually the first thing she goes for – even before the kettle.

We nattered away as women do in kitchens, talking about everything and nothing as breakfast came together. I'd been feeling pretty gloomy since Bryn's funeral, and I tried not to let that show. A looming flight home didn't help. I don't think Kate ever quite grasped how melancholy I could be at times, and I tried not to go on about it too much. I tried always to be cheery with her.

'You're looking very beautiful this morning, Whit.' (This kind of thing always helped.)

Over the years Kate had slowly infused me with the confidence, love and wisdom that brought me to life, and I still looked to her in the moments when things felt shaky. She had an invincible sort of optimism about her, and I had always found it to be contagious. You couldn't help but leave her company feeling better. . . even if you hadn't talked about The Thing, whatever it happened to be at the time.

She was evidence – like Parker and a few other older women I have known – that the kindness you show people in the quiet moments can affect their lives in profound ways. These women have a twinkling in their eyes that hints at stories I may never hear, of lives remarkably well lived, of decisions bravely made, of luck and of gratitude . . . But most importantly, they know how to keep going no matter what.

Kate was a woman who knew how to live, and that life was infinitely improved by the little things – picnics, flowers, candles, cushions, sailing, sunshine, little presents for no reason at all, spontaneous hugs and bubble-blowing and fireworks just because, wearing green for emotional comfort, taking tea back to bed in the mornings, liberal use of butter, chocolate as both medicine and travelling companion . . . One *always* bothered with the little things. These were the parts of life you could control, and they would keep you cheerful and strong. Delight and beauty were always there to

221

be found if you were looking for them, and you had a duty to, really. You owed it to yourself and to the people around you.

And if you couldn't see any sunshine, you made your own. Earlier in the summer when things were so messy with Jack, Kate let me come up to her house to spend a day alone, away from his space, while she and Richard were out so that I might get my head together. I arrived to find a note on the kitchen table welcoming me. Beside it, a child's plastic container of bubbles with a wand inside. She left me some whimsy. I went straight out to the lawn and filled the air with sparkling orbs, and I laughed as I had not laughed in weeks.

Knowing I was leaving soon, and all too aware of how much death had come to my world this summer, I wanted to tell Kate as I watched her frying the eggs how much I loved her, how grateful I was to her . . . for everything. I didn't – she would have been so embarrassed – but I smiled at her back and thought to myself how thankful I was that she came out in the rain all those years ago just before Jack and I might have driven away. I *almost* missed her.

Timing is everything, as she has often reminded me.

Rhogo

Blackberries began to ripen along the lanes and hedgerows of Beulah as summer turned to fall. It was a time of year I had come to adore, and though the arrival of the blackberries has come by coincidence alone to signal that it's almost time for me to return to America (I so often leave just after I've made jam), its significance to me had become something far more. I felt it in my core. There were deeply felt pulls of seasonal rhythms and migrations.

Each year, I set out on my ritual trek, picking one, eating one amongst the brambles 'til I have either made myself ill or filled my pots to overflowing – usually both. I rambled, searching, down the lanes and footpaths that September, cut and poked by thorns, stung by nettles. My clothes were snared, my fingers stained. I was in my element, and the twin blows of summer slipping away and my leaving were softened every time by these wonderful little berries, just waiting in the hedgerows.

For me, blackberry time in Wales ranks above Christmas, and this may be precisely because it is the antithesis of commercialism. It was just endless, free joy. I relished the surprise of each berry's individuality. And I relished the slow, simple, attentive cooking of the jam as much as the adventure of the picking . . . lovingly filling my jars, thinking of the people I'd give them to . . . Every part of the process was important to me.

As my berries macerated on the counter overnight and then simmered into that season's first batch of jam, I reflected on the last few months of work and play, all the changes and lessons. I drifted back to other times I'd cooked down these little black orbs in Jack's kitchen, stirring methodically, picking out the tiny white larvae that inevitably surface on the burbling liquid. (No one said beauty came without a price.) Blackberries always made me acutely aware of the passage of time, but also put me in mind of a sort of continuity. They tuned me in to the seasons, which I had come to cherish way back in my kitchen days and nurtured on the farm the next year. That love had never left me, and still I savoured each period of plenty as it came and went.

Whether I was taking a jar of jam to Rose in London to give her a dose of the wild countryside she so desperately needed, or simply sharing it with local friends too busy to pick their own, I was spreading the love and wonder I had so carefully gathered in my travels. In especially abundant years, I might even appear on a friend's doorstep with a pile of gleaming berries in hand, fresh and raw, and they gazed at me like some wonderful, wild creature who had performed a magical feat. All it took, really, was time and determination.

As autumn settled upon us, Jack and I pushed hard up on Rhogo. My departure sped towards us, and we needed to get as much done as possible. The gorgeous panoramic views that had been such a treat in the summer were the same

224

reason Rhogo would not be a pleasant place to work in the winter. With the view comes the weather. A cold wind would soon howl across that hilltop, blowing rain and maybe even sleet and snow sideways at any who dared to be out. Jack knew he did not want to be there if he didn't have to.

In a marathon slog, we stripped out and rebuilt a huge straight stretch that ran down the south side and towards some boggy ground. The foundations of these walls had baffled us both all summer, with so many huge stones tipped down into the ground at wild angles. Always assessing investment and return on our energies, Jack was often content to leave them be after a bit of exploration with a pick if it seemed they would take too long to dig out and reset. I, on the other hand, was like a terrier, determined to get at my buried prize, and I would not stop until I had won it. The happiest photo I have of myself from that job – any job, really – was from this stretch of days. I am squatted in a trench in my filthy overalls, pick resting on my shoulder, as I glory over a stone, newly uncarthed, that weighs more than I do. Jack sometimes got irritated at my obsessive digging and grunting and yanking, but he was so delighted by my satisfaction and my physical strength in these small moments of triumph. He just laughed: 'You're a *mad* bugger! You know that?' He knew he had to photograph this one.

The stone, as it had been all summer, was an unlikely mix of beautiful slabs and strange, faceless, lumpy shapes. With so much to rebuild, my skill level had grown enormously by virtue of practice. I could fly now, confidently improvising my way with even the oddest of shapes and random coursing if necessary. There was no use wishing for better stone or moaning about it. Good walls could be built of almost anything if the waller were skilled and focused enough. Jack still fussed at me about pins and lines, but that would never change. (He didn't help his case by always presenting me with a rat's nest of string each time we had to roll out the line. It never took me – and it was always me – less than fifteen minutes to find and free the end.)

The weather turned as we built on towards the finish on our final day. The short sleeves of foundations had turned to cosy layers and camouflage waterproofs for the copes. Rain dripped from my oversized hood. My gloves got cold and soggy. I stepped carefully through the rushes, my field of view partly obscured by the hood, as we hunted out the last of the remaining stone to pile on top. Rubble copes for this one. This wall was to be the last thing I would build in Wales that year, and we had reached its end: with the last copes up, my big summer of restoration was over.

I set up the tripod and with a timer shot photos of us standing proudly by this newly completed run. The sun came out. Jack stands slightly at an angle in his fisherman-looking waterproof bibs, leaning one hand on the wall and giving the camera a sideways, satisfied gaze. I stand opposite him, my hand on the wall, too, with my camo waterproof trousers hanging loosely over my canvas overalls and layers of black fleece underneath. We both wear hats, smiles, ruddy cheeks. I squint at the sun.

A few days later I was at the Wyeside to watch a National Theatre broadcast, and I chatted over the interval to a friend of a friend. Upon learning that I was a dry-stone waller, he was quick to say, 'Oh, you really must see the work happening on the Rhogo. It is absolutely *exquisite*.' Swelling with pride (and much to our mutual delight) I had the pleasure of telling him that this was my handiwork. I felt so happy knowing that people were watching the restoration, not to mention took pleasure in what they saw. My work mattered to more than just me and the farmers. People saw beauty in it, just like I did.

Blaen Cammarch

October arrived, and I dreaded leaving Jack. I had been in Wales five months, through the hottest, driest summer on record, two restoration projects so dreamy I won't see their likes again in my lifetime, and a conversation about marriage that didn't go the way I had imagined. I'd had a bit of money in my pocket for adventuring. I'd learned to sail. I'd been wined and dined, snuck spliffs and rollies out under the stars, gazed up lovingly at the moon with one of my best friends, swam and sunbathed nude without a care in the world, picnicked near and far, seen heaps of good theatre, travelled to Europe three separate times and London even more. In some ways they had been five of the most challenging months of my life, but without question they had also been five of the best and most extraordinary.

I had just returned to his place – *our* place, no matter how the marriage conversation went a few months before – from a whirlwind few days in Italy and London, and it felt particularly good to come home to him. I could scarcely believe it was about to end. I remember so clearly, so strongly how at home, at ease, in love I felt with him on the Sunday night I got back from my adventuring. I sat with him, bundled in my heaviest wool jumper and jacket, as he tended the last big tree trash bonfire in the fields next to the house. Those heaped tangles of branches had been waiting since he'd had the two huge ashes cut on Kate's seventieth birthday the year before.

It was serene, cool and damp that evening. I remember the sounds of the river, the feel of the heavy, chill air and the radiance of the fire. I remember feeling cwtched and protected there among those secluded hills with only him as my quiet, contented company. I remember watching him through the haze of the smoke as he raked the fire, broke sticks and tossed them onto the pile. And then he plunked his big shoulders, his long back, his stiff legs down beside me, squeezing onto the remaining corner of one of his overshirts, cast aside as the heat of the flames grew, and being so big that our shoulders touched automatically, unobtrusively, sweetly as we sat together in the warmth of his fading fire.

Our relationship had always had a hint of November about it, perhaps one of sunset. Both approached that night. It was a perfect moment, but we also knew it had an expiration date. I would go back to America before long – the place I called 'home' with less and less certainty. Jack had always been old, at least on paper and compared to me, and though I had rarely noticed in life, his age was becoming more apparent to me now. (I began to realise that ageing sometimes begins to accelerate without warning after years of little change. Like time, age is elastic and progresses inconsistently.) There would always be an ocean in the middle of our romance, which, however improbable, had been one of the most sustaining bonds of my life. He had given me all that I hold sacred: my work, the countryside, love, beauty and an understanding of genuine peace. We accepted our lot early on, and we chose to savour the time we *do* have, perhaps because of the expiration date. Those kinds of moments – by fires, on windy hilltops, falling asleep in tents, as we finish the last of the wine at our candlelit dinner table, usually with my feet in his lap, and think of perhaps reaching for the bourbon as a nightcap – were always bittersweet, and we protected them. For years, each time we parted we wondered silently if this would be the last time. None of us can know whether we will see our loved ones again after a goodbye, be it trans-Atlantic and indefinite or out the door for a routine day at the office, but the cards had always been stacked a bit tougher against Jack and me.

That last Sunday night in Wales, life felt so pitch-perfect, so poignant that I refused to ruin it with dread. We simply kept tending the fire because focusing on the immediate is often the best thing to do when departures loom large. Jack and I do chores, usually involving wood and saws and axes. But in those moments with him there was always a hint, something on the wind or in the trees, that eventually, inevitably, winter will come. I knew it was there even if I refused to look in its direction. We knew.

I loved him so intensely that evening.

All those years, I had been trying to hold the overwhelming, chest-swelling beauty and love that have so often crossed my path in Wales. Blackberries and journals are as close as I have come . . . Jot it down, seal it in a jar, and with any luck, return to it later. It will get you through leaner days.

Meadows of Dan, Virginia

As I was driving home along the Blue Ridge Parkway one afternoon that November, my vision started to go blurry . . . sort of shiny, sort of sparkly . . . unclear, in any case. It started out as a splotch in the centre of my vision and then grew further and further outwards. It was sort of like my annual migraine, which arrives like clockwork as the seasons change and the sinus pressure ratchets up, but I had caused this one myself.

This could be a bad sign, I thought. I was not well versed enough in head injuries to know.

I had been joyful in shirtsleeves and sunshine that day, euphoric after so many frigid workdays and painful, frozen fingers. I had been *so* cold during this project – miserably, infuriatingly cold – that I swore aloud all day about it, almost like a disturbed homeless person muttering on the street. *Every day*. Mainly, it was the wind. I had no shelter at all on that bare hilltop.

My vision was scaring me. I wasn't sure I was seeing well enough to drive the rest of the way home, but I was close . . . ten minutes left? And what else could I do?

It was one of those reality-check moments that those of us who work and live alone have from time to time that lead us to wonder what the fuck we are doing. I wondered why I subjected myself to such pain, such risk. Why was I working such a physical job alone in such a remote area, far away from my home and support network? I was building a 40-ton, dry-stack gateway at the entrance to a 130-acre farm, and I had stood up from a squat, where I'd been working on the foundations of a column, only to ram the crown of my head straight into a piece of steel I already knew was there. I had just watched the damned thing being welded on, but the welders were gone now, back down the mountain and across the state line to Mount Airy. I had been careless in my movements, my attention.

Would I wake up in the morning? Which friend could I bother, possibly worrying them needlessly, but possibly needing them to keep an eye on me for concussion symptoms? Or worse . . .

The nurse I managed to phone after scouring the back of my health insurance card through squinted eyes told me that I should beware of loss of consciousness and confusion, and to definitely go to the hospital if I started vomiting blood. She thought I was *probably* fine, but just in case . . .

I don't like to be dramatic about these things. I can't afford to be, or I can't go to work. I didn't think twice about whacking my head until my vision went funny. It was a stupid mistake and a headache up to that point. But it did give me pause. Vomiting blood? Loss of consciousness? I was *alone*. What was I supposed to do if either of those things happened? Who would know? How long would it take someone to miss me?

234

My work is dangerous with or without power tools, tractors, heavy lifting or shards of stone flying into my eyes. There are trip and slip hazards, smashed fingers, sprained ankles and wrists, lumpy, purple shins, sore backs, sunburns, dehydration, sunstroke, hypothermia, long-term hearing loss, clouds of cement dust up my nose . . . lots of options for pain, disfiguration, disabling injuries or even death. Physical work is risky, plain and simple, and this bell-ringer was an excellent reminder.

Why do I do it? Because I am a dry-stone waller, and working a dangerous job alone in a remote place is what we do. God knows Jack has told me his share of near-death experiences and close calls over the years.

There was the time he had a hole in his Gore-Tex, got hypothermia because of the cold, heavy rain he couldn't feel soaking in and was on the point of The Big Sleep when his mobile (which rarely has any signal on the hill) happened to ring and wake him. He was able to get home and warm up in the proper way, but only just.

Or the time he got pinned by a slab in a frigid river around Christmastime, only to be rescued by the farmer's wife who happened to come by.

Or the time he sneezed in an awkward lifting position, dislocated his neck, wound up paralysed on his knees with his head in a puddle, and it started to rain. Hours later, he would fall asleep with one nostril above water assuming that he would never wake again, but in the morning he did. The farmer's wife (who normally didn't) happened to take a walk by that day and found him. She phoned emergency services to come out. But he was too big for the Air Ambulance once it arrived, so two ground crews had to be dispatched to walk him out of the fields on a stretcher, poor things. He is a mountain of a man.

Believe it or not, there are more stories than this. Jack is *so* lucky to be alive. My brush was comparatively silly compared to what he has experienced, but it was enough to make me think. Are we crazy to keep on? Maybe. But we love what we do. If there is risk, we accept it willingly because we simply don't know how else to be.

Perhaps I was having a small existential crisis that evening as I hoped I didn't die alone at thirty-one of a head injury sustained as part of this absurd job I'd chosen . . . I welcomed any and all distractions from my immediate fear of death and blood-vomiting, and I let my mind drift back across the ocean to a lush green valley that has always brought me comfort. I floated, almost as if on drugs.

I found myself on a familiar hillside above the River Cammarch. It was vividly colourful, but somehow removed from time and words. It was images, feelings, memories. I stayed there a while floating around, disparate scenes from all the years in that place somehow mingling together now into one wistful, animated collage of longing . . . Some subconscious stuff surfacing for a moment, perhaps. It was beautiful, if nonsensical. My mind eventually moved back towards a slightly more verbal and logical space, and I thought for some unknowable amount of time about Jack, his age, my age, the ocean in the middle, what it meant to be together and apart . . . I came to no conclusions.

Wait, was I about to die? Was this it? Was I confused, like the nurse warned? Oh, God, *seriously*, did I have a concussion? Or was it just that my life at that time always felt a slightly incoherent swirl of here and there anyway, and I really had no idea where I lived?

I don't remember anything else from that night apart from the fact that I was too nervous to go to sleep for a very long time. I delayed going upstairs to bed for as long as I could.

Luckily, I did wake up the next morning. My friend Eliza – the equally oddball and fiercely independent orchardist – had been on death watch half an hour away. We had arranged that if I didn't get in touch with her by 9 a.m. she was to come over and check on me. One can only ask certain people to potentially come in and find one dead, and Eliza's general fearlessness made her a reasonable candidate for such a task. We were the kind of friends who drank home brew under the stars and fired shotguns into the wild mountain air, and she'd given me my first motorcycle lesson earlier in the year.

In the end, thank God, I was absolutely fine, and I felt silly. I sent the 'I am alive' text, adding in some self-deprecating bits to laugh off the worry that had plagued me all night. Eliza congratulated me with dependable humour.

Orchard Gap, Virginia

I admit that it's sometimes a lot of fun to stand out. It's been amazing the number of people who want to cheer me on for precisely the same reason that others leer or judge. Men talk to me at the hardware store in a way that shows they are slightly awestruck. Some DIY-ers ask my advice if they catch me in the masonry aisle looking knowledgeable and authoritative in my overalls. Men and women alike sometimes exclaim 'You go girl!' if they catch me wielding a sledgehammer or even just loading 90-pound bags of cement into my truck, one after the other. Much to my embarrassment I often wind up dominating the dinner table conversation at parties once people find out what I do for a living. Older women often can't get enough. They fought and waited for me to have this.

I'm not particularly comfortable being the centre of attention, yet I seem to attract an awful lot of it. Despite my rather commanding physical presence, underneath it all I am still *painfully* shy, even now in my thirties. The truth is,

I occupy an odd space, and I mean something different to everyone.

On a job site in the mountains of Virginia, clad in my overalls and the six thousand layers of clothes I wore to try to keep out the bitterest, most unrelenting wind I'd ever experienced, I met with all sorts of characters, good and bad. There were welders bearing moonshine, a truck driver called Cootie Man who brought my stone deliveries and tales of felonies long past, and a neighbour who asked me the worst possible question, but we'll get to him later. It's the good guys I want to talk about first.

It was on this job that I began to realise how my overalls function as camouflage. They communicate differently in every context, sometimes causing offence, but sometimes letting me jump rank in education and class.

At times, my overalls caused me to be treated as 'less than'. Labourer's attire usually does in urban areas. I got my first taste of this in DC when I transformed from office monkey to steel-toe-clad Mall rat during the festival. I rode public transit in both costumes, and the contrast was a bit shocking. People in their nice, clean suits looked at you very differently when you ceased to look like them, and not in a good way. No one wanted to be near you, and many looked right past you like you didn't exist at all. It was the same when I really started working construction and went into Whole Foods in my overalls looking . . . utilitarian, let's say.

But my overalls were doing me good service out here in the mountains. I began to find that people opened up to me in ways they probably wouldn't if it were more obvious that I'm a world-travelling ex-academic who might have some sort of judgement to pass on their intellect or experience or politics. I didn't want to hide who I was, but I also didn't want to be prejudged about it. In my overalls I just looked like someone who knew hard work and liked to be warm, and so I got to hang out with welders and truck drivers, which is a whole lot cooler than you probably think. They have hilarious and sometimes harrowing stories (and they might just bring you moonshine, which happens to me much more often than you would think).

The more education I received and the more I moved through circles comprised exclusively of highly, formally educated people, the more I realised what a divider it can be – socially and economically, yes, but also within families and communities. I pondered things like genuine confidence versus snobbery and exclusivity, curiosity versus pig-headedness. Though the majority of my friends were in North Carolina, where I'd gone to graduate school and found my people for the first time in my life, I left precisely because I was fed up with living in a bubble . . . only to come home and find that I hated being surrounded by conservatism outside the walls of my own house. I have always been caught in the middle – a bridge, an ambassador. It can be a wearying position, representing America to the world, the left to the right, the right to the left, the academic world to the labouring one and vice versa.

It was painful for me to come home with a Master's degree and listen to people without one prefacing their comments with things like, 'Well, I'm not educated like you, but . . .'. I hated listening to people begin statements as if I were waiting to declare them stupid. Graduate school – in addition to edifying and expanding – also teaches one that there are a lot of people who just learn to jump through hoops very, very well – who actually aren't broadly intelligent at all, but very specifically so – and many of them will die starving in the woods if and when the apocalypse comes because they are so devoid of practical skills. I wanted to wear a sign saying, 'The fact that I have a Master's degree does not mean that I think this is the only way to be an intelligent human being.' Instead, my overalls kind of do this.

In a way, my education had made me an outsider in some circles. Education was an answer to my curiosity, not a way to put myself above anyone else, and I felt very sad that anyone might think the latter ... particularly when I knew just how lucky I'd been. I hadn't wanted education to be a divider, and perhaps that's one reason I was eventually so happy to travel through the world in dungarees and steel toes. Overalls advertised humility, approachability and practicality. They looked friendly. No one assumed in my overalls that I was a snob, the intellectual elite, et cetera. That came as a great relief.

I couldn't decide whether I had more in common with my well-heeled clients – who have all but one been extraordinarily kind, generous, interesting people – or with the welders and the truckers, but I was so happy that I sort of got to tap dance in the space between the two.

My overalls hid or advertised a lot of things, but I could never hide the fact that I'm woman – nor would I want to.

It's funny: in the early days, it's almost as if *I* didn't realise that I was a woman. Or, I didn't realise that it mattered. I had simply never thought in those terms, and I certainly didn't have an agenda when I started walling except to be happy.

When I was younger, I was smarter, stronger and taller than most of the boys, so that didn't come into play at recess or in class. My father treated my brother and me equally, and my otherwise very traditional grandfather, who told me constantly how pretty I was, loved it when I put on his old Army kit and ran around in the yard playing soldiers with my cousin Aaron (who really did become one). I'd never felt held back by my gender in any way, which is perhaps why that

241

infamous graduate committee member ripped into me for – among many other things – being so ignorant about the women's movement. She was right about that part – I hadn't studied it. Where the great power struggles of the twentieth century were concerned, I'd spent my time studying Civil Rights and Black Power. I got my feminist education later as I got to work.

It wasn't until I picked up the hammer full-time that I realised I was sometimes treated differently because I am a woman. Sometimes I get more help than I should, and sometimes I'm not given a chance at all. Sometimes my advice is not heeded. Sometimes my male clients feel guilty or uncomfortable that I am moving enormous quantities of weight while they look on. (I remind them with a laugh that I'm not volunteering.) I get asked more often than I would like whether I am married, have children, have a boyfriend . . . what, exactly, are the circumstances of my life outside my overalls?

Perhaps it was sheer luck that these annoying feminist lessons kindly left me be until age thirty-one. By that time I had enough respect for myself and my skill that stupid personal comments had *really* started to piss me off. I was tired of explaining to friend and foe alike who I was and what I did. Sometimes you just get to a moment in your life when you are sick of breaking down your existence for examination, enjoyment or critique by anyone else for any reason. It's not from insecurity, but sheer fatigue of repetition and scrutiny. I have seen people's eyes glaze over as I have talked. I have watched judgemental expressions creep across faces. I have served as the dinner party spice over and over again. I have listened as strangers have asked me personal and presumptuous questions, as if they have a *right* to know simply because I happen to be a bit unusual and start all my conversations with a friendly, open tone.

242

People who stopped by the job site out of curiosity often assumed I wasn't working alone – that I must have some male co-worker hiding somewhere. Or they spoke as if I had a boss, and that he was a man. He was *always* a 'he'.

A neighbour came over from across the street to tell me that 'y'all' were doing a great job. He said he'd been watching me that last month or so and that it looked good. I'm usually happy when people tell me they've been keeping an eye on my work, but I couldn't help wondering to myself why he hadn't noticed there was never anyone else around but me?

And then, though he was not asking me out on a date, having just referenced his wife, he asked, 'Have you got a husband or anything?'

Was I a lesbian? Would a man let me be out here working like this if I *did* have one? It was such a loaded question. I just told him no and left it at that.

He invited me to church, too. He meant well, I knew, but I was reminded yet again that as long as I lived in my native region of America, I would never escape the Evangelical Christianity and invasive moral judgement that seem always to be waiting for an opportunity to pounce. (In Britain, if someone approaches you randomly, they probably want money. In Mexico, they want to sell you something. In the South, nine times out of ten, they want to talk to you about Jesus. Nothing against Jesus, but I know the drill. When I was young, we were in church every time the doors were open – or else.)

You had the guys like Brad and Roberto and Cootie Man – my welders and truckers – who accepted that you were a bad-ass lady worthy of their respect on the job site, and then you had dummies who would turn up and say annoying things like this. The difference is that people who work physical, creative jobs know quality and hard work when they see it, and that instantly engenders respect for the person doing the work. Jack had always teased me about being a woman, but he had respected me from day one.

Some people were annoying and a bit clueless, but I have also experienced outright harassment. Curiously, the worst comes from those who never say a word. I have had successive pick-up trucks of men drive by leering at me while I'm unloading pallets or rubble from the bed of my own truck at the dump (obviously, where I look my most attractive). The nastiest ones ride by slowly and kind of snarl-smile because they're thinking about taking my clothes off. It's so obvious it's pathetic. They never actually speak to me – they're far too scared. I don't even mind a bit of playful banter in the right scenario – I can hold my own – but the leering and lip-licking sends me into blind rage. I experience a lot of admiration and borderline harassment in my job . . . both are familiar at this point. Plenty of men have been lovely and admiring and respectful, but these guys are just disrespectful trash in oversized, overpriced trucks they don't need to tow their dinky-ass trailers of mulch. It's unfortunately very familiar. And if they are stupid enough to think I can't throw concrete that far, they haven't been paying attention to the right attributes. I could, and my aim is brilliant.

The thing about insulting conversations or the occasional fury-inducing incident of harassment is that I often have to take valuable time out of my workday for them. I can't build well and talk at the same time. Building is a non-verbal headspace for me, and conversation distracts me. Extremes of heat, cold and frustration likewise do not help my willingness to chat. Lastly, I'm not known for my polite language on the job site (I conveniently blame Jack for this), and visitors leave me trying *so* hard not to cuss like a sailor because I've just smashed a finger again that I'd already smashed last week.

And if it's a leering-at-the-dump kind of incident, I am so angry I literally can't see straight, which is not a productive state of mind. People have said dismissively, 'Oh, don't let them get to you.' I'm sorry, but I have a right to be pissed off at some idiot staring at me so boldly, as if I am a piece of meat for his enjoyment. It doesn't happen often, but it makes my blood boil.

I get it: I threaten some men. It's not intentional. I'm just trying to do my work and get by in the world. But I'm in what they feel is their territory, and a lot of the time I'm doing the work better than they might.

Shouldn't anyone with a brain be able to look at one solitary, super-strong woman in the middle of 40 tons of stone and realise that she deserves some respect?

Meadows of Dan, VA

The world turned white overnight, and it stayed that way for a while. It had been cold all along, never breaking freezing some days, but now, progress simply stopped.

As I sat in my temporary quarters at Jim and Silvie's place waiting out the ice storms, I had a lot of time to think. Too much, really. I needed to get back to work. Being cooped up always led me to near-insanity before too long. Why had I agreed to do a project in the mountains this time of year when I was so likely to suffer in cold and be delayed by snow and ice? (Because my client nagged me into it, and I was too weak to force her to wait. Note to self: weakness results in suffering.)

I had been in business about two years by then, and I felt like I was forever chasing my tail, trying to catch my breath, racing between darkness and meetings and rainstorms and freezes. I was hardly ever up to date on my tax deduction spreadsheets and mileage records. I always had an estimate or two that I should've written up yesterday. Most days, small business is the feeling that you aren't getting any piece of it quite right, that you are always letting someone down (possibly yourself), that you could definitely be doing it better if only you were a little more organised, a little more brilliant about design, a little more charming with clients. I almost always felt like a *slight* failure.

The truth was, I had never thrown myself wholeheartedly into developing my US career beyond a few projects here and there to keep me going. Jobs kept appearing, and I worked like hell on the walls wherever I was, but I bumbled my way along in business, and that side of things just happened to become legitimate and sustainable over the years. I was lucky. It seemed to happen almost without my trying, and more than anything else a successful business at home felt for a long time like a tie to a place I didn't want to be. I did my work because I loved stone and had a real need for it in my life, but also because it was the only way I could ever make enough money to get back to Jack and to Wales without taking a proper full-time job with five stingy seconds of vacation per year. Self-employment meant I absolved myself of letting anyone else down when I decided to take off again. I stuck with it for that reason as much as any.

I still wasn't paying rent or a mortgage, and I had no car payment, so life – at least in that sense – was easy. But I could see why traditional craft and small business simply aren't sustainable for everyone . . . I was confident and established, and I was certainly never bored, but I still felt I was struggling to stay afloat, and I was beginning to feel a bit ragged. The work is one thing, but it's the stress that is truly exhausting.

On the other hand, I knew that when I did completely nail a project, nothing was more happy-making than my small business. It was addictive. I almost always came out on top, but it still somehow surprised me. I just felt a lot of stress in the meantime. I was definitely still at the phase in my career where people were asking me constantly to do new things. Perhaps construction is always like that: each job different and challenging in its own ways, unless you're throwing up cookie-cutter houses in new developments ... So I had to learn to fake confidence ('Oh, yes, of course! That shouldn't be a problem ...' [thinks to self, WHAT ON EARTH DID I JUST AGREE TO?!]) and then figure it out, and usually I did. I rang Jack occasionally for advice on technical matters, but mostly, I had simply learned to trust my ability to wing it, and that was where my confidence grew.

When the weather finally broke a bit and I was back on the job site, half frozen in an unrelenting wind, my mental state shifted to survival, to the immediate, to physical suffering and logistics. There simply wasn't the energetic bandwidth for philosophising when my face was numb all day, apart from perhaps wondering in coarse language about the sensibility of my life choices. I very consciously spritzed expensive perfume under my overalls each day simply for morale, and off I went again.

There was a strange, crystalline mud-ice on site where once there had been puddles and claggy clay, and I had to be very careful to avoid slipping with big stones in my hands, potentially getting pinned or hitting my head on one of the many stones littering the ground. I cursed my aching, burning hands as they adjusted to the cold before my core temperature and circulation increased with the heat of my labour. I wiped my nose endlessly, and my eyes watered so much from the wind that I wore safety glasses all the time to help shield them.

I sheltered from the wind in my truck at elevenses and lunch and in any other moments when I simply couldn't take it any more.

When I got home at the end of the day – or sometimes the middle of the day if it turned out just to be too cold and miserable to carry on – and I stripped off all the layers of my spacesuit (my affectionate nickname for my full winter get-up), I had great rings of dirt between where my hat and neck gaiter had stopped and my glasses had begun, almost like oversized spectacles made of filth. Anything on my face that was exposed was grimy and wind-battered. My cheeks burned red and numb-ish for the same reason, and the colour stayed the length of the job no matter how much of the thickest moisturiser – my bear grease, as I had taken to calling it – I slathered on morning and night. I took embarrassingly long showers, dropping my dust-cloud overalls in the hallway and leaving them there in quarantine until the next morning when I suited up again. My trusty overalls had come home from Wales still bearing dirt from the last days on Rhogo, and I had vowed I would not wash them until I finished this job. (It was a vow I could only get away with in such freezing temperatures when I was not sweating like a horse.)

The stone selection on this job was particularly challenging. In the three deliveries Cootie Man brought me, I bought something like 60 tons of stone, and I had to sort through it all to find the 35–40 tons I needed. Buying stone is a bit like buying a mixed bag of jellybeans. There are some pieces in there that you really want, others that are perfectly acceptable, and inevitably plenty of crap that you just don't want at all. Each project has different taste buds, let's say, and this project was particularly picky since it had so many corners. And curves – there were no perfectly straight runs outside the columns. Everything was a swooping S-curve. That meant that this project only wanted the red and orange jellybeans . . . maybe an occasional purple one . . . but no whites, NO greens, and no yellows. (Licorice goes without saying and should be banished anyway.) There was a lot of stone that I just couldn't use for this structure, but you have to buy the whole bag of jellybeans . . . In fact, you have to buy *enough* whole bags of jellybeans so that you have enough reds and oranges to do the whole, huge project, and each bag, of course, is a little different. It's tough to do this kind of precision improvisation – what dry-stone walling is, really – without a lot of leftovers. Field walls are one thing, but formal entrances with complex shapes are quite another. Plenty of jellybeans just don't make the cut.

Though visually the top lines of the walls would sit at the same height, there was a significant drop – something like half a metre – from one column to the next, which meant on one side of the gateway I was building to a much greater height. Because of the way most women's body mechanics work out, our strength lessens as the load rises above shoulder level. There were some stones that were so heavy I simply could not dead-lift them to that height. Some I simply could not lift at all. I had to be smarter than that. Sometimes I flipped big stones, end over end, onto an empty pallet and then dragged that behind me with a tow chain I inherited from my grandfather. Then, I rolled them off the makeshift sled and up the existing wall, using it as if it were a ramp, to their final resting places. I had to be sure the stones would sit where I wanted them, for it was a lot of energy wasted if they did not. I rarely missed, and I celebrated each good placement as enthusiastically as the first. I loved to get it right.

I would have to use huge slabs to cap my columns, for the weight of the top of a well-built stone structure is what really holds it together. For this, I would need the tractor. I put the forks on the front-end loader and spread them to the right width for each slab as it came time to move it. First, I laid out my caps on the ground in hot-pink boxes spray-painted onto the grass in the exact dimensions of my column tops. It took a while to work out what would go where from the pile of big, heavy pieces I'd saved for this exact purpose. Laying out on the grass also helped me see any differences in the levels (thicknesses) between my capstones (each side would take three or four slabs depending on my exact selections) so that I might sort those out beforehand. I didn't want to be fiddling about with pinnings any more than I had to once I heaved the slabs off the forks ... I'd be standing on the forks by then, using them as a step ladder, so any lifting I did I'd have to do myself at that stage. There was a lot of hopping up and down, checking and double-checking that I'd put the brake on tightly so the tractor couldn't roll away or – worse – onto me. Even with the tractor, it was a hell of a lot of work, but I was so pleased with how clever I'd been. I took a few minutes to sit atop my columns in celebration when they were complete. These were my first, and I had worried over them for months beforehand. It was almost like passing my walling exam all over again.

I would not finish that project without my share of tears – stopping to whimper or shout or throw things every now and again on the job site, in the truck, and at home – but I kept going. This was the most beautiful thing I had ever designed, and by far the biggest and most complex dry-stone project I'd ever undertaken in America. I was really pushing myself this time, and I *had* to come out on top. There was a lot riding on my success. I had made a lot of choices in my life that I needed to justify to myself. To my credit, I had at least passed the point of caring what anybody *else* thought about how I was living my life, and that had taken a long time.

After a lengthy slog through sub-freezing temperatures, ice storms, road closures and good-old-fashioned backbreaking work, I completed my gateway in early February, finishing

251

clean-up one Sunday night in driving rain and darkness, with only tractor headlights and a mountaineering headlamp to show the way. It was *brutal*. There had been tons and tons of spare stone – all the crap jellybeans – left scattered about on the ground that I had to collect and move three-quarters of a mile deeper into the property with the tractor bucket, but I had to load it by hand. If I loaded it too heavily, the tractor would tip forward going downhill or over big bumps, so it took a while. My gloves were full of holes. My hands were sore and wet, my back tired. But I'd done it.

Soggy and frazzled with the heat on full blast, I drove away up the Blue Ridge Parkway that night with my truck bed piled precariously high with wooden pallets and wire mesh. I prayed that nothing would fly off, forcing me back out into that miserable weather again and keeping me even a second longer than necessary from a hot shower, a stiff drink and bed. Stick a fork in me: I was *done*.

I went back the next day, clean, dry and a bit more rested to stand back and marvel at my creation – something that remains one of the greatest pleasures of my job. As I drove up, I almost couldn't believe what I saw.

It's never possible to understand exactly what you've done until the ground is completely tidied up and there are no remaining visual distractions from the lines you have wrought in stone. I'd been so furious in clean-up mode the day before that I forgot to look up and see what was beginning to emerge, and then I'd left in darkness. I was returning to see it as if for the first time, and it really was magnificent.

I instantly wished that I had charged more – for its beauty, for my suffering. That is an ongoing lesson.

Greenville, South Carolina

Back home in South Carolina, my parents greeted me and my tools warmly when we came down the mountain, just like always. It felt good to be home and have a bit of money in the bank, and now, I could rest. It had been a long, cold, heavy job these last two and a half months away.

In the bath one morning that first week home, I heard my father down the hall telling a friend on the phone about what I'd just done and how impressive it was. I was proud, and Dad was, too. But the distraction of another major out-of-town project was now out of the way, and I found myself crammed once more back into my childhood bedroom, suddenly face to face with the wreckage of the last few years.

My room was crowded with antique axe heads and pitching hammers, hawthorn stumps from trees I hacked down by hand, bits of broken pottery and rusted old iron, random stones from this memorable job site and that special hilltop, expensive wellies I didn't particularly need in South Carolina, bags I'd only sort of unpacked, piles of mail and receipts I hadn't quite dealt with yet, stacks of books I intended to read, a calendar stuck on a month long passed. It was a collage of relics and responsibilities. I had moved back into that room three years before when I came home from North Carolina – an entire house into one room and the rest into storage – and there I was still.

I began to realise just how dishevelled my world in America had become, existing somehow out of time and space. Sleeping amongst this chaos in this little room forced me to reckon with the state of my life even if I could not bring myself to reckon with the stuff. To the outside world who never saw this scene, my life looked OK. I was having a big adventure, it seemed, and in many ways this was true. To me, now in the thick of the backstage chaos, my life looked slightly horrendous: sloppy, disorderly, irresponsible, over-whelming . . . And that's without the humiliation of the fact that I was nearly thirty-two and still living with my parents – I'm just talking about the actual mess. There was hardly room to walk. I suspected that to a trained eye my space looked like some form of mental illness.

I had been living back and forth between America and Wales for six years by then, and living and working out of my car most of the time that I was in America. Six years of follow-ing my heart and bouncing back and forth across the north Atlantic and the Blue Ridge mountains . . . Six years of eccen-tricity and love and absolute self-indulgence which, fortu-nately, had seemed to charm a sufficient number of clients to keep me going, but it had also produced this disconcerting space . . . the yang.

On paper I had got what I asked for: a busy life with one foot firmly planted in America and the other in Wales. I had wonderful people in my circles in both places, and my world was filled with love and support. My days were filled with stone, overalls were my uniform, and I had enough work and enough money for the first time. I'd just completed with great success the most beautiful and technically challenging job of my career. I'd finally been able to buy the $30 square-nose shovel that I couldn't afford two years before, which to me indicated that I had arrived. I felt I could finally say with certainty that I was successful at my chosen career and living a nice life (even if my room was a little messy).

But something bad was slipping up on me. A quiet sense of dread was soon with me all the time. My chest felt heavy. My mind became restless. I luxuriated in long baths and wrapped myself in silk and roses as I tried to recover from the brutality of the last job, but something wasn't right, and I couldn't keep it from rising to the surface. It was in my throat all the time, threatening to choke the life out of me, or to suddenly spring from my mouth as fumbling words followed in short order by salty tears. I wasn't sure what the problem was, but I realised I would not be able to ignore it much longer with the hope that it would simply go away quietly.

By most accounts, my life was a success, yet things still felt difficult, unsettled. I remembered it warmly, but I was almost haunted by the summer of 2014 with its endless sunshine and constant adventure. I knew something big had just passed me by.

That summer I'd got used to living a rural life full-time, to having Kate as my neighbour, to opening my window at night to the sounds of rivers, to people who loved theatre and classical music and great art, to public rights of way that led out my door and up the mountain, to tea as ritual, and to a physical and spiritual freedom I had never once felt in America ... Now, I was without that, and I didn't know quite what to do.

255

And the marriage conversation with Jack had posed as many questions as it answered. I would not be moving to Wales permanently, as it turned out, so what did I want from my relationship with Jack if not a marriage?

I knew I had been deeply affected by the experiences of the last year or two, but I hadn't yet had a chance to stop and take stock of what it all meant. I hadn't had time to process any of it. I wasn't sure where I was any more, but I was no longer allowed to shut out the world and any of its problems (or mine) and simply focus on my work. Everything was in my face. I had to acknowledge realities big and small, near and far.

To wrestle with all of that in a small, chaotic space was near impossible for me – not to mention I hadn't seen it coming. I was a woman who was used to being on the open hill. To be back in a tight suburban *pied-à-terre* with lots of television and talking was not easy for me by then, but I hadn't left myself any other choice. All my resources had gone into being with Jack – all that back and forth, all those $1200 plane tickets that I could never quite get over the guilt of – and I had no home of my own. In some ways, though working on the road was tiring, it at least let me be alone in quieter places. My clients had private guest quarters for me, and those had been my haven when I was not in Wales.

I had come home from Virginia feeling triumphant, but before long I pitched into a major nosedive. I'd had to muster my adrenaline and drive for so long, and I was still in the habit, yet it now had nowhere to go. Though I was physically flattened, I still felt restless because suddenly I had no purpose, no obvious channel for my mental energy. My brain remained in a state of anxiety and frustration no matter how many rose-scented baths I took, and I couldn't even focus my mind enough to read a book.

Eventually, I didn't want to get out of bed. I had crashed.

I was bewildered about why I should be feeling this way with all I'd just accomplished in the last year. I was angry that I wasn't stronger, happier, able to just *be* for a bit without some sort of entertainment to serve as distraction from what I now realised was my quiet, creeping misery. Before long, I wasn't interested in anything, and I didn't have the energy to fake it any more.

I was no stranger to depression. I had been cut down many times in my adult life. I'd had rough patches due to romance gone afoul, trouble at work, insecurity over my academic prowess, fights with (those I thought were) close friends, and just because of winter. I had only ever been in a dangerous place once. When I was twenty-two, I hit rock bottom for the first time, and it frightened the fuck out of me. There was one night that I wanted it to be over. I had never been to that place before, so disconsolate and hope-less and alone, and I did not know that it had an end – that it was a cycle. I was terrified that this might be my new real-ity. I never took any steps to end my life, but I remember being aware of the kitchen knives in a way I never had been before, and that night I lay face-down on the floor of my apartment, burying my hands under the protective weight of my body and weeping uncontrollably until I was too tired to cry any more.

I made a phone call the very next morning to arrange to see a psychiatrist as soon as possible, and I got the help I needed. I had scared myself sufficiently the night before and knew I had to do something. Besides, the cracks were beginning to show at work – I could barely not-cry, let alone get through my tasks. The doctor I saw was cold but efficient, listening with absolutely no expression and almost no reaction. He prescribed one pill that was a combination anti-anxiety/

antidepressant and another that could be used to spot-check myself if I was having a panic attack. I hated pills, but I was grateful for them at this point. He said he could also refer me to a psychotherapist. I told him I just wanted to get back to work and get on with things – that I thought work was what I really needed, not talk. He just looked at me with his face of concrete and explained a bit more about the medication, never pushing therapy, which I feel in retrospect was a mistake. As he was wrapping up the diagnosis and prescription talk, I remember he said, 'This will happen to you again over the course of your life, and it will probably always be triggered by stress.'

He was not kidding.

In later – and always less severe – episodes, mainly because it had become less shocking with repetition, I had been helped along by a variety of things: amazingly caring friends who chose to listen with love; plenty of exercise and fresh air and sunshine; the wisdom of older and wiser people (especially those who have been brave enough to say, 'me too'); throwing myself into physical work; hot baths; hours and hours and *hours* of writing in my journal. The great Joan Didion once wrote, 'Had I been blessed with even limited access to my own mind there would have been no reason to write. I write entirely to find out what I'm thinking, what I'm looking at, what I see and what it means. What I want and what I fear.' And while she wasn't talking specifically about mental illness and anxiety, I don't think she would disagree with me. The pages of my journal were a safe place for all that scary, choking, black energy to go.

By now, I had been to the bottom and back more times than I wanted to remember. I knew the ropes. There are always warning signs, but I am very good at ignoring them and pretending I am fine until I am *drowning* in sadness and anxiety and lethargy. And then I think, 'Shit. Really? How did this happen AGAIN?' Depression creeps up on me, hurls me to the ground and sits on top of me, and then I spend a while being miserable in various ways and stages until, one day – and I never know quite when it will be or why that moment exactly – I somehow get my fight back and turn the corner.

This time it was different. The corner I needed to turn was a very, very long way away – possibly on another planet, never to be located. What I felt was despair coupled with a fatigue from some deep, unreachable place inside me that – I didn't realise until it stopped functioning – had kept me going, working, able to deal with the world and maintain a resilient front. That winter I became intimate with a new variety of depression particular to those of us who undertake intense, project-based, creative work of the sort that exhausts mentally, physically *and* emotionally. As a waller, my physical exhaustion was something extra special, let me tell you, but I had not understood the emotional price of my work and the patterns of my life until now. This was a moment of reckoning.

When depression hits, I forget all the nice things I bring to the world because, basically, I just feel like an embarrassing mess of a human being. I don't feel I can deal with people without crying or otherwise revealing that I feel horrible, and believing they might judge me or just not understand, I hide when I can. I had always found the slightest bit of comfort in reminding myself that I was like Virginia Woolf. Like Winston Churchill and his 'black dog'. Like lots of other world-changing people. Like plenty of close friends of mine. But in the moments when you really can't bring yourself to face the world, there is little comfort to be found except perhaps if you can manage to sleep. I often can't.

Those who have never been depressed don't understand how exhausting simple conversation can be – even with people you really enjoy on a normal day. You can't imagine how unappealing everything is – even the things you love the most. And you are *tired*. Even when you know good and well what you need to help you survive as you wait on the storm to pass (sunshine, exercise, interaction with loved ones, adequate sleep and good food), you can't always muster the will to make it happen, and that makes you feel even worse – a failure. It can be a vicious cycle. It becomes a difficult resting momentum to break, and meanwhile you may be slipping deeper.

When it hits, you pull back from people because you cannot believe in that instant that anyone could possibly want to know or talk about how shitty you feel. It is embarrassing. You feel guilty. You don't want to worry people. And no one could possibly love you when you are a mess, so why bother telling anyone that you're not OK?

It was somehow more frustrating this time because a lot of people in my life seemed to think that I led such a magical existence that I had no problems. (Insert rant about how social media encourages false impressions.) I wanted to yell at all these people who believed that my life was as good all the time as the pictures they had seen on the internet, who told me how lucky I was, who weren't struggling over their existence like I was – over complicated love affairs and being sort of homeless and not able to live where I wanted to live and, well, *everything* . . . Followed by more crying, or perhaps simultaneously with the yelling. I was just being crazy, I knew. I felt so isolated by my anger, so embittered by the fact that people believed the wonderful parts of my life came without a price.

Even I continued to ask self-critically and, frankly, a bit bemused *what*, exactly, I had to be unhappy about. On paper, nothing. I was living the life I'd asked for, and I'd just finished building something beautiful. I had a man who loved me and lots of friends, as well as shelter and food and my health. The sun was still coming up, and the moon and the stars were still as beautiful as ever. But that's not how this works. Depression is not logical. When I'm in the thick of it, I can sit in my bed in the dark fighting tears and do my best to remember genocide and female genital mutilation, civilian casualties of war and rape victims, slavery and people with debilitating physical illnesses – all kinds of stuff that should engender perspective and make me feel like my life is OK by comparison. Logically, I know this. But I still feel like crap. One cannot will away one's feelings.

I was losing my mind, losing my ability to face the world, and I didn't know how to talk about it, or even who I *could* talk to about it. My journal was not enough anymore. Anyone at home was too close, too embarrassing. I needed privacy, yet I didn't want to be alone, yet I didn't want to inflict my miserable self on anyone else. I was floundering, and I needed back-up.

I wondered whether Rose might understand. From the start we had talked honestly with each other about our worries and our 'wobbly bits', as she endearingly called them. She had always shown me a wonderfully indulgent sensitive side, easily slipping into the role of loving older sister, and in that moment I *so* wanted to be petted by someone I trusted and admired.

Lonelier than I had ever been in my life, I finally got up the courage to write.

'Girl,' I began, 'I fell off the surfboard this week, and it was *not* pretty.' I poked fun at my misery in an attempt to make it more palatable, but she read between my lines, spotting all the pain beneath. Ever fearless, Rose dived right in after me.

261

'Hooray, she's human!' her email began. Still spluttering seawater, I laughed.

She didn't start a fresh message, but interspersed her responses throughout my original, as if we were actually in conversation. The effect was both hilarious and deeply kind, full of balm but also exclamation marks. She was thousands of miles away, but she couldn't have felt any nearer if she had knocked on the door and sat down beside me on my bed.

I told her how hard I'd been working, how exhausted I was . . . I'd been going 100 miles per hour at maximum stress for weeks on end, and I'd stopped cold turkey, and I was not OK.

'Does that make any sense?' I asked. 'Have you ever felt that way? (Are you smacking your forehead RIGHT NOW?)'

Most of her message was sweet and funny – I would have cried if I hadn't been laughing so hard – but towards the end she wrote me a handful of impassioned, crystal-clear lines telling me that I was not weak, but an artist and a human and – beautifully – a woman. She knew exactly what had clob-bered me: the post-creative crash – the postpartum portion of the cycle – with a heavy dose of winter on top.

I had known from the start that Rose was not going to be the kind of friend I could ring up to help me move a sofa, but this kind of deep empathy and spot-on humour in the midst of some of life's most complex and painful moments were her superpower. She came through for me that day in a way no one else could have.

She encouraged me to be patient with myself and the process. 'The exhaustion just has to work its way through,' she said. 'The sun always does come out, as you know.'

And then it actually did.

South Carolina had a freak summer day that week that brought the sun out and took the temperatures near 70

262

degrees. I knew this was priceless medicine, available for a limited time only, and the beautiful, glowing orb in the sky inspired me at last to break my resting momentum. Even at my lowest, I cannot resist the sun and would not dream of wasting a gorgeously warm winter day by hiding in bed. The universe seemed to be conspiring in my favour as the miserable days of February dragged on and I battled to right the ship.

I ventured outdoors for yoga with a chaser of therapeutic bikini-clad sunbathing and beer. This would not be the end of my struggles, but it buoyed me for a time and reminded me – for a couple of hours, anyway just how good I was capable of feeling. I was utterly sun-stoned, and I dreaded nightfall, but I tried to hold on to the gratitude of the day.

I wrote to Kate that night in delighted astonishment at the surprise gift of warm sunshine, knowing the precious feeling of contentment might linger a while longer if I shared it, and she always appreciated a tale of good fortune. She knew that I had been feeling low lately, so when I told her of my divine weather luck, she wrote encouragingly, 'Definitely continue to *carpe diem* (even if curiously close to crap diem, too, as I discovered on typing fast just now).' She went on to reassure me, as Rose had, that coming down after any big bout of work, when you've truly stretched and given yourself, is bound to be a really low, shaky, emotional time, and in exact proportion to what you've given and stretched. As ever, I trusted her.

I had never thought about it before. I hadn't witnessed it in people I knew, but also I hadn't known a lot of people with jobs or personalities like mine, and I reasoned that this was not the kind of thing one necessarily experiences in the nine-to-five jobs most people have (and I used to). I hadn't thought of my work as a creative process either, but of course it was, and a heavy one to boot . . . All that nervous preparation, then the long, draining act of building, then facing the client's pleasure or displeasure with it, and then saying goodbye to it and moving on. I realised that I had never pushed myself quite like I had on this last project. I asked a lot this time, and this was the price I had to pay now. This crash – this horrid, listless, dysfunctional lull I could not seem to shake – was simply something that *artists* go through when they are depleted in the wake of a big project. I was not a freak, and I was not alone, and this would not last forever. I felt so relieved and reassured by the messages from Kate and Rose that I read them over and over again that week.

There would always be some aspects of my job that threatened to send me into dark periods of depression, but coming to understand the cycles of the creative process made all the difference. I began to know and accept as best I could the soaring highs, the bottomless, depleted lows, and the utter fucking crashes. I learned them the hard way, which, unfortunately, is the only way I've ever let myself learn anything.

Thankfully, I did it this time with wise, kind friends looking on. They helped me understand where I was, and that it was temporary . . . that they loved me no matter how black it got, and that there was always something left to laugh about. I was coming to understand what an individual and sometimes lonely path I had chosen for myself, but I knew I had people at my back who believed in me and loved me even when I could do neither for myself.

I began to return to the world.

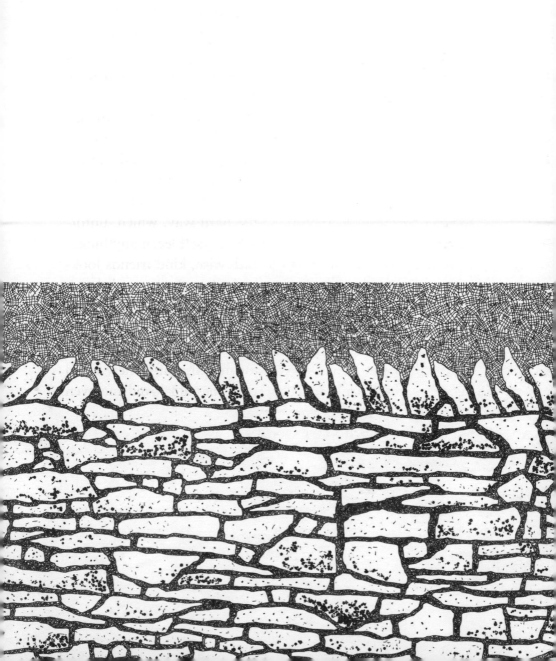

Durham, North Carolina

Why was it, I wondered, that every project I have is terrifying up until the moment I physically dig in and get started? Was it a lingering fear of failure? My perfectionism?

The commencement of the actual manual labour has always been the antidote to my worries. It is the most therapeutic thing in the world for me. It shuts me up and keeps me busy, shifts my brain from all the questioning to simple, arduous physical movement. I am always relieved to get out the tools, move heavy stuff, make stacks. Put a mattock in my hands or a multi-ton pile of gravel before me to move, and the ship will right itself. It has been that way since day one.

If my work was in one sense what had laid me low over the winter, it would also be the thing that brought me back to life in time.

The next project was *anything* but straightforward, and I was nervous about it. All winter, I'd known that by March I was scheduled to be teaching walling workshops for the first time – just intro-level stuff at a community garden in North Carolina – but to think of facing people as an authority of any sort always intimidated me, and I was still a bit wobbly after that last run-in with my ornery brain chemicals. I would have to drum myself up to be clever *and* cheery. There were plenty of logistical and technical components of the design that I needed to figure out as well. The only answer was to get out there and do it. I could always hear Jack's voice in my head: 'Just get on with it, woman!'

Have you ever heard someone say that they didn't realise how much they knew until they had to teach it to someone else? That was exactly my experience when I got my first workshop students. I knew I was good at my job, but I had forgotten how naturally suited to it I am. I comprehend shapes, body mechanics and tool-use. I have a physical constitution that lets me handle with relative ease and grace a lot of weight. I understand design and process, can visualise how things come together in pieces to form a whole. (Thanks for all the Lego, Mom and Dad!) One realises very quickly in teaching others that some have these understandings hardwired in them and some simply do not. Many can learn a bit, but some – frankly – have no hope. Jack had always referred to the latter category as those with 'shape dyslexia'. Others simply lack the physical coordination to pull it all together.

The project was a big one of terraced retaining walls and slab steps, and though parts were so technical I'd have to do them myself, I was able to get several groups of volunteers building with reasonable proficiency on the straight sections. Watching my students, I began to understand how far I had come in six years, and I felt grateful for the patience it must have taken for Jack to teach me. I found myself cringing often as I watched my students struggle to get it right, and there were times when I could have taken off every single stone that someone laid down, but I didn't.

It was heartening for me to see in the eyes of a few of the young women I taught the very same wonder and excitement that I felt towards Angharad and Jack when I first met them. I was on the other side of it now. I was the first highly educated craftswoman they'd ever met, and it shook them up a bit. They were all bright, successful girls, bound for medical school or graduate school or dental school, and like me, they would never have considered manual labour. I think they were shocked to discover how satisfying and empowering it is to, say, spend a day building a wall. They all wrote to thank me afterwards, and most of them friended me on Facebook. One wrote, 'You are probably the coolest lady I've ever met.' I wasn't sure about that, but I do know the feeling.

Crashing with old friends as I worked in North Carolina, I began to remember that I had a life at home, too . . . That the friends I'd collected were pretty amazing, and that everyone was really coming into their own in different ways. They were buying houses, marrying each other, doing wonderfully creative and inspiring work. I wasn't the only one who was changing – I was just the only one who'd run away to do it.

North Carolina was a shot of much needed positive energy and enthusiasm. With the help of my old committee chair from grad school, I snuck into a sold-out conference at my old university. It was a multi-disciplinary affair, all centred on North Carolina foodways, which had been my world. There were so many wonderful and familiar faces there from my time as an academic, a cook and a farmer. There were mentors, friends, young folks I'd helped bring along in my wake. I could hardly walk ten feet without being interrupted and hugged (the best kind of interruption, of course). It felt like home.

My old professors introduced me to students as a wonder, not someone who limped over the finish line and then jumped disciplinary ship. The students looked at me with according awe. Those introductions were such a validation for me . . . an absolution of sorts, too. No one ever gave me any shit about walking away after my MA, but I suppose I felt a bit guilty deep down. To know these brilliant professors were proud meant the world.

It was interesting to be back in my old academic territory and among my old grad-school colleagues as a successful waller – one now considered so successful by outsiders that she is asked to instruct. Our paths were in some ways so divergent by then. We had all been scholars, and now most of us were working in creative pursuits of some sort. I still had friends from the food business, too. In some ways I felt a bit of a traitor – like I had abandoned much of what we shared (food, wine, scholarship) – but actually I had taken those things and run with them. They were about beauty and tradition and meaning, and those were still the things that drove me as I travelled with my hammers.

Importantly, though Jack was still a huge part of my world, I wasn't just chasing love any more, but my craft and excellence in it, as well as a deep cultural richness and people who wanted to share in that. I had been looking for – and now was living – a hands-on, curious, creative life. It made perfect sense to these people. Interdisciplinary scholars of the humanities whose research was intimately tied to people's stories and creativity; journalists; chefs; writers; wine-importers; poets; organisers; farmers . . . All deeply curious, experience-driven people themselves.

My friends couldn't figure out what on earth I was doing for a few years, but that was because I couldn't . . . And now that I was firm about who I was and what I wanted, they were right there with me. I didn't need their validation, but I certainly welcomed it when they offered it. It made me feel less lonely to return and see that we were all carving our own paths.

270

Blaen Cammarch

In June, Wales was full of tall, creamy cow parsley in blossom on the verges, and hedgerows so gloriously deep and overgrown that they sometimes slapped your wing mirrors as you drove along the crooked single-track lanes. Lush and fragrant, the whole of Powys felt like my personal secret garden.

I'd put Jack on a plane home from America on the sixth, and I followed five days later. My relief came like clockwork. Lingering over tea for ages in my dressing gown in the mornings, driving the lanes, wandering in my wellies . . . It was always a multi-day exhalation . . . a moment to be still, to watch and listen and smell . . . to get rained on . . . to feel the sun's gentler warmth soak down into my bones.

I had truly settled into a full, international life. I flew back and forth at least once a year, always knowing that I would be back before too long, and I had grown comfortable with one foot firmly planted on each side of the Atlantic. In Britain,

I had gorgeous friends, satisfying work if I wanted it, rest when I didn't, enough money to rent a car or a hotel room when I felt like it, and confidence on the left-hand side of the road . . . I had become, I guess, culturally ambidextrous.

I survived the race through my spring projects in the US – in part because I'd flown out the cavalry when I got short on time – and now, back in the eastern half of my life, I put my stress out to pasture for a minute. I had an enormous amount of work waiting when I got home again in July, but it's remarkably easy to forget the outside world when summer is in full swing in the beautiful, bewitching lands along the banks of the River Wye. This would be a short trip – only three weeks – but it gave me a moment to catch my breath. I had no plan except to love the sun, the hills and my friends.

Wales had never felt anything to me but absolutely extraordinary, yet high summer in the hills was a time of magic and revelry and love . . . a time apart. Every second of life felt a little more breathtaking and wondrous in the light of June. Time seemed to slow down. Moments stretched on, dreamy and generous as the twilight. The world was suddenly awash with powerful sensory cues, reminders of a time just out of reach. All around me now were the same old birds, plants, smells, sounds, light and particular laughs and smiles that had been with me through the indelible summer before . . . All winter I had thought of it with reflection and longing. I began to wonder with a mix of worry and gratitude whether I would be chasing that halcyon summer for the rest of my life, and whether it had become something bigger than it really was. I was, I knew, cripplingly nostalgic at times.

One night Jack and I walked down the track through the lower fields as the bright sky finally began to soften. I loved these hills any time of day or year, but June was almost unspeakably magnificent, and to be out in the twilight was to have them exclusively to one's self.

I had put the question of marriage out of my mind the year before, and though I felt no more settled about where we were going, we just carried on. I simply enjoyed his company in the time that I had it. Quiet moments like these evening walks were precious. We avoided the big topics, stuck to the familiar and the immediate: the state of the land around us, the growing pestilence of pheasants lurking in the hedges, the state of restoration of some old piece of farm kit, some interesting ripple on the hillside above, illuminated in a way we'd never noticed before.

The weeks we'd spent in Virginia in May had been close, with lots of long, slow dinners out under the trees and plenty of wine in the moonlight, but I couldn't help noticing we weren't as at ease with each other now as we had been on the other side of the ocean. It unsettled me, but I tried not to let myself make too much of it. Something wasn't right, but it never did me any good to dig where he was concerned. If Jack did not want to talk, he wouldn't, and pushing only brought anger and a widening of the gap.

The little things buoyed us. Both careful observers, we tried always to find the humour and beauty in the details of the world around us. In all my years in Wales, the only wild hedgehogs I'd ever seen were the ones that lay dead on the road. (Once, I petted one called Harry that a rescue group brought to Beulah Show, but I don't count him. He was delightful, but hardly in his native habitat while hostage in a pop-up tent and wrapped in a blanket.) Jack was determined that he had them in his garden – there was cat food about, after all – and that I would see one this summer.

I was dead asleep, and he woke me. He had never done this in all the years I had known him. I assumed something was dreadfully wrong. My heart pounded, and he'd dragged me from one of those parts of the sleep cycle that is so deep one wakes completely confused if disturbed. 'There's a hedgehog outside!' he whispered.

'What?' I ask with bemused annoyance.

'Get up! There's a hedgehog in the garden. I can hear it. Hurry!'

I finally figure out what's going on, drag myself out of bed, go downstairs with Jack following, and make my way to the front door with its big window that looks out over the front garden. Jack flipped on the outside light like a spotlight during a prison break, determined to catch what he was after.

There was nothing there.

'Sorry . . . I was sure I heard one.'

'It's fine.'

We shuffle off to bed. Just as I get back to sleep, he nudges me again.

'It's back! I'm *sure* it's a hedgehog. Get up!'

Same routine. Downstairs, flip on the light, and it's the cats. At their own bowls.

'What the fuck? Seriously?' I ask.

'Oh, *sorry*, love.' He put his hand on my back. He really was. 'I was *sure* it was a hedgehog. They *are* about. I know how much you want to see one.'

Finally, we sleep.

He has never lived it down.

Cwm Elan – Elan Valley

Rose texted me one morning that July to announce at the last minute she was coming to Wales. Could I pick her up at the station? She was an elusive creature for most of the year, so it was very special when she surfaced, especially if we happened to be on the same side of the ocean when she did. I set off in Jack's Land Rover that afternoon in a flurry of excitement.

Elusive or not, Rose had become one of my closest friends, and by then there wasn't a thing in the world I wouldn't have done for her. She had come to me as if by magic that April weekend two years before, and since then, she'd brought me a solidarity and sense of belonging I had neither experienced nor expected. She'd brought light and hope, too, in the black days of winter when I was slipping away. In every way, she made the world a much happier place to be.

My heart swelled as I saw her step off the train, effortlessly glamorous as ever, at the far end of the platform. She was in a sleek straw fedora (what we affectionately called her 'town hat'), a white linen top, a rosy, embroidered skirt that hit just below her knee, and matching leather sandals that wrapped delicately up her ankles like an espadrille. If it weren't for the lush green hills and mobile phones around us, it could have been the 1950s in the South of France. She was always like something out of a film . . . sort of on a separate plane from everything and everyone around her because she always looked so perfect and romantic in any scene, and she moved with a timelessness and grace that no one else seemed to have. She could be breathtaking, and she didn't have a clue.

We hugged long and hard before walking down the platform, arms around each other's waist and both laughing about 'how London' she looked.

We'd been texting about a picnic. I asked her if she'd like to go to the Elan Valley. I had the perfect swimming spot there. We'd been swimming together in wild and wild-enough places many times by now – it was our ritual – but never here. She didn't know quite where I was taking her, but Rose had an unmatched spirit of adventure, and I knew she'd be game.

I was keen to see my sheepfold again, too – to show it off, really. Friends almost never get to see my work. It is like a state visit when I can drag one of them into a field punctuated everywhere with sheep shit. And this was one of those spots so pristine and wonderful that I really needed someone else in my life to understand how lucky I had been to toil in such a scene for a time.

We stopped in a nearby town on an enthusiastic search for picnic provisions, and by the time we finally got to Pen-y-Garreg, a thin layer of clouds hid the sun. We parked the Land Rover in the wide spot at the bend before the bridge and set out for the stile at the edge of the woodland. We pushed our way through chest-high bracken, descending into a secret world as we hastened down to the water's edge.

I undress quickly and splash right in, as is my habit. She hesitates, looking exquisitely beautiful on the shore as she reconsiders her resolve, as is hers. I tease her from the cold, crystalline water. She hems and haws dramatically for what feels like ages, watching me as she paces back and forth over the grey, stony beach. Slightly breathless, I tell her it's not so bad . . . it's not as cold as the last place we swam. I shame her for being a poor excuse of an Englishwoman, weak of nerve and unjustifiably wary of this bracing water.

'You were born for this!' I called. 'Don't be a pussy!'

I couldn't believe I'd said that word to her. I didn't mean to.

'*Don't* call me a pussy,' she chides . . . only it's more like a coo. Her vowels were always so velvety. Eventually, with an eyebrow raised and a playful grin widening across her face, she admits she'd be much braver if she were alone – this production of fear and trembling is mostly for my benefit.

The sight of her there on the shore will never leave me . . . her hair wild and beautiful, her face soft and carefree. She always watches me with such warmth in her eyes before she wades in, and always with her arms hugged tightly to her ribs to swaddle herself from the cold for as long as she can. It is the most remarkably intimate thing.

Finally, I persuade her in. She shrieks on first splash and tells me I've *lied* to her – it is most certainly *not OK*! It sounds, for a moment, as if she is being murdered . . . expletives, gasps, splashing, nonsense noises. But I know her, and I know it *is* OK. I laugh as I watch her settle in, and soon we shiver and shout and swim together, just like always. Within a couple of minutes, she is yelling her thanks to God for how beautiful this is, how much she loves this lake. Her voice rings out over the water like a song. Anyone within two miles would have heard her, and I felt sure that God had heard her, too.

A lake is where my friend looks happiest, and I was lucky to have her with me that day. Rose had given me so much in the time we'd known each other – far more than she would ever understand – and this brief respite was an offering of love and gratitude that I had never managed to articulate. Her swim began with trepidation and expletives, but she soon relaxed into a moment of perfect, unguarded joy that was deeply moving to behold. She was living in that moment all that Wales is to me – all of its transformative, healing power – and she beamed so innocently as she glided through the water, talking to God.

Not much else matters when you are afloat in a beautiful lake. It is a reminder of just how perfect life can be, but also how tiny and ephemeral we and all our worries really are. The shock of the cold will do that to you. The immediacy brought about by that sensation strips you to the barest essentials of your existence: breath, movement, sight, sound. It clarifies. It distils. Time almost ceases to exist. Wild swimming is, for me, one of life's most sublime and restorative sacraments. It is an incredible privilege to share that with someone you love – that conscious, elemental communion, however fleeting, with all of creation.

Swimming with Rose was like holding a tiny, sleeping baby, or perhaps relaxing by the fire late at night in the arms of someone you love ... total togetherness, marked by a heartbeat of almost unbearable tenderness and beauty. This was a sacred space for me, a feeling of home, a place to return to ... same as Wales, really. And though these moments found me over and over again, they never lost their magic. They left me feeling every time as if my chest might explode with love.

Moved though I was, I kept it to myself. I usually do. Our laughs and jokes rippled back and forth across the surface, one swimmer to another, though my eyes might have brimmed over had I let them.

She swam for the shore before I did, greeting me with a towel in her outstretched hand by the time I walked out of the water. Side by side, we dried and dressed, still sighing from the exertion and exhilaration of the cold. The magic was subsiding already.

We climbed back up through the bracken to the real world and poked around my sheepfold for a minute, but we were too chilled to linger in the breeze. We would go to a tea room just below the dam, skipping our picnic after all. We drank local wild-foraged teas made with things like red clover and raspberry leaf. We devoured scones with clotted cream and butter and fresh strawberry jam that passed muster even for the annoyingly discerning ex-chef and ex-farmer in me. Hands around our steaming cups of tea, we still shivered a bit under our wet hair, but we were glad of our swim, we agreed. We talk about property, love and what's for supper – the usual for us. Her eyes sparkled still.

Wye Valley

One night late, just before I went home, Kate and I made our way out to the front bench after dinner, whisky in hand. We lit the candles and the citronella, and rolled a couple of cigarettes we didn't really intend to inhale. They were supposed to be midge repellent as much as anything, but I found cigarettes powerfully atmospheric on balmy nights such as these ... a ritual slowing, savouring, sharing. I never smoked thoughtlessly or in places that weren't beautiful, and there was something quietly but undeniably spectacular about the blue smoke swirling slowly around us, drifting up towards a big, friendly summer sky only just beginning to darken.

Kate is *heaven* in these moments – completely present and attentive, and always full of wonder. She was beautiful when she smoked, and she sat beside me looking elegant and content. I tried to memorise it all without her noticing.

As we waited expectantly for the full July moon to show herself over the lawn, we talked about love and sailing ... the way the sea forces you to cede control, or at least the guise thereof ... We cannot control the tides, the winds, the weather, nor time. In some ways that was a relief – permission to simply relax into what is rather than what might be. She told me stories from the time just after university when she sailed across the Atlantic in a 22-foot sloop – the swells, the doldrums – swimming at the end of a rope that kept her attached safely to the boat and having the sudden realisation that the ocean was so vast it could simply swallow her and her tiny little boat without even noticing or meaning to ... She marvelled over how small you felt, how lucky. Every day you realised this, she said, and every day you wake up at sea you do so with tremendous gratitude. She told me this last part as if I would one day know it for myself.

Kate was a funny one, I had learned: you couldn't always get a story out of her when you wanted one, but sometimes she opened up on her own in the loveliest and most surprising ways. You never knew, for instance, what she might decide to tell you out of the blue over a pot of boiling potatoes or a basket full of beans. A few weeks earlier, I prodded her girlishly for stories about her old boyfriends, and though she was laughing at herself even as it happened, she closed up like a bank holiday. 'You'll have to get me much more drunk before I'll tell you any of that!' You couldn't interrogate Kate. You just had to let her unfold in her own time and her own way.

There was something incredibly refreshing about this – a stronghold of old-style British dignity and reserve – in a world where oversharing and high drama is now the norm. I had grown up in a world of direct questions and open curiosity. I sometimes blundered innocently enough into the boundaries of my friends' personal histories, and questions were politely batted away, topics shifted with grace. Once, as I wondered aloud over these differences, Kate laughed to me, 'Whit, you have to remember, we were brought up to speak in the third person!' Some of it, she explained, was just generational. Facebook was introduced when I was at university, and we all know what happened to the world after that.

I told Kate as we sat out that night that I felt I was on the edge of something big. I felt powerful, as if the world had something important waiting for me soon, like there might be some sort of sea change. She always loved it when I got like this – hopeful, a bit mystical. 'You're just coming into your power, Whit. You're not even in your prime yet,' she said, turning to look at me. There was something in her eyes then . . . some foretelling of wonder.

'Although I suppose whatever age one is, one feels one is in one's prime . . . except at seventy-two,' she conceded. 'There are some nice things about it, but you know you're crap at other things.'

The first star appeared about 10 p.m., and the moon was on the rise.

There was scaffolding across the front of the house while its roof was being repaired. Kate wondered aloud whether we should go up to look at the view out over the moonlit valley. It was a tantalising thought . . . but as much as I adored this woman's eternal spirit of adventure, I knew this was not necessarily the best idea for a seventy-two-year-old a couple of whiskies deep with a slightly disobedient right arm (there'd been a bad break a few years back). To my relief, she soon changed course: 'Do you know, Whit, I don't feel *quite* strong enough tonight. Maybe another time.' The *potential* mischief was enough to make us both laugh.

As darkness finally arrived, a chill came over us, and we retreated into the warmth of the kitchen. As she laid the table for breakfast and I made us peppermint tea to take to bed, she said suddenly, 'Never underestimate love at first sight.' I looked up to see her smiling at me knowingly.

'That sounds like the voice of experience,' I said.

'It is.' I knew not to ask, so I simply smiled back, delighted as ever by the mystery of her.

I hugged Kate downstairs and up that night. She and Richard would leave early the next day for an event over in England, so we would say goodbye just in case I wasn't awake in time in the morning. It was the last time I would see her that summer, and I dreaded these moments. I'm bad at goodbyes ... messy, earnest, too talkative. Kate, thank God, is much more elegant and composed every time. She gets me through them.

She wakes me early anyway, peeping in with more peppermint tea. She sits on the bed with me for a very long hug. It is a moment of sleepy sweetness. As she gets up to make her way to the door, she turns back for a moment. 'We'll keep . . .' (Types fingers as if on a keyboard.)

'Of course.'

Shouting down the hall, she nudged lovingly, 'There's plenty of hot water for a nice bath!'

'OK.'

And she was gone. I hoped to see her in the autumn, but I couldn't be sure.

I stayed on at the house a while that morning alone. I turned on Radio 3, made myself the same fried eggs and toast that she would have, and then took her perch in the kitchen, back to the Rayburn, to write a while in my journal before I went back to Jack. I clung to as much routine as I could. I always do in leaving moments, and there was so much from the night before that I wanted to remember – big life stuff as well as lovely atmospheric details. I knew that bit about the scaffolding would make me laugh down the road.

As I sat writing that morning, I pondered what it meant to long for a place while you are in it – to constantly feel as though it's slipping through your fingers. The Welsh had special words for longing, so ingrained in their culture was it. *Hiraeth* doesn't have a single-word translation in English. It is a deep, nostalgic ache – a sort of homesickness. I once saw it described as 'a longing to be where your spirit lives'. It might be a longing for the way things used to be, or even a place that was only ever imagined. It is, then, unanswerable – the sense of peace and relief unattainable. One could never get the thing one longs for.

These were tender days, filled with gratitude as much as longing, sadness and uncertainty. It was the same old uncertainty, and I'd been living with it for a long time now ... whether I would ever feel still and settled anywhere.

Benson

Jack and I made our way east towards Heathrow a little earlier than usual, deciding to camp along a riverside in Oxfordshire. As we pitched our tent – always a tense ten minutes no matter how well we know the drill – I thought about how independent we both were, how used to doing things ourselves. We each instinctively start on our own poles, setting out to accomplish tasks independently when actually the objective requires us to cooperate and communicate. We need to work together and cede a little independence, or it's not going to end well. I wondered if we would have been the same in a marriage, struggling against each other all the time . . . especially if we lived together all year, every year. I knew that one of the reasons this relationship had worked for us was precisely that we weren't together all the time. There were big breaks, and even in the long stretches we could console ourselves if we were annoyed with one another that it wasn't forever – that we ought to enjoy it because we'd be missing the other before we knew it.

Jack had always said to me that he wished he could have had a marriage like Johnny and Jenny's, so close and inter-dependent and long, but he knows he's just not wired for it. We could not have been more intimate, but I wondered the same about myself. Was I a day-in, day-out, long-haul kind of woman?

We had a long, wine-soaked dinner by the river that night at the marina café. Lulled by the booze and the beauty of the Thames on a perfect summer's eve, Jack suddenly confessed how sad he was that I was leaving, how he couldn't under-stand why I wanted to be stuck with him when I had so many adventures before me and should really go and find myself a younger man. 'I'm old,' he said. 'I'm miserable. I'm not going to go off on a crazy boat trip with you. This is ridiculous. What is it *about*? Why do you bother?'

I could see he was genuinely puzzled, and this was a rare moment of straightforward sincerity. He did not open in this way often.

'You have to understand,' he said, 'that I'm walking a plank blindfolded. I know I will fall off eventually and lose you, but I don't know when it will be, and you have to forgive me if I find it all a bit terrifying. I know you love me, but it's obvious to me that the people and things that bring you pleas-ure are increasingly elsewhere . . . and that's OK, but I know this has an end. You're going to go one day, and that's it.'

It was interesting: I hadn't said so to him, but while I had been away in Italy the week before I felt – just as I had the previous year on a quick holiday with Rose – completely absorbed in where I was, that I'd rather be in Italy than anywhere else on earth in that moment. Italy had, in some ways, stolen me away from Wales. Wales had become more complicated – a place where real life had taken root – and Italy was a place still filled with wonder and hope rather than expectation. There, I missed nothing and no one, and in fact it simply felt like the rest of the world didn't exist. And somehow he knew that. We had always been able to feel one another across the ocean – you may read that with scepticism, but it's absolutely true – so what was a Channel and a few Schengen borders? He knew. Of course he knew.

He'd only been distancing himself in anticipation of what he felt was his inevitable hurt. It was the same reasoning that prevented him from marrying me the year before.

I explained to him that I knew the same – that we had an end – and all that he'd just told me were the same reasons I felt more and more that I was a burden to him. But also that no one on earth made me laugh like he did, and that it was incredibly wonderful to have such a low-maintenance, highly attuned lover (I finally felt glamorous enough to use the word) to come home to when I wasn't off adventuring . . . that I felt very lucky. I also made sure to tell him he wasn't holding me back from anything, that I wasn't looking for another serious relationship because my life increasingly pointed to exciting work and lots of adventuring – lots of being on the move, and for that reason I wasn't eager to be tied down right now.

He said he wanted to be sure I knew it was coming – that I was aware and, if possible, prepared.

As if any of us can be, I thought.

He talked about ageing, growing physically weaker . . . that *he* didn't mind so much for himself, but worried I'd be silently thinking, 'Oh, my God! I've got to get away from this old man! Help!' He hated that thought, he said. 'I'm not as strong as I was . . . I've got some of the old man mannerisms now, I've noticed.'

I knew that in some ways he was a very different man from the one I'd met six years before, but I wasn't horrified like he thought I was . . . and it's not like I was suddenly surprised by his ageing. How many years had I spent thinking about it as I worried over marriage?

We'd both been thinking about essentially the same things, only from different sides: age and the complexity it brings. We faced it differently now that we were past the marriage question.

'I don't feel there is some big decision to be made about what happens now,' I said. 'We are fine as we are, and yes, things are changing, but at least we have said it aloud now. The future *is* uncertain, as it is with all people and all things, but at least we're facing it with an awful lot of love between us.'

I felt confident about what I was saying, but I'm not sure which of us I was trying most to convince that we would be OK.

I felt shaky packing up camp the next morning. The day had arrived. I hated this day. Every. Fucking. Time.

Dugspur, Virginia

I landed gently back in America after an idyllic few weeks in Wales and Italy, returning to the mountains of Virginia to stay with friends, write, and reacclimatise myself to the pace of my American life. I felt in that moment as good as I could remember feeling about myself and my life – like I had finally reached a place I'd been working towards for years ... Like this was a reward for struggling through the hard parts and surviving.

It took about five minutes for stress to swallow me up again.

Before I knew it, I was scrambling all over the place to try to wrap my exhausting non-profit project in North Carolina that, while beautiful, had dragged on since spring, and I was also facing the design and construction of a highly technical, highly priced smoker for loyal clients who had been waiting patiently as my schedule evolved in its usual bizarre way ... and all in the miserable heat of August. I was building better than ever, but I was under a lot of pressure. And surprise! I had a return flight to Wales booked, too. I had one eye always on the calendar and one on the weather forecast.

Down in North Carolina, it was unbearably hot. Within an hour of starting work each morning, I was soaked through my heavy dungarees and every other stitch of clothing I had on, as if I'd jumped into a pool. The humidity was *suffocating*. I soon fell ill with some sort of bizarre summer cold, further sapping my energy and my strength with fever and congestion. Dripping with sweat, I was drinking at least a litre of water per hour. I was utterly exhausted and on the verge of overheating, but I had to work through it. There was no time to be ill, no time to be off for any reason at all. I had to get back to Virginia to finish my smoker, and then I had to get on a plane.

I managed somehow to build beautiful garden stairs, finish the long, tiered retaining walls, and even construct a clever, snaking bench into one section despite the heat and my cold. Triumphant but utterly exhausted, I raced up the road to Virginia. Mercifully, it was a touch cooler there, but the work that awaited was far more complicated. This project had a lot more tentacles than just stone, but I had teamed up months before with a blacksmith down in South Carolina who had been smoking meats in steel smokers most of his adult life. Jeff and I solved a lot of the gnarliest problems together, often aided by a combination of cold beer and sheer redneck ingenuity, and he always managed to make me laugh. Mostly, though, I was tense and tired.

When I was working in America, I always kept Jack updated with photos from my job sites. He enjoyed watching my progress, especially if I was building something unusual. This smoker collaboration was definitely that. It was a demanding project, but it was beginning to shape up nicely.

One morning, while Jack and I were on the phone as I drove to work, he decided to announce to me that what I was building was going to fall down – that my walls were too thin – and he wanted to know what I was going to do to fix it. I felt like I'd had my legs cut out from under me, and it was only 9 a.m.

Calmly, I told him that I agreed – that I might do it differently and make the walls thicker if I ever did it again, but I had to go with what I originally designed this time. The project was too far along. I was *way* above foundation height, and that determined how thick the walls could be.

'You've been seeing photos all along,' I said. 'If you were concerned about this, why didn't you say so *weeks* ago? There's nothing I can do about it now, and this is not helpful.'

He was insistent. 'There's no way that can work. They're going to fall over. What is holding them up if not their own weight?'

'I understand what you're saying, but I'm the one here on the ground, and I'm telling you it's going to be fine.' My observational powers told me that it would be. I was there and could yank on things, test their strength. He had seen an iPhone photo – that was it. I was starting to feel really offended that he had so little faith in my abilities and my judgement after all this time. I explained as calmly as I could a bit more about the structure and various design elements. He wasn't taking me seriously or even listening. He didn't like that I didn't want to take his word as law, and he growled at me as he never had done in all the years I had known him: 'Well, of *course* you know best! I don't wish to discuss it further!'

Then, he hung up on me.

If this scene had been a cartoon, there would have been steam coming out of my ears and my nostrils. I was *fuming*. I threw a hammer. I might have thrown a second hammer. I don't remember. I have a lot of hammers. And then I sat down on the tailgate of my truck and I wept. Thank *God* my clients were out of town and not there to witness the mess.

This was all deeply unsettling. It wasn't like him to lash out, to hang up. I was livid, yes, but I started to worry. Had the old bastard had a stroke? Was there something going on that he wasn't telling me about? Was he ill and stressed and didn't want to break the news to me until we were face to face? Stress always made him distant. I was unspeakably annoyed to be an ocean away. I just wanted to turn up on his doorstep – our doorstep – and sort it out by the fire over a drink. Nothing ever got fixed in an email.

Later, I sent him an angry email. He didn't respond for a week, but when the message came, it said I should probably find somewhere else to stay on my upcoming trip.

What?

I lay in the bath, stunned. My nerves were raw. I was exhausted. I had been under tremendous pressure with two different projects and yet another looming flight, and always going to and from Jack. And now Jack was being an asshole.

Rose rang up from New York, knowing I was in an ugly moment. I put her on speakerphone, terrified to drop her in the bath. I'd already sent her a ranting, outraged email. My rage now spent, I brought her up to speed about how pitifully weary I was, how full of tears.

'Darling,' she said gently, 'I don't know *anyone* who asks as much of themselves as you do. I'm not surprised that you're exhausted. And you don't have to keep doing this if you don't want to . . .'

This had never occurred to me.

'What do *you* want to happen?' she asked.

I told her I wanted to cancel my trip, but my friend Ashley

294

was flying over to film Jack and me at work on the hill. Ash already had her ticket and was so excited about the project. I had been, too, but now I just couldn't stop crying. I was too tired, too muddled, had too much work to do.

I told her that maybe I just needed this all to be over, but that I knew I was so tired I wasn't thinking clearly. I had been with this weathered and wonderful and poetic man for years – one who really knew and accepted me even in my ugliest moments, who worshipped the ground I walked on, who was always the first to call me on my bullshit and get me to laugh at myself – but also I was coming to realise that I wanted to marry, and I wanted children – or at least the opportunity for them. I knew that suddenly now after a long time of *not* knowing it. And we just didn't seem to be getting along like we used to. Things were changing. He wanted to read and nap, potter with his antiques. I wanted to sail and go to dinner parties and drink in the world. I wanted him with me for all those things, but it wasn't what he wanted for himself.

She promised me with tenderness in her voice that it would be OK – that I would be OK . . . that I needed to figure out what was best for *me*, and that maybe it was time to make a change. This was a moment to step back and re-evaluate.

'Try to get some rest . . . Darling, I *insist* that you take a few days off! Can you? Just get through this project, and then see how you feel when you get there,' she said.

I gave myself a couple of days off. It may have helped my body, but my mind kept spinning. I spent yet more time crying endlessly in bed, almost paralysed by fear and sadness. I felt it *bodily*. I wondered with a lump in my throat if this was it with Jack. With all that had changed, I still couldn't imagine my life without him, and I was terrified I would lose the whole of Wales if I let go . . .

The smoker was a triumph, but I was wreck.

Wye Valley

When I arrived in Wales, Kate picked me up from the train and took me in for bit. She kept me fed, left me to sleep as late as I could, and kept telling me how beautiful I looked (despite the fact that I had bags under my eyes the size of Texas). I did yoga, sunbathed, pruned trees and built a wall for her, trying to keep busy and calm, and she gently reassured me that it would all be OK in the end, come what may. We sat up late a few nights drinking whisky, and she let me talk it out while she sewed by the fire. I had cried so much in Virginia that I didn't have any tears left. I just rambled at her in a daze about what on earth I was doing with my life. I must have seemed half mad by then.

Jack couldn't bear to see me, which left me drifting between the houses of my friends for weeks. Embarrassingly, it continued even once my friend Ashley arrived from America to begin filming. I felt terrible that she had come all this way and now couldn't get the footage she intended of the two of us working together on the hill, but he did at least take her out with him to show her his old walls here and there and do a bit of building on camera. He and I didn't speak properly for weeks, and he began to do dramatic things like send every letter I'd ever written him back to me, though maddeningly, he would not cough up my wellies – the one thing I actually needed.

It felt like things were really and truly over, and I began to accept that I would never see him or the house ever again. The longer it went on, the easier it became to stomach that thought, though I still didn't get a decent night's sleep.

Life sometimes turns on a dime.

Late one night, I got an email from him asking me to come back and spend my last week with him. This was all too hard, he said. I told him I wasn't sure that I could, and I cried myself to a pitiful hour or two of sleep. In the end, I agreed to meet, but I was undecided about coming to the house. I had made my mental goodbyes already. I didn't know if I could bear to open the door again.

When we finally did see each other we decided to meet for a day in Hay-on-Wye, one of our favourites: antiques, books, coffee at the Old Electric Shop, lunch at the Granary . . . We had an amazing, normal, happy day, and I could not have been more relieved. My weariness by that time felt so heavy I couldn't imagine how I would ever manage to be the same woman I had been, ever sleep enough to recover and get on with life . . . but suddenly, back together, everything began to feel OK again.

On the way home, we stopped on a mountain road and pulled over to have tea and coffee from his flask, just like always. The views were incredible, and the sun was shining so brightly. I felt at ease for the first time since we'd fought on the phone the month before. We were on a beautiful hilltop, alone together in the wind, and *everything was OK*.

At Jack's behest, I went back to Blaen Cammarch for the last week of my trip. I slept like the dead that night. I was finally home.

But then sometimes there is *another* dime, and life turns sharply again. Just as things had begun to get back to normal, the rug was jerked out from under us. Jack was evicted from the house that had been our home.

The storm that had been brewing in the ether – connected, I'm sure, to the foreboding rumblings in our relationship – had at last broken open. It would prove destructive, cutting a path right through us.

I can't describe our shock.

Perhaps, Jack observed, it was just as well that we were going: what had once been a wonderful place to live now seemed to be on its way to ruin. But he felt terrible that I was losing my sanctuary, for he knew how much the place had meant to me. It had been sacred to us – the woods, the hills, the streams and rivers. Everything seemed to be under threat, and I'm not sure either of us could have borne it had we stayed. Jack had spent his life in conservation, and what was happening was hard to watch. Pheasants, pheasant pens and gamekeepers were everywhere, a veritable plague upon the land. Excavators had been tearing their way through unspoiled ground, imperiling SSSI woodlands. Huge piles of trash accumulated here and there around the estate. New roads were sliced through ancient fields. The land wasn't ours, but we knew it intimately, and to see it change so drastically was heartbreaking.

Blaen Cammarch itself wasn't an especially nice place, but it had a certain beauty about it, and it was private, and it was ours. We didn't realise until Jack moved out just how mouldy it was, for instance. With the carpets pulled up and the walls bare it looked pretty dilapidated, but it had been paradise for me. Luckily, I didn't have to see that part. I was already home in America, and though I wish I could have been more help to him during that stressful time, I was glad not to have the memory of the place spoiled.

It was never particularly comfortable as a house, yet I had never felt more comfortable anywhere in all my life. There was no central heating – only a wood stove, the occasional space heater if we felt like splurging on electricity, and an oil-burning Rayburn in the kitchen that was often too expensive to run. Draughts blew around the doors in their frames. Many of the windows were old and leaky, with the plaster rotting away beneath. In the cold months, condensation built up on the inside of the panes as we slept, and if it got cold enough in the night it turned to indoor frost. (This was not as uncommon as you might like to imagine.) Once, we left the milk out on the counter overnight and found it frozen by morning. Jack kept the house a bit warmer if I were there in the winter, but often when we spoke on the phone he'd be wrapped in a sleeping bag and hat by the wood stove in the middle of the day.

The floors creaked, and the plaster was split in places in the old vaulted ceilings upstairs. I memorised all the cracks and beautiful contours of those ceilings as I lay in bed, staring up in the morning light as Jack still slept. Some of the doorways were at a height high enough for me to get through barefoot and fully upright, but low enough that the occasional combi-nation of boots and forgetfulness meant I whacked the top of my skull as I tried to pass through. It was muddy as hell outside almost all the time, and the track to get to the house would assault the vehicle of any over-eager driver who approached, not knowing the worst potholes and ruts by heart like we did.

But the spring water was gorgeous, and the wood stove was warm, and the privacy and the stars unrivalled in my experience. I'll be dreaming of the roses over the front door for the rest of my life. That house, tatty as it was in parts, was heaven to me. I had never thought of its flaws as flaws – just character.

Not long before I would leave for America, knowing the end was near in a more final way this time, I set out in my favourite wellies up the big hill behind the house. It is the one I walked up my first-ever day in Wales, and a place to which I have returned with reverence many times since. I deliberately left my camera behind this time. The pace of a walk is different without the agenda of a camera. You pause for different reasons when the pause is to look rather than capture. Your gaze is more deliberate. You memorise rather than relying on the mechanical lens.

I stood on the trig point at the top for a long while, remembering all the times I'd done it before, taking time to revolve and look out in each of the four cardinal directions. I lingered. I wanted to remember it forever. The light was sharp and golden as it is come autumn. I literally said thank you each way I looked. I blew kisses. I closed my eyes, almost prayerfully. It was a lamentation, but a moment of celebration and thanksgiving, too. That hill had given me an awful lot over the years. I could come back, but never setting out from Jack's house as I had always done before.

This was it: a point of no return. The spell was broken.

Somewhere over the North Atlantic

Ididn't know what would come in the next year. We'd lost the house and been through a series of huge emotional upheavals, and I just felt *exhausted*. Jack and I were sturdy people who built sturdy things, and our whole world felt so fragile now. I mulled it over on the plane. I watched the Elan Valley pass below us, then Ireland, then the ocean. I wrote for a while, then stared out across the glistening water with dramatic music in my ears. (Probably Tallis.) I had a good seven hours to think with no technological disruptions, something I had come to appreciate as I came and went over the Atlantic in those years.

I knew that a turning point had crept up on Jack and me . . . so much had shifted in the last year. He was ready to retire and at the age when technically he could. I was stronger and more confident than ever, ready to pick up the hammers when he decided to put them down. It was that year that I first undertook some of Jack's jobs for him while he wasn't quite well enough to work. (Was it a healing incision from skin cancer removal? His knee? I can't remember now.) I worked alone for his customers, which felt strange. I work alone most of the time in America, but I had never before worked alone on what would have been his job. I mended a gap that had developed in a wall across boggy ground that he'd restored some twenty-plus years ago. He sat on the hill behind me, watching from a distance. (Eventually, he couldn't resist, and he got up to fetch me hearting to build with.)

As I stripped out the collapsed piece of wall, I found something that caught me off guard: his glove. A relic. The leather had dried and hardened over the years it lay hidden in that wall. Jack often leaves old, worn-out gloves in the wall he's working on. I never thought I'd be the one to find one, nor did he. We always expect when we leave things behind that it will be someone in a distant generation uncovering them later – as distant as we are from the seventeenth- and eighteenth-century men who smoked clay pipes and left the broken ones in the walls we repair today. I was hit with the sudden realisation that Jack and I were in a torch-passing sort of moment, and though I observed it with delight and laughter, calling him over to see, it hit me in my core.

These walls were his legacy, and I was reminded how uncertain my future is with this work – even as his customers panic over his upcoming retirement. I wondered, same as those farmers, who will tend these walls when we are both gone. I felt twinges of deep sadness, but kept working – kept putting stone on stone. It's what we do. No one is more sentimental than the two of us, but there's no time to wallow. We have to get on with it, and as Jack always says with a laugh, 'Each stone you put on the wall is one less you have to put on the wall!' (Bless him, he is rarely as serious as I am.)

I have always known that my working life in Wales had a time limit. I just didn't know quite what the expiration stamp was. It never mattered much in the beginning. As I've said, who on earth could have guessed this would turn into a career for me? I didn't think I'd still be coming back seven years later. I wandered on blindly, trying not to think too much about what might lie ahead, but I was beginning to hear the ocean roaring below the cliff. I became aware of each step I took.

When I did allow myself to think about it, I knew full well that I had access to these sublimely beautiful hillside restoration jobs only as long as Jack was working and in my life. But his retirement loomed large, and there were moments when it was clear that we were unravelling. Maybe we would hang on a while longer, and maybe Jack would take an occasional walling job if something especially appealing came along, but he'd said to me not long before that his body was showing its age – it was time to be done. He was tired now. First, it was one knee. Now, the other. His neck is stiff, and he's had enough rain in his face.

I knew that one day all I would have would be what remained in my mind's eye plus scant snippets in my journal if I happened to write after a particularly moving day, perhaps close to my departure for home when, like clockwork, I get wistful and words come as plentifully as Welsh raindrops. There would be a photo or two stolen along the way, hastily shot after tossing aside my leather gloves for just a moment because I'd been so struck by what I saw when I looked up from my work that I couldn't bear to let it slip away. Jack never looked more right than he did out on the hill, between stone and sky, quietly content in his work.

Time spent working on the hill – methodically, day after day, and in all weather – is a beauty few of you will ever see.

Even my photographs can't give you the evocative scent of grass and lanolin in your nostrils, the tireless song of the lark swirling high above, the plaintive bleat of separated lambs and ewes, the tractor pushing along just over the hill, or a car whooshing past on its way to one village or another. It is an incomplete picture without the smells and sounds that mark the atmosphere of Mid Wales, and to build in a spot is to know it intimately.

My jobs in America netted me far greater profits than anything I could do in Wales, yet it was still Wales I longed for most days. I have never managed to escape the romantic pull of the thousands of miles of dry-stone walls that criss-cross the Welsh countryside. I suspect I never will.

Washington, DC

By its end, 2015 had been nothing but a blur of stress with only a few bright moments here and there to break the darkness. I'd almost lost my mind, almost lost Jack ... and losing the house had been so disruptive that I had failed to plan my spring projects for 2016. It takes a lot of thought, logistics and extensive communication to wrangle even the most eager clients, and though I had a list of requests from various people, I hadn't had the bandwidth to push any of them to timely fruition that winter. I couldn't think of anything but our loss.

Luckily, an old friend asked me out of the blue to come to work in DC for him that spring. His timing could not have been better.

That friend was Tyler Nelson, the newly promoted Technical Director for the Smithsonian Folklife Festival. T's first festival, back when he was a low man on the tech totem pole, had been my last – the one where I met Jack back in 2009. Amazingly, thanks to Tyler, I now found myself back on the National Mall where Jack and I first came together all those years ago, only this time it was *I* who was building a dry-stone wall. Jack flew over to see it. This would bring us full circle, he observed. The whole experience was slightly mystical for me, as if it had been written all those years before. This wall felt predestined – a gift, a moment for reflection and gratitude, a healing of sorts.

When I had finished heaving up the last of my copes a few days prior, I swelled with a sense of triumph unlike any I'd ever experienced before. I couldn't remember being more exhausted in all my life – my body was like an overcooked noodle by then, and my heart full to the point of bursting – but I'd done it. I had worked six twelve-hour days on that wall in unyielding 90-degree heat and sun, essentially building it in double-time, in the midst of twenty-two consecutive days of work. That is the kind of gruelling schedule it requires to get the festival open on time each year, and it had left me absolutely physically and emotionally depleted. Still, I wouldn't have been anywhere else. The festival gets in your blood, exhausting though it is, and it calls us back to the Mall each year like a seasonal migration. This time I was able to give back to it from a gift it had given me seven years before.

I stepped back to see that my top line was consistent enough for me to declare the wall 'done'. What a *beautiful* thing it was – far more beautiful than I thought I'd be able to achieve given my exhaustion and the time constraints of our production schedule, which included a lot more than this wall. My wall would only be there temporarily, and it was such a small piece of what we were doing, really. All along I knew that I only had to build something passable and safe for the public to approach, maybe to lean on while they ate their gelato from the next-door stand, for the next few weeks. But I saw

306

immediately that afternoon that through my sheer stubbornness and unwavering obsession with beauty I had built something quite special, even with the odds against me. It would have fitted perfectly as a permanent structure in the lushest and most sublime of gardens. It was one of the best I'd ever built anywhere. It didn't matter, of course – it couldn't stay no matter how wonderful it was, and only I would have known the flaws anyway – but it meant something to *me* that it was so beautiful . . . So 'tidy', as the Welsh might say by way of classic, enormous understatement of admiration.

Overcome, I stopped in my tracks as construction zoomed on around me, and texted Jack with tears of joy and relief and exhaustion in my eyes to tell him that if ever I had loved him, it was that very moment. Of course I had loved him in a million places and as many moments, but he had given me this life, hard as it was, and I was simply overwhelmed with gratitude.

I also knew that only one other person on earth could relate to what I had just experienced: building a temporary dry-stone wall on the National Mall, coping with heat, humidity, dust and the pressure of time and curious tourists, knowing all the while that that wall would come down in three weeks' time. He had done it, too.

My message of love dispatched out into space, I turned to find a toehold on my wall and make my way to the top. One knee up, then another, then carefully to my feet, where I stood towering on my metre-high cope stones with the Capitol to my right, the Washington Monument to my left, and the National Gallery before me. I couldn't believe what I'd just done, so I simply did my usual: climbed up to the top of my creation and revelled in it. But I knew this was a big one – a significant moment, and one I should relish. I was too exhausted to process it, really, and though I didn't know it yet, I had pinched a nerve in my spine as I built that wall, one result of which was the discovery of some long-term, degenerative spinal problems that had been lying in wait for years. By the time Jack arrived in Washington a few days later, I'd be waking before dawn each day with numb hands and sleepy eyes full of tears, wondering whether I might be facing the end of my career when just seconds before I'd been at what felt an apex. It was a terrifying and magical time, and there was no one I wanted to see more. Only he understood what it all meant – what I had done, what I might lose.

Jack is still treated as a dignitary in Washington, beloved by all who were there at the 2009 festival, and before too long, by those who've just met him, because he is truly that special. He was welcomed with much excitement and fanfare. My parents, whose early reservations about him have transformed into gratitude for all that he has given me, were there to greet him warmly and make sure he thought I had built a decent wall. Interns looked at him with awe just like they had in 2009, but this time it was because he was mine – my mentor, my man, a mystery of sorts – and it was me they looked up to now.

I hadn't realised until then that in the intervening years, I'd stepped into Angharad's shoes – a tough, hardworking, yet still beguiling woman who leaves most men flabbergasted and most women inspired. In yet another poetic turn, I had done all the welding on this year's festival, too. I had accepted a four-month position on the festival's Technical Crew, working as a builder this time instead of my former administrative role. I built the wall, and I worked the metal, and lots of people had been watching me. Like Angharad, I had just been going about my job, but work and age and luck have changed me. I carry myself differently now. People always notice. A crowd of women cheered loudly as I pounded steel with a sledgehammer, each blow ringing out like a great bell, in front of the National Gallery one day (not knowing I was only doing so to correct something stupid I'd done a few minutes before). A troop of Girl Scouts smiled widely and talked to me as a female colleague and I worked in harnesses and hardhats as we operated heavy equipment to erect the largest structure on the festival site that year. Female interns hovered nearby, watching shyly. Every middle-aged woman who had ever been pissed off by men at work – especially in technical trades – seemed to want to give me a nod and a 'You go, girl!' that summer. I was so worried about my hands by then – they would determine my future – but I also felt more powerful, more grateful than I ever had in my life. These moments were the final stage of my feminist awakening: I was learning what I meant to other women.

From Jack's presence to feminism, it was a moment to savour, if a little bittersweet.

I still wondered at times whether I had failed at parts of life . . . still living with my parents, having no prospects of buying land or a house any time soon, being unmarried and childless and perhaps remaining that way because of my work and travel schedules . . . but this was a moment when it all made sense. Each of those 'failures' seems like a blessing depending on the day, and every time I work through another spell of shaken confidence I find something utterly magical waiting on the other side.

I got what I asked for, which is an amazing thing to be able to say. Doesn't mean I won't ask for something different in a year or even tomorrow, but it's incredibly reassuring to know that we can have what we want . . . It just doesn't always look like what you think it's going to, and you may not get it all at one time.

Down on the Mall, with the festival closed and Jack long gone back to Wales, a Bobcat dismantled with diesel what I had built with muscle and bone. It rammed and pulled until my wall was nothing more than a pile of rubble. By then I was miles away, driving a forklift in the festival warehouse because driving equipment is what broken construction workers do, so I didn't have to see it, thank God.

What a strange thing it was for a dry-stone waller to be asked to build something so ephemeral.

I tried to be Buddhist about the whole thing, letting it go peacefully, and appreciating what it was . . . also that people respected it, respected me. I felt slightly gratified, too, when I heard later that the men had been miserable heaving the stone into and out of the dump truck as they cleared the Mall of my ruins – that they'd said they weren't surprised I'd been injured! Moving several tons of stone by hand in a day is not for everyone.

I found a piece of that wall when I returned to the Mall about six months later. One little chip, just bigger than a quarter, lying on the ground by the park benches now back in place where my wall once stood. I picked it up, kissed it and put it in my pocket. Just another relic in my collection of moments passed.

Epilogue – Patrick County, Virginia

In the final month of my thirty-third year, I bought my first house. It felt like destiny.

It also felt like a miracle. (I had wondered where the miracles were in the year so many of my fellow Millennials refer to as the 'Jesus Year'. Mine had not yet come.) It's not as if I suddenly came into a hoard of money overnight. My parents announced without warning when I casually began to look at property that they would give me the downpayment, and I couldn't have done it without them.

But I chose well, too. It was a house built before the Great War by a family not long gone before my 2017 arrival. It clung to the side of a mountain high in the Blue Ridge, looking down over Rock Castle Gorge. It had pure, frigid spring water, and my floor joists were hand-hewn chestnut. The chimney leaned, and nothing in the entire house was square, but it was sturdy and had so far stood the test of time. It was full of mice, but also full of promise.

There was something about it, and I embraced the beauty of its imperfections.

That spring I watched the lilacs and trillium and columbine come, then the flame azaleas and mountain laurel, and a lone antique rose outside my white clapboard springhouse. It was pink with the intoxicating smell of only the oldest, sturdiest rambling roses – a real wild thing. The trees got their leaves back as I watched from my porch with tea in the mornings and wine at twilight. I was delighted by nightly displays of the most incomparable fireflies and stars I had ever seen, mesmerised by the sight of my washing billowing in the mountain breeze as it hung drying on the line in the sun. When I wasn't ripping out 1960s plywood panelling or repairing my haphazard water system, I spent hours on the back of a jet-black Tennessee Walker, riding across mountaintop meadows and lush river bottoms, gently trespassing in places no one goes. In so many ways, it was perfection, but it was not a time without tears.

I had cried my first night in the house because it all felt so wrong all of a sudden, though this was all I had wanted for months. I had cried in happiness and relief only a few weeks before when I found a passage, now more poignant than ever, in my old journals as I researched my own life in the process of writing this book. Three years before, on a sunny September hillside in the early morning light, while my beautiful friend still slept just inside, I wrote about a home I wanted, only it felt out of reach. I had been refining what I wanted over the course of the years ... Stars, privacy, quiet, fire, green, sunshine, peace, good food and the space to care for myself as well as return the warm hospitality I'd been shown in all the years I'd been a nomad. Church bells tolled down the valley, and a tractor began to make its way steadily about its work in a nearby field. We were in Italy then, and full of hope. It was a heavenly stretch of days, and I was deeply moved by everything I was experiencing. I thought back, too, to the farm in North Carolina, to all my years in Wales, to all the old houses I had come to adore, filled with the lovingly worn and storied possessions of lives so beautifully lived . . . These places had all given me a clue to what I needed.

So many people had given me refuge in their homes, but only one person ever pushed me to give *myself* a home. It was Rose, the friend I'd been with in Italy that day. She was the reason I finally stopped telling myself that I couldn't. I could, only I had never made it a priority.

It wasn't until I returned to DC two years after that journal entry for four more stressful months of festival work, full of traffic jams and back injuries and unfriendly concrete surroundings, that I realised the mountains of Virginia were the only place in America I felt any peace, any connection with the universe and its stars and our earthly seasons. On the drive from Washington home to South Carolina, when I was finally free to leave the city, I stopped for two nights with Jim and Silvie, my first Virginia clients, who had quickly become my friends. I slept like the dead on their mountaintop, with the windows flung wide open and quilts piled high even in July. I woke to birdsong. I'd watched the sunset alone on the porch and greeted the moon as it rose over the hills. Wales felt close.

I knew.

Virginia lowered my blood pressure. It inspired me. Importantly, my sense of beauty was constantly stimulated, and I had room to breathe. It was easy to find solitude and quiet. As a teenager or even a twentysomething I had not understood that I had this need, but by my thirties, I was *desperate* for beauty and simplicity and peace. These things are my daily balm . . . the only way I can really keep going as

313

an oversensitive soul in a rough, hyper-connected world and a woman in a grinding job. I was weary then – physically, emotionally, and spiritually – after so many years in motion with no base of my own. And my body was broken. My fingers still were not right from the summer's injuries, and I didn't know yet whether I would ever make a full recovery and be able to continue my building career. It felt even more important to give myself space and rest and love. I needed to care for myself in the way that Jack had once cared for me. I knew what I needed, and I could deny myself no longer.

By the time I found my sweet little house, Rose was gone from my world. She walked away with no warning, no explanation, and no goodbye the autumn before, and it nearly crushed the life out of me. She went as mysteriously as she came – a bit like Mary Poppins, I guess – and though I cried I knew what a gift she had given me . . . the will to do it, the recognition of the need. We had talked so many times about being citizens of the world, at home in many places, but we'd also talked about root chakras and the need for sanctuary, however humble. With the memory of her arm wrapped tightly around my waist, the determined look on her face, and the best kind of bossy big sister confidence that was in her voice in these moments, I knew that I could give myself that at last – that it was time. I may never see her again, but in that house or in a beautiful lake, her love is with me always.

Jack, too, in our last meeting – a few months after we'd split for good – excitedly told me to go for it. I'd shown him the real-estate listing, almost as if I needed his approval. He knew – as did I in my heart – that it had to be mine. It already was, save the paperwork.

And there on that Virginia mountain, without Jack, I began to rebuild.

I had talismans from Wales, from Italy, from festivals long

put to bed. They were some of the first things I brought with me when I came up the mountain, along with books, sheets, towels and toilet paper. The trio of little ceramic geese in flight that Carwyn gave me many moons ago down in Cardiff. Stones from the tops of important hillsides. Egg cups from a favourite spot in Hay-on-Wye. Bone-handled knives that Jenny had spare. The secondhand jumper that had become my second skin. A shard of a plate I broke in Italy at the end of a perfect night up in the olive grove.

And I had the moon, which always made me feel connected to Kate . . . the same moon shining on us both, even if one of us was sleeping, an ocean away. Luminous and magical herself, Kate had stood at my side as we admired the moon together on so many unforgettable nights in the Wye Valley. As I looked up at the sky one night from the quiet of my front porch, I knew that she was with me, and that she always would be . . . even if, like the moon, I couldn't always see her.

It was a huge seismic shift to lose Jack, who had been my rock and my respite for years. I wasn't sure anymore who I was without him, but I realised I needed to remember, to stop and regroup. Maybe he was the great love of my life, but the complications of our age difference were inevitable and in the end, insurmountable. We had always known. It's just that things never fall apart in quite the way we imagine, and the end was a whimper rather than a bang. I had grown up at last, and he had suddenly become an old man, though still with bursts of mischief and youth, and always with a brilliance that fanned out over the hills around us. My body cried out louder and louder for children, but the biggest thing was that he had refused to marry me, and that turned out to be more important to me than I had ever imagined. Bring it down to a practical level, and it left me with all sorts of immigration concerns. I couldn't simply be there in Wales and see

315

what happened. I never had more than six months' visa, and beyond that, his refusal left me homeless, adrift.

There is a price for the kind of storied life I have led . . . I once thought it was only financial, but it has taken a toll on my body and on my heart. I have lost many of the people who fill this book, and my heart shattered with each one gone, but that pain does not negate all the wonder that came before.

For all that I have lost, I do not believe that my love was for nothing. I lived better, searched deeper and loved harder in eight years than many will do in a lifetime, and for that, I have suffered greatly at times, but grown even more. I would do it all over again. My gratitude is something I could never adequately express – for my luck, and for those who loved me and pushed me, fed me and housed me. It was a time so marvellous and improbable that I knew even in its midst it could not last – that it was something perfect, something to be savoured. I was determined that I would not forget. I wrote it all in hardbound paper journals, in endless letters that took flight on beautiful stationery scribbled with blue-black fountain pen ink, and in email, too. Now, here on these pages, a bit distilled for the world. Thank God I wrote. It's over now, and the golden light that shone on it all has slipped out of my grasp like perfect, predictable clockwork. Were it not for my words – my relentless obsession with not forgetting the beauty and the good fortune of my own life – it would be gone already. What I have left are my love, my sense of wonder, and at last, an understanding of my own power, and I will carry those things with me the rest of my life. Wales awakened them all.

This book is both love song and elegy to those gorgeous years and the people and mountains that filled them.

An Abbreviated Walling Glossary

Many of the following terms are simply the words I have known, though – like building styles – walling terminology varies greatly from region to region in Britain and Ireland.

Batter The slope (taper) of a wall, expressed as an angle or as a ratio of horizontal to vertical dimensions. A wall is generally widest at its base and narrows as it rises until it reaches copes and coverbands.

Batter frame The wooden frame we use to run our lines, helping us keep the correct batter and height when building.

Bedding plane The layers within a stone, formed when it was still sand or mud, along which it tends to split. These can be highly regular, as in roofing slates, or highly irregular, as in the sedimentary fieldstone varieties found in some areas of Mid Wales.

317

Cock-and-hen A form of coping that alternates large and small upright stones along the top of the wall. Also known as buck-and-doe.

Copes The line of stones along the top of the wall which protects the structure below. The downward force of their weight and the tight arrangement of their placement helps hold in place all that lies beneath.

Course A layer of stones in the face of a wall. Depending on the regularity of coursing, you might think of these as 'levels'.

Coverband A layer of throughstones placed on top of a double-faced wall to anchor it, help keep rain out of the middle and provide a base for the copes.

Dry-stone wall A wall built without mortar, and such that the amount of precipitation penetrating its interior is minimised through careful building technique.

Face An exposed side of a wall; also, the side of a stone that shows once it is placed into the wall.

Foundations The lowest course of stone in a wall; its base.

Gap A breach in a wall due to defect or damage; also, a verb, which is to repair these breaches. Sheep love to get through these if they can.

Head The smooth, vertical end of a wall, perhaps for a gateway. Also known as wall-head, cheek-end.

Hearting Small, irregular stones placed between the two faces of a wall to pack the space between them.

Joint The space (hopefully minimal!) between two adjacent stones in a course. These should be as tight as possible unless one is purposely leaving space for a bird to nest in the wall.

Letterbox A large space between stones into which one could slide a letter or perhaps even a hand! These most often happen to inexperienced or inattentive wallers, and they are weak spots in the wall.

Lintel A stone slab or wood or metal beam placed over an opening to bridge and support the structure above. These sit above windows, doors and fireplaces as well as lunkies and smoots.

Lunky A rectangular opening at the base of a wall built to permit the passage of sheep or geese from field to field, though small enough to keep cattle in place, which can be blocked with a large stone. Geese were often permitted to roam free to help control the liver fluke population.

Masonry Stonework characterised by the use of cut and trimmed stone.

Pinnings Small stones wedged into spaces in a wall face. (Jack always said that too many of these indicated sloppy walling.)

Retaining wall A wall built across the face of a bank or slope to keep the soil from slipping. Single-faced.

Rip seam A series of joints not crossed widely enough (*minimum* of two inches each side, ideally much more) in successive courses, leaving a vulnerable spot in the wall. These tend to be vertical or near-vertical and of three or more courses in height. They occur most often in the walls of inexperienced builders, but can happen to anyone who is inattentive. Also known as a running joint.

Smoot Smaller than a lunky, it is a rectangular opening that allows rabbits and hares or water courses to pass beneath a wall.

Stile A set of steps over, or an opening through, a wall, designed to allow the passage of pedestrians but not livestock.

Throughstone A large stone placed across the width of the wall to link its sides together.

Acknowledgements

Writing this book has been the most emotionally exhausting thing I have ever tried to do. I have not been able to say all the things I thought I would – to describe the full beauty of these places and the people who animate them. There is never enough room for all the magic I see in the world.

I could write in equal length to the manuscript to thank all the people who made this possible through their incredible kindness. I will try to be brief, but this is my Oscar moment, and when you live on the road as much as I do, you have extra people to thank:

My parents have been entirely supportive – even in the moments when they weren't terribly sure about what I was doing. Endlessly giving and patient, they endured late-night and early-morning airport runs, my sometimes very grumpy temper, heaps of tools and books and leftover stone and half-unpacked bags. I will be eternally grateful. Oh, and for that house downpayment . . .

My brother – ever generous and hilarious – helped to arrange flights, whisked me away for adventures, texted me nonsense when I've needed a laugh and offered advice when I've needed that. All I wanted when I was a kid was to be like him, which is part of the reason I've worked so hard. And now, as he would say, it's all white meat AND a biscuit!

My family endured years of long absences and seemingly strange priorities and still welcomed me home with open arms *every* time. I can't thank them enough for their acceptance of me, wherever I roam, whoever I become.

My grandparents knew struggles that I have been lucky enough never to face, and I have been spared largely because of their hard work and moral strength. Proctor and Hazel Phillips Brown. Carl and Ilene Ingram Ellison. Their names deserve to be in print. I hope I have made them proud.

If Bert and Jennifer Medlock ever thought I was crazy, they never said so to me. They gave me work when business was slow, shelter and food when I needed it, the occasional stiff drink and a lot of laughs and encouragement as I built a business.

Chandler Robinson was the world's best tech support (particularly when my laptop died just before my edit deadline), and I owe him bottomless thanks for all the cold beer and laughs when I turned up on his doorstep, frustrated and thirsty.

In a moment when I felt unsure, irresponsible and guilty about my life, Martha Lynn Robinson told me I was right to try to enjoy my life *now* instead of putting it off 'til retirement. She proved that not long after in a battle with cancer that she would eventually lose. I never forgot her words, and I'll never forget her.

Teachers have mattered *so much* to me. I am grateful to all, but to three in particular: Nancy Neal in music, Cynthia

Tisdale in literature and theatre and Brenda Benton, who brought history to life in a way no one ever has since. Your work made my world so much more enticing and beautiful than it might have been otherwise.

Bill and Marcie Ferris, two of the best professors (and indeed humans) the University of North Carolina will ever have on its faculty, encouraged my writing from day one. Long after I jumped the great academic ship, but long before it was clear I'd make it over here in this other boat, they always told me they were proud of me, and it made me cry *every time*. Their friendship and support have been vital.

David Cecelski first drew my attention to quiet rural brilliance and began to break down my unexamined stereotypes about geography, class, education, intelligence and politics. He paved the way for what I would find in Wales and what I would eventually become.

Kathy Roberts brought the study of material culture to life for me . . . vernacular architecture, the handmade, the patina of place and of objects. She gave me a new lens on the world, and Wales was all the more beautiful for it.

Ayşe Erginer, Executive Editor of *Southern Cultures*, was my first serious editor and set an extremely high bar for all who come after. I am grateful for words and wisdom, for clarity and cheerleading duties, for endless enthusiasm and encouragement (and for exceptional emoji prowess).

Ayşe and my friend Ashley Melzer were my brilliant volunteer proofreaders, tone-checkers and hand-holders in the final stages.

Nia and Liz Bevan made sure I was doing right by the Welsh language, as well as celebrating with me in London and hosting me warmly in Pembrokeshire.

Anna Malzy (whose real name is Acorn), for her tireless

323

good humour, easy friendship and vital manuscript feedback.

Carlene Stephens first brought me to the Smithsonian as an intern, fed me so many more times than she had to, and was sensible enough to tell me that law school was a very bad idea. Thank God for her.

Kim Stryker, patron saint of lost twentysomethings, said, 'Yes! Of course you go!' when I wrote wondering nervously whether I ought to say yes to Jack's invitation. Together with her husband Eric Astor, Kim gave me my first paying job as a waller in America. They have celebrated and supported me from the beginning.

My Folklife Festival family are always waiting back in DC to greet me warmly, lend a hand, cheer me on, offer work and celebrate late into the night. Special thanks to Tyler Nelson, Marquinta Bell and Claudia Telliho, who regularly made miracles happen, and to Dorey Butter and Betty Belanus, who brought Wales to life on the National Mall.

Diana Parker has been a crucial sounding board and support as I stretched and floundered and finally grew . . . Another mother, a loyal friend.

Doug Moody is my oldest and best friend, and I love him like a part of myself. If I hadn't had him through this and everything else, I would have cried a lot more than I laughed. Rock, comedian, R&R director – whatever I needed, he has been.

I have a huge North Carolina posse, past and present, but thanks especially to: Emily Wallace, Katy Clune, Kate Elia and Nick Williams, Kate Medley, Jack Reitz, April McGreger, Mimi Logothetis and Pete Yeganian, Jay Murrie, Sheri Castle, Nancie McDermott, Jeff Currie, Malinda Maynor Lowry, Sarah Blacklin and Ben Horner, and Kim and Dan Marston.

Glasses raised to my London friends, whose support,

laughter, enthusiasm and willingness to house and feed me have been so crucial: Caroline Donaghue, Sarah Thomas, Claire Brandow Jones and her husband Theo, Jen Avila and Paul Dadomo.

Helen Owen's tea shipments quite literally kept me going.

Diane Flynt opened a door for me in Virginia that took my career to a place it might never have gone on its own, and she has been a friend in every sense.

Thank you to my Virginia clients who've now become friends and neighbours: Jim Newlin and Silvie Granatelli, Walter and Sally Rugaber, Gary Stone and Lorrie French. Your kindness, generosity and enthusiasm have truly changed my life.

And to my other amazing neighbours in Virginia, who have been a huge support and a reliable laugh: Gary Moore, Theresa and Brian Palmer, Eliza Greenman, Sammy Malavarca, Rachel and Steve Van Sutphin, Lee Chichester and Jack Russell, and CG the Tennessee Walker.

Chip Callaway is probably the kindest and most delightful landscape architect on the planet, and I'd pick his table at any dinner party anywhere.

Jeff Hatfield is a fine blacksmith, collaborator and friend. He was optimistic and encouraging at every turn and always ready to make me laugh when I was stressed to my breaking point . . . or pour me another whisky, which sometimes helps, too.

My chef gave me a chance when I knew nothing, taught me everything she could, and endured me in the years when I demonstrated at least as much attitude as promise.

Thanks to my stone yards and their wonderful teams of people – *especially* the delivery drivers: Super Landscape Supply (now Big Rock) in Greenville, SC; Stone City in Greenville, SC; Quality Stone in Marion, NC; Arrow Stone in Christiansburg, VA; Scott Stone in Greensboro, NC. All these folks always greeted me with the greatest enthusiasm (and sometimes answered a lot of stupid questions as I learned to do my job).

Diolch yn fawr to the people of Wales, who welcomed me every time with open arms. And especially to Dai and Nelda Davies, Nicola Browne and Hayden Owen, Derrick and Sarah James, Kath and Eddie Phillips, Carwyn Evans and Lowri Davies, Tom Pearce, Gwilym Pearce Jones, Bryn Pearce Jones, Ellie Pearce Jones, Maria Carreras, Del and Roger Ho Sang, Liz Fleming-Williams, Ray Woods, Toby Small, Roger Capps, Emily Chappell, Julian Lewis and Jackie Sampson, Beth Billingsley, Joyce and Nigel Gervis, and Henry, Harvey and Cai Morgan-Gervis.

Thanks to all the farmers whose walls I was lucky enough to work on: Ivan and Mrs Grafog, Huw and Mary Dafadfa, Jeff and Kate Rhandir, Brian and Sorcha Troedrhiwdrain, and especially the Davieses of Upper House (Gareth, Jo, Will, Johnny and Bruce). I am grateful for your kindness, respect and good humour.

Emma Beynon gave me my first fountain pen, took me sailing, and always believed that I was a writer. Her love of language, of woollens, of the stars and of the gritty parts of life have endeared her to me over and over again, and her friendship has been a crucial one during my years in Wales.

Without the inspiration and support of Angharad Pearce Jones I wouldn't be doing any of this – the building or the writing. Thank you for cutting a path for me, and for always welcoming me back warmly no matter how long it's been.

Thank you, thank you to John and Jenny Morris, whose generosity and hospitality know no bounds. They welcomed me from the start, kept my glass full and fostered a true understanding of life beautifully lived.

Laughter has been a survival strategy as I have worked on this book, and top comedic honours go to Tim and Deb Bunker. In addition they gave me shelter, food, therapy animals and the kind of creative understanding and kinship that only artists can. (They would rather I insult them profanely than be sincere, but they'll have to suffer the latter this time.)

It was Deb who pointed me to my cover artist, Sarah Ross-Thompson, whose work embodies all that I love about the landscape of Britain, and who seems to understand dry-stone walls in a way that few who don't build them can. I am grateful for her keen eye and gorgeous prints.

I am grateful to Sue Viccars for expert and patient copy editing (a Herculean task where this book was concerned), Bekki Guyatt for design, Beth Wright for publicity, and Meryl Evans for legal review.

Tim Bates, my agent at Peters Fraser & Dunlop, wrote me a letter of enquiry out of the blue in 2015 during the horrible period of depression described in this book. I was sceptical at first – it seemed too good to be true – but he has worked tirelessly to get me where I am today. I had been writing in my journals and saying aloud for about a year that I'd like to find a direction and a home for my writing, and lo and behold, he appeared. I am eternally grateful to Tim and the staff at PFD.

My editor Claire Chesser has been an amazing shepherd to this project from day one. Her clear, calm good sense, her humour and patience, and her sheer enthusiasm have been such a wonderful thing to have as I have struggled to bring this book to life. I cannot thank her enough, and I hope we will have the chance to work together again in the future. At the very least, I think I've made a friend I'll keep.

Rose brought an extraordinary, intoxicating magic to my

life that I will probably never find in another. She believed in me and took me seriously as a human being and an artist long before it ever crossed my mind to do so, and that made all the difference. We coexisted beautifully for a time, and the warmth, bravery and true sisterhood of those days will live on in me forever. Not a day goes by that I don't miss her.

I can't write about Kate without tearing up. She is quite simply one of the most important people I will ever meet – one of the brightest lights on this earth. All that she has given me and all that she has meant to me I still haven't managed to do justice to on the page, but I feel it every day as I move through the world. I couldn't bear to let her down – ever – and I worked harder at everything I did because of her. Her support and enthusiasm have been invaluable, and I hope I have made her proud.

Jack said to me years ago, 'You should write our story when I'm dead.' When I got an agent out of the blue and then a contract with a publisher, he was still very much alive and we were still together, and he was so excited for me. So much of this book is deeply personal for us, and it feels important to tell you that he, too, knew we were living an amazing tale. I have tried to reflect our love, our humour and our struggles as fairly, honestly and beautifully as I could. He only ever asked that I change his name, and that I have done.

And to all the others who offered a kind word and a helping hand along the way: I know better than anyone that I did not do this alone. Thank you.